Septimius Severus and
the Roman Army

Septimius Severus and the Roman Army

Michael Sage

Pen & Sword
MILITARY

First published in Great Britain in 2020 by
Pen & Sword Military
An imprint of
Pen & Sword Books Ltd
Yorkshire – Philadelphia

Copyright © Michael Sage 2020

ISBN 978 1 52670 241 8

Printed and bound in the UK by TJ International Ltd, Padstow, Cornwall.

Pen & Sword Books Limited incorporates the imprints of Atlas, Archaeology, Aviation,
Discovery, Family History, Fiction, History, Maritime, Military, Military Classics,
Politics, Select, Transport, True Crime, Air World, Frontline Publishing, Leo Cooper,
Remember When, Seaforth Publishing, The Praetorian Press, Wharncliffe Local
History, Wharncliffe Transport, Wharncliffe True Crime and White Owl.

For a complete list of Pen & Sword titles please contact

PEN & SWORD BOOKS LIMITED
47 Church Street, Barnsley, South Yorkshire, S70 2AS, England
E-mail: enquiries@pen-and-sword.co.uk
Website: www.pen-and-sword.co.uk

Or
PEN AND SWORD BOOKS
1950 Lawrence Rd, Havertown, PA 19083, USA
E-mail: Uspen-and-sword@casematepublishers.com
Website: www.penandswordbooks.com

Contents

To my Darling wife Judith for all of her help and encouragement.

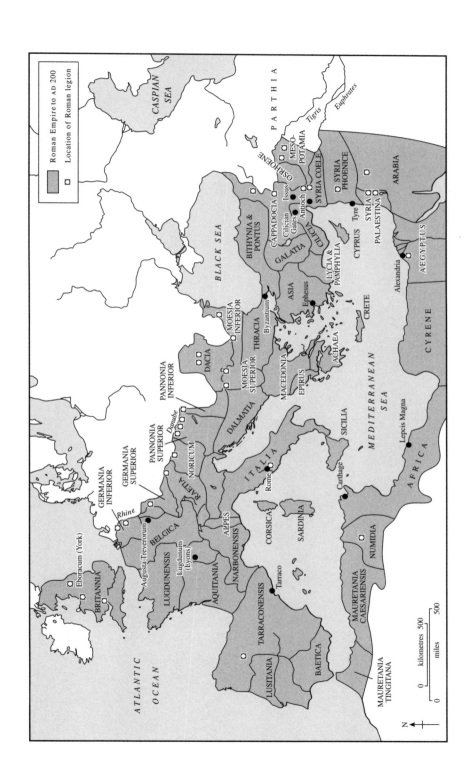

CASPIAN SEA

P A R T H I A

Tigris *Euphrates*

OSROENE

MESO-
POTAMIA

CAPPADOCIA
Cilician
Gates
Issus
Antioch
CILICIA
SYRIA COELE
SYRIA
PHOENICE
ARABIA

BITHYNIA &
PONTUS

GALATIA

LYCIA &
PAMPHYLIA

ASIA
Ephesus

CYPRUS
Tyre
SYRIA
PALAESTINA

BLACK SEA

Byzantium

THRACIA

MACEDONIA

EPIRUS

ACHAEA

CRETE

AEGYPTUS
Alexandria

CYRENE

MOESIA
INFERIOR

DACIA

MOESIA
SUPERIOR

PANNONIA
INFERIOR

DALMATIA

MEDITERRANEAN SEA

SICILIA

Lepcis Magna

PANNONIA
SUPERIOR

Danube

NORICUM

GERMANIA
INFERIOR

GERMANIA
SUPERIOR

RAETIA

ITALIA
Rome

Carthage

AFRICA

Rhine

BELGICA
Augusta Treverorum

Lugdunum
(Lyons)

ALPES

NARBONENSIS

CORSICA

SARDINIA

NUMIDIA

ATLANTIC
OCEAN

Eboracum (York)

BRITANNIA

LUGDUNENSIS

AQUITANIA

Tarraco

TARRACONENSIS

LUSITANIA

BAETICA

MAURETANIA
CAESARIENSIS

MAURETANIA
TINGITANA

N

kilometres 500

miles 500

0

0

Introduction

The Emperor Lucius Septimius Severus, whose reign bridged the transition from the second century to the third centuries AD, was an important figure in the development of the Roman Empire. His rise to power was marked by a prolonged civil war in which he defeated two other rivals for the throne. By doing so, he restored imperial stability and provided Rome with a dynasty that with a brief interruption lasted for a further generation. When that dynasty ended in 235 the empire faced a period of increasingly serious external threats and increased internal instability that lasted until the end of the third century.

Severus enlarged the empire's boundaries in the East where he created the new provinces of Osrhoene and Mesopotamia and may also have stabilized the Roman frontier in Britain. He divided the province of Syria into two parts to weaken potential threats from its powerful garrison, another trend that would become a general development by the end of the third century. Of more importance are his military reforms which improved the terms of military service, reformed the Praetorian Guard and increased the military garrison of Italy.

His reign marks another increasingly important development, the growing importance of men from the provinces in positions of power in the central government including serving as emperor. This trend first appears in membership of the Roman Senate. It begins the entrance into the Senate of new Italian families, then followed by men from the European western provinces, then by those from the African provinces, and finally senators from the eastern half of the empire. For instance, in AD 69–79, 17% of known senators had a provincial origin, coming mostly (70%) from the western provinces. By the reign of Septimius Severus, over half of known senators came from the provinces; almost three fifths of these were from the east, and over a fifth came from north Africa.[1] By 200 they outnumbered all senators from the western provinces except for those from Italy.[2]

Senators of African background had reached the highest office, the consulship, by AD 80, although few Africans served as consuls over the next three decades.[3] But their numbers increased in the course of the second century, with Africans playing an increasing role especially in the fields of law and literature. Marcus Cornelius Fronto, consul in 143, from Cirta (modern Constantine in Algeria) in Numidia, served as a tutor to the future emperors Marcus Aurelius and Lucius Verus. He used his high position to advance other Africans in imperial service.[4] Africans even married into the imperial house.

Although North Africans seem to have been formally accepted, there does seem to have been some residual sense of them as foreign. So Fronto, in one of his letters to the young Marcus Aurelius, calls himself a Libyan nomad in obvious self-deprecation.[5] Likewise there seems to have been some disdain felt for an African accent. The biography in the *Historia Augusta* calls attention to the fact that Septimius Severus spoke Latin with an African accent.[6]

One can see the rise of Septimius Severus to the position of emperor as a further consequence of the acceptance of Africans in the course of the second century. It was also the result of another trend: the changing geographic origins of emperors. By the end of the first century Trajan, whose family came from the colony of Italica in Spain had ascended the imperial throne. Hadrian, his successor, also came from Italica. It is likely that their families were in part transplanted Italian colonists, but they also developed local roots. Hadrian's successor Antoninus Pius's family had its origin in Latium and Nîmes in southern Gaul. While Pius's successors, Marcus Aurelius and Lucius Verus, had diverse backgrounds. Marcus's family originally hailed from Spain and Lucius's belonged to the Roman aristocracy. Even at the summit of power, the Italian core was losing its importance as men from the provinces came to dominate the central government. Severus was part of this trend. Although the only emperor of African origin, his dynasty produced one emperor born in Syria and another from Phoenicia.[7]

As had happened so many times before in so many other places, it was war that brought Rome to Africa. In this case it was the three separate wars with Carthage, the other major power in the Western Mediterranean, that extended from the mid-third century to the mid-second century BC. The first war, lasting from 264 to 241 BC, decided which power would control the strategic island of Sicily. There was a Roman invasion of Carthage's territory in what is now Tunisia in 256 BC that ended in the total defeat of the invading force. It was a series of surprising Roman naval victories over what had appeared to be the most powerful fleet in the western Mediterranean that ended the war and ejected the Carthaginians from Sicily.[8] The second war grew out of the first. After the loss of Sicily, the Carthaginians attempted to expand in Spain. It was a move that aroused Roman fears. Unable to put up with Roman demands Hannibal invaded Italy in 218 BC and inflicted enormous casualties and destruction. The war was finally decided by Roman victories under Scipio Africanus and ended in 201 BC. Its result was far more significant for Rome's presence in Africa. A Roman client, the Numidian prince Massinissa, was installed on Carthage's western borders. Confident of Rome's support for him and its distrust of Carthage, he began attacks on Carthaginian lands at roughly ten-year intervals. Given the terms of the treaty that ended the second war, Carthage could only appeal to Rome for arbitration, which consistently favoured the Numidians. The situation came to a head in 151 when the Carthaginians fielded a large army to resist Numidian encroachment. The army violated Rome's treaty with Carthage and gave her politicians the justification they felt they needed to finally destroy Rome's hated rival. Even though Rome's vastly greater power made the outcome inevitable it took three years to totally defeat and destroy the city and enslave its inhabitants in 146 BC.

In the aftermath of the war the Romans decided to permanently occupy North African territory. In 146 as well they created the province of Africa out of the lands that had been Carthaginian and installed a praetor as governor. He resided in Utica to the west of Carthage. Africa was a small province of about 5,000 sq. m. It lay northeast and east of the Royal Ditch or Fossa Regia dug by Scipio Africanus in 201 BC after his victory over Carthage in the Second Punic War to separate the land allocated to Carthage from the territory of Numidia to the west. Although it seems to have attracted few Roman colonists, the area became a crucial granary for supplying Rome. It remained the largest supplier of grain for the city until the annexation of Egypt in 30 BC.[9]

A century later another war widened Rome's imperial presence in Africa. The civil war between Caesar and Pompey expanded into Africa. Despite the death of Pompey in Egypt in 48 BC, his Republican supporters fought on. They gathered a substantial army that had the support of the king of Numidia, Juba I. Caesar landed in Africa in 46 BC and in the same year overcame his opponents at the battle of Thapsus.[10] After his defeat Juba committed suicide and his kingdom was annexed by Caesar and formed into a new province, Africa Nova or New Africa. Its first governor was the historian Sallust who provided a less than stellar example for his successors. Caesar also created the first substantial Roman settlements in Africa, including the resettlement of the site of Carthage which had been vacant for the last century after the failure of a colonial venture in the late 120s.[11]

Caesar's assassination prevented the implementation of many of these ventures. It was under Augustus, Caesar's adopted son, that substantial changes took place. Between 35 and 27 BC the old African province and the new one created by Caesar were joined together to produce a sizable entity, Africa Proconsularis. As its name implies it was given to a senior governor, a man who had held the consulship, and developed into one of the most prestigious posts, normally held at the summit of a senatorial career.

The area that had been annexed was, like the rest of North Africa, an ethnic and cultural mosaic. The original inhabitants were the Libyan peoples, the ancestors of the modern Berbers. They usually lived in small villages under headmen and were organized in tribal groups of various sizes. By Roman times, many of these groups had an economy that mainly depended on pastoralism, although there were sedentary agriculturalists as well.

At times they coalesced into larger groups of which the largest was the kingdom of Numidia, located in northwestern Tunisia and northeastern Algeria. It arose as a consequence of the Second Punic War when the Numidian prince Massinissa was established in power by the Romans. He forged a kingdom by unifying a number of tribes which did not always join willingly. It was finally terminated by Caesar when he created the province of Africa Nova.

Several important tribal groups, often coalitions of smaller tribes, bordered the southern boundaries of Roman occupation. In the east, south of Tripolitania, were the Garamantes. They occupied the oases of the Fezzan in southwestern Libya. They often raided the Roman province and were the object of several campaigns under Augustus. To their west was a collection of various native peoples that the Romans called the Gaetuli, whose area of occupation stretched westward to the Atlantic Coast from the Gulf of Sidra on the northern coast of modern Libya. Gaetulian cavalry units were later incorporated into the Roman army.[12]

There were smaller tribal groupings which were of significance, the Nasamones and the Musulamii.

The Nasamones were a semi-nomadic tribe who moved between the semi-arid coastal area along the shore of the Greater Syrtis or Gulf of Sidra in Libya and inland oases and created serious problems for the Romans. Under Augustus they were temporarily subjugated but only loosely controlled. They supplemented their meagre resources by raiding passing caravans.

Mauretania, annexed by Claudius after the local dynasty ended in chaos in 44, was divided into two provinces, Caesarea bordering Numidia and Tingitana to its west extending to the Atlantic. The Gaetulian tribes to its south included the Musulamii. They occupied a large territory spanning the border between Algeria and Tunisia with its centre around Theveste (modern Tebessa) in Algeria, and also bordered the province of Mauretania Caesarea.

Towards the beginning of the first millennium BC the arrival of newcomers in North Africa had led to crucial changes in what had been primarily a land of towns and villages, dependent on small-farming and pastoralists.

Previously in the second millennium BC the Phoenician cities along the coast of modern Lebanon had become important trading and manufacturing centres, especially the cities of Tyre and Sidon. Not only did they boast excellent ports, they were also located at the junction of a number of Near Eastern sea and land trade routes.[13]

Probably in the ninth century BC, the Phoenicians started establishing colonies in the western Mediterranean. Their main competition came from the Greeks, who were also founding colonies at the same time. The Phoenician colonies were probably successors to earlier trading posts. The lead was taken by Tyre which had eclipsed Sidon in importance. There were early settlements in Spain and in North Africa as well as elsewhere in the western Mediterranean. Most of the settlements were probably founded in the course of the eighth century. The most successful of them all, Carthage, seems to have been established in the first half of the eighth century BC.

The colonists brought their language, institutions and culture with them to their new homeland. Numerous colonies organized as city-states dotted the coastline of North Africa. Colonies were founded along most of the coastal area, stretching from modern Libya to Morocco. Their inhabitants spoke Punic (Phoenician) and their political institutions mirrored those of their Phoenician homeland. They were initially independent. Their coastal locations offered excellent trading opportunities both for their own manufactures and for goods from neighbouring African peoples where they served as middlemen linking local economies to the wider Mediterranean market.

Carthage, because of its magnificent harbours (one commercial and the other military) and its extremely fertile hinterland, emerged as the dominant city. It expanded in two directions. Within Africa, it built up a large empire. By the mid-third century BC it controlled the coast of Africa from Cyrenaica in the east to the Atlantic Ocean.[14] Carthage's empire and influence extended outside Africa as well. Carthage drew extensive tribute from the local Libyans and also from the other Punic colonies whose inhabitants were labelled Libyphoenicians.[15]

The cultural effect of these city-states was to deeply implant Punic culture and language in much of North Africa. For instance, Neo-Punic, the later version of Punic, continued to be spoken and written in Tripolitania until the end of Roman rule. Extended Punic texts are very rare both in public inscriptions and on private monuments after the end of the first century, but are not quite unknown, while brief formulae continued to be inscribed until about the end of the second century.[16]

After the end of the civil wars of the first century BC, the Emperor Augustus established a number of colonies in Proconsularis. He sent settlers to the two most important cities in Roman Africa: Carthage and Cirta. In addition, he founded six new colonies in the province. Mauretania to its west, which included all of North Africa west of modern Algeria, was after 33 BC governed by Roman administrators until Augustus entrusted it to Juba II, the son of Caesar's opponent in 23 BC. In the decade of direct Roman rule twelve further colonies were founded there. In the course of his reign Augustus founded eighteen new colonies in North Africa and in addition resettled Carthage and Cirta.[17] The motives for the foundation of these colonies varied. Some were military and others were founded for commercial reasons, while still others provided new land for those Romans who had suffered from the civil wars and for demobilized soldiers. It was from these transplanted Italians that the first African consuls came.[18] Often the prime motivation was protection against pressure from the local tribes which had been displaced by the colonies.

The need for such military measures is clear under Tiberius, Augustus's successor. There had been earlier troubles, perhaps prompted by continued Roman immigration often unsanctioned by the central government. The continued unrest came to a head in the rebellion of Tacfarinas under Tiberius. Tacfarinas had served with the Romans before deserting and turning against them. In AD 17 the Musulamii, part of a federation of native peoples in Mauretania called the Gaetulians, rose under the local chief, Tacfarinas. They fought the Romans for seven years before Tacfarinas was captured and the revolt put down.[19] Even after Tacfarinas's capture sporadic violence continued. Perhaps, the main problem was the increasing encroachment of Roman settlement and colonies on Musulamian land.[20]

The murder of the Mauretanian king and the annexation of his kingdom led to a decision to impose direct Roman rule. Widespread revolt broke out in response among the native tribes in AD 41. It was put down by 44. Two new provinces were created, Mauretania Caesariensis and Mauretania Tingitana.[21] Colonies of veterans were established at the capital of each province. Claudius, following earlier practice, granted rights to local communities, including grants of colonial status and Latin status.[22] Despite the colonization, the number of Romans along the North African coast remained small.

Claudius's successor Nero greatly increased the imperial presence in Africa. Later writers claimed that he confiscated half the land in Africa, which must refer to Africa Proconsularis.[23] Pliny claims Nero executed and confiscated the property of six landowners who possessed half of Africa. This is an exaggeration. It would have resulted in land holdings far beyond any others known to be in private hands. It points to the previous concentration of wealth which must in part have been due to the need to produce grain on a grand scale for Rome.

Nero's reign ended after a series of revolts against him and, after his suicide in June 68, in a further series of struggles between contenders for the imperial throne. In Africa, the commander of the sole legion, III Augusta, Clodius Macer, rebelled against Nero, but was soon suppressed. After a great deal of bloody fighting Vespasian who had been in charge of putting down the Jewish rebellion of 66–73 emerged as the victor at the end of 69. He was the first emperor to have direct experience of Africa, having served there as governor in 62, and his wife Flavia Domitilla had family connections to Africa. Given the chaos caused by Nero's confiscations he set up a regional bureaucracy to manage Africa's extensive imperial properties, which seems to have also accomplished the reorganization of the African provinces. Although the emperor founded few colonies in Africa, he was active in reinforcing existing settlements with veteran colonists who could provide some measure of military aid in the event of either internal or external threat. There is little direct evidence for the activities of Vespasian's successors, his sons Titus and Domitian. Nevertheless, there is evidence for continued troubles with local tribes, especially in the Mauretanias. Given the imposition of taxes and restrictions on the use of traditional lands, as well as other exactions, the continued unrest is easily explained.

The emperors of the second century seem to have paid little attention to Africa. The first, Trajan, never set foot there. His successor, Hadrian, who spent much of his reign travelling through the provinces visited it only once. This indifference lasted until the end of the reign of Commodus, Marcus Aurelius's son.

This general indifference did not mean an end to Roman attempts to push further south and west from the coastal area. This push had taken place under Domitian and continued under Trajan and Hadrian. Indicative of this move forward was the relocation of the camp of III Augusta from Ammaedara (modern Haïdra) in western Tunisia to Lambaesis (Tazouit-Lambessa) in modern Algeria, probably in the 120s under Hadrian. Earlier, Trajan had founded a veteran colony in an existing native city, Timgad (ancient Thamugadi) not too far from the legionary camp at Lambaesis. It was veterans from III Augusta that provided the first settlers. It also presumably provided some support to the camp in case of a threat.

However, despite the apparent lack of imperial interest in Africa, its tribal and nomadic populations became increasingly sedentary and so easier to control. More than five hundred towns in the older areas of Roman occupation in Africa Proconsularis were established.[24] Some had Latin rights[25] and some were given full citizenship, such as the great centres of Proconsularis Carthage, Utica and Lepcis Magna. This was also a period of extensive building in these towns. The cities were far from uniform. There were existing cities like Carthage and Lepcis Magna with their own civic traditions. Then there were towns that functioned as tribal capitals and are indicative of an increasingly sedentary population. Also, in the interior of the province there were towns that served as market centres and engaged in small-scale craft production for the surrounding rural populations. Finally, there were cities that grew out of the settlements that were adjacent to the military camps, built on the land assigned to the legion, which the Romans called *canabae*. Initially they housed the merchants and traders who supplied the troops with food and other goods and offered various services. As the legions became more sedentary in the second century, the soldiers formed liaisons with local women who then lived in the canabae with their children. They often grew into sizeable towns and occasionally into cities. At Lambaesis, the canabae near the camp developed into a town with Roman citizenship and eventually became the capital of a new province, Numidia, carved out of Proconsularis by Septimius Severus.[26]

The situation in the west, in Mauretania, was more unstable. A rebellion broke out in AD 122–3 which was successfully suppressed. However, the province remained unstable with outbreaks of resistance from various local tribes. In 145 several years of troubles in Tingitana came to a head with a more violent upheaval which was only put down in the 150s. It was serious enough for troops to be summoned from other provinces and for a senior commander to be put in charge.

Mauretania continued to be restless, especially its mountainous south. Probably in 172 a number of tribesmen took ship and launched a raid on the province of Hispania Baetica in southern Spain with its capital at modern Cordova. A few years later, in 177, another Moorish raid was made into Spain and finally destroyed by Roman forces from Tingitana.[27]

Despite the restlessness evident in the Mauretanias, Roman Africa did not face serious threats. The garrison consisted of a single legion, III Augusta. As mentioned earlier, under Augustus it was moved westward twice. It was finally established at Lambaesis under Trajan or Hadrian. The legion was temporary disbanded in 238. When it was reformed it returned to its camp at Lambaesis. Its relocation there is indicative of the fact that the perceived source of trouble was now to its south in the Aurès Mountains of Algeria.

Under Augustus and Tiberius the legion had been commanded by a senatorial proconsul. Caligula removed control of the legion from the proconsul and entrusted it to an imperial legate. This step can be seen as the removal of an anomaly, since the proconsul of Africa was the only senatorial official in charge of a legion. Added to this was the fact of Africa's prime importance as a grain growing area for the city of Rome. It was crucial that the central government maintain control of the major military forces in the province. As has been pointed out, the division of military and civil responsibilities led to later difficulties.[28] Interestingly, the action anticipates the steps taken at the end of the third century when such a division between imperial military control and a civilian administration was applied to almost all the provinces.

Recruitment for the African legion followed a pattern which was general in the legions of the imperial army. During the first century the soldiers of the legion were non-Africans, especially Italians and Gauls. At beginning of the second century Africans appear, but a large number of foreigners still served. These came from different provinces than those of the first century. There were Bithynians, men from the lower Danube and Syrians. By the end of the century, Africans were in the majority.[29]

The legion was supplemented by auxiliary units.[30] Little is known about their locations or composition in Proconsularis. The Flavian emperors created additional units, many drawn from local tribal groups. Based on known units, it is likely that many of these units were mounted as it was the nomadic tribes to the south of the province that caused most of the problems.

The situation in the Mauretanias was probably the same. It has been estimated that approximately 5,000 auxiliaries garrisoned Tingitana and double that number were stationed in Caesariensis.[31] The other African provinces, apart from Egypt and Cyrene in the east, were very lightly garrisoned given the large extent of territory that the Romans controlled. This is an indication that the threats they faced were for the most part of low intensity. Adding the troops of the III Augusta would mean a total garrison of approximately 25,000 men for Roman North Africa. They had to cover the vast distance that extends from the western border of Egypt to modern Morocco.

The far eastern area of Tripolitania in Africa Proconsularis was the only area that directly bordered on true desert. Although it was bordered by some major tribal confederations, like the Garamantes, and there was sporadic fighting, the threat to the province was never serious. To its west, the section of Proconsularis that included the former kingdom of Numidia had its southern border along the pre-desert area to the north of the Sahara, where there was sufficient rainfall to permit some dry farming, that is farming without the need for irrigation. Southwest of the mountains, running from parts of modern Libya to the Hodna valley in Algeria with its harsh climate, there ran a series of forts and earthworks begun under Hadrian. Remaining in use for centuries, they were not a continuous line, but seem to have been used as a form of border control. The same arrangement occurred further west in the Mauretanias. There the line of the frontier ran further north of the desert and was designed to control the tribes of the mountain areas in the Aurès and to channel and police their annual migrations in search of pasture for their flocks.

The frontier zone, a more accurate term than frontier, worked for the most part in Africa and elsewhere, but it was not a defensive line.[32] Given the manpower available in Africa it could not have been. Rather, it was a zone of transition which could, when necessary, be defended. The tribes and other groups that bordered it to the south were never united enough to pose an existential threat although they could as they did under Tacfarinas wage an effective guerilla war. Deals could be struck with local leaders to help in the policing of the frontier. The tribal leaders could also use their connection to Rome to gain Roman support against their rivals. There is an inscription of 168–9 recording and affirming a grant of Roman citizenship to a Iulianus Zegrensis and his family. He was the headman of a local tribal group, the Zegrenses who lived on the high plains of the Atlas Mountains on the southern boundary of Tingitana. It praises Zegrensis' devotion to Rome as the reason for the grant: and the hope that Zegrensis' grant would inspire the same conduct in others. The exchange of mutual favours between local elites and the Romans for mutual advantage emerges clearly in the wording of the inscription.[33]

Roman control of the North African provinces was underpinned not only by political means and by the ultimate sanction of military force, but also by the effects of the Roman presence on the region's economy. In Africa as in the ancient and medieval worlds in general the economy was based on agriculture and trade.

Carthage had owed its prosperity not only to its empire but also to the fertility of its countryside and to its wide-ranging trade, especially in the western Mediterranean. Agriculture was also the key to the high level of prosperity the provinces reached in the second century. The two crucial crops were cereals and olive oil.[34]

Grain growing was concentrated in the province of Africa Proconsularis. The Roman writer Pliny in the first century expressed amazement at the fertility of African soil.[35] As Pliny stresses, that fertility was due not only to the quality of the soil, but also to use of irrigation and other techniques. The Roman government recognized the need and Augustus, as well as other emperors, initiated a series of hydraulic projects to irrigate suitable farmland.[36]

The increase in grain production was driven by the demands of the city of Rome. By the end of the second century, one estimate is that 200,000 tonnes of grain were required to feed the population of the city of Rome.[37] According to one source, Africa supplied two-thirds of Rome's grain requirement while Egypt provided the remaining third.[38]

Africa supplied more places than Rome with grain. Based on finds of red African burnished ware, African grain seems have been exported throughout the Roman west.[39] Grain importation was of first-class importance to the emperors. The population of Rome had grown far beyond the capacity of Italy to support it. Egypt and especially Africa were crucial in maintaining peace in the city. Failure or dangerously low stocks of grain could lead to violence and the threat of the loss of power. Under Commodus, Marcus Aurelius's son, the threat of a failure of Rome's grain supply was cleverly used to bring down Commodus's chief advisor Cleander in 190. The situation was so threatening that even Commodus feared for his personal safety.[40]

The importance of the African grain supply was further underlined by legislation by Vespasian and Hadrian to encourage grain production by offering incentives to cultivate vacant land. In addition, the emperors created a subsidized grain fleet. The state itself did not own the ships, rather they were privately owned. Once again, incentives were put into play. Under Claudius, the merchants who bought and sold the grain were offered full compensation by the state if the cargo was lost.[41] But there was state intervention, as there had been under the Republic, in the construction of new port facilities and in the building of roads to link the interior to the ports on the coast.[42]

The other pillar of the economy was the olive whose cultivation expanded dramatically in the early empire. Its cultivation had been concentrated in the far eastern portion of Proconsularis, Tripolitania. The area was dominated by three large settlements: Oea, Sabratha and Lepcis Magna. They had been colonized directly from Phoenicia but over time became subordinated to Carthage. Even subordinated to Carthage, they had been rivals of one another. The coming of the Romans did not change that. In the chaos of the struggle over imperial succession, in 69 war broke out between Lepcis Magna and Oea. The hard pressed Oeans called in neighbouring tribes and the conflict was only settled by Roman intervention.[43]

Tripolitania was the region best suited to olive cultivation. It is a dry area sandwiched between the Mediterranean coast and the Sahara Desert. It does not in general have much fertile soil. However, the olive is a suitable crop for it as it can grow in extremely dry conditions. It has a further advantage that once it starts to bear fruit it requires little attention. Its oil was far cheaper to transport to market and was employed for a wide variety of uses.[44] The port cities had been involved in its cultivation under the Carthaginians and it had created a municipal aristocracy of fabulous wealth. The coming of the Romans did not alter that. The Romans did not displace this local aristocracy. The relative stability of Roman rule and the opening of new markets for olive oil greatly increased the aristocracy's opportunities to amass wealth, and they were quick to capitalize on them.

The advantages of olive cultivation were obvious. Although centred in Tripolitania it was cultivated in all three of the African provinces, with a particular concentration in the dry southern areas of Proconsularis.[45] It was especially suited to areas too dry for cereals.

Both cereal cultivation and olive growing were done on large estates, with most of the population owning little or no land and working as tenants of the landowner. Large amounts of land were converted into imperial properties. Probably the most important reason was as a way to assure the grain supply for Rome. But given the wealth of Africa, its taxable potential must have been appealing. Large private estates were held by senators and equestrians of non-African origin, but over time as Africans entered the senate and held equestrian posts, they came to dominate private land ownership.[46]

Although the wealth of Africa was primarily agricultural it also benefited from trade, especially the trans-Saharan and its shipping connections to the rest of the provinces. Artisanal production contributed to this economy, but it played, as was typical of the ancient world, only a small part.[47]

By the second century, Africa, thanks to its exports, had become one of the wealthiest of the western provinces. The major city of Proconsularis, Carthage, was the second most populated city in the western half of the empire. It had a population of perhaps 150,000–250,000. In the west only Rome was larger.[48] There had been continuing foundation of new cities spurred by the increasing level of wealth. The prosperity of the province also encouraged the giving by the Roman government of grants that raised the status of many African cities. The native elite who had been the main beneficiaries of the new prosperity were engaged in building and beautifying their home cities.

Chapter 1

Sources

T he life and reign of Septimius Severus and the members of his dynasty until its end in 235 are relatively well-served by the literary sources, which must form the basis of any detailed discussion of his reign. Although history writing in Greek continued into the fourth century, in Latin history morphed into biography, which by the fourth century had shortened and became less detailed. It had become summary entries on figures from the long-dead Republic or short biographies of emperors. Unfortunately, the Greek historians who wrote after the 240s survive only in quotations in other authors or exist solely as names.

Among the three large-scale accounts of Severus and his reign, most scholars give preference to that of Cassius Dio.[1] The historian's full name was Lucius Cassius Dio. His family, which was clearly wealthy and important locally, came from Bithynia in northwestern Asia Minor from the city of Nicaea (modern Iznik), which lay astride an important military route into the interior of Asia Minor. His father Marcus Cassius Apronianus pursued a successful senatorial career at Rome. He governed provinces in Asia Minor as well as the province of Dalmatia, part of modern Croatia, becoming consul in an unknown year.

Most of what we know about Dio is drawn from his history, which contains a number of personal details.[2] He was born in the early 160s and seems to have spent much of his youth in Rome. From about 180 he mentions that he is describing events in Rome as an eyewitness.[3] He probably held the praetorship in 194 or 195 and the consulship twice. The first time was under Septimius Severus, probably in 205, and the second consulship came in 229 with the honour of the Emperor Severus Alexander as his colleague.[4]

Dio and his father were part of an increasing number of senators who came from the Greek East. During the imperial period a growing number of senators came from outside Italy. In AD 69–70, 17% of known senators came from the provinces and most of those originated in the western half of the Empire. By the reign of Septimius Severus that number had risen to 58%. Of those from outside Italy, 57% were from provinces east of the Adriatic and about one-quarter originated in North Africa.[5]

The greatest of Roman historians, Cornelius Tacitus, probably completed his last work, the *Annals*, in the early 120s.[6] After Tacitus, the only other historical work written in Latin that we know of was by Annius Florus under the Emperor Hadrian (118–38.) He wrote a summary account of Rome's wars from Romulus down to the reign of the first emperor, Augustus, based mainly, but not exclusively, on Livy. He ends the work with Hadrian's predecessor Trajan (98–117), whom he praises for renewing Roman expansion. There is no evidence for a large-scale history in Latin until Ammianus Marcellinus, a Syrian Greek by origin, writing at the end of the fourth century.

In the west, history was abandoned for biography. Its foremost author was Suetonius, also contemporary with Hadrian and a member of that emperor's bureaucracy. He wrote a series of the lives of emperors beginning with Julius Caesar and ending with Domitian, who was assassinated in AD 96.

His lives are structured according to various aspects of the subject's life, with sections focusing on character, accomplishments and attitudes towards the Senate, and details of the imperial family. The use of anecdote and the lack of chronology makes it difficult to use him as a historical source.[7]

From the 130s until the end of the second century, no historical works are recorded. Literary works in Latin continued to be written, especially by men from the provinces, and in particular North Africa, perhaps the most culturally active area in the western half of the empire.

This historical desert is in contrast with histories written in Greek. For instance there was Arrian, who came from Bithynia and the same aristocratic milieu as Dio. He was consul c.130 and as governor of Cappadocia in north central Asia Minor commanded troops in battle. He wrote a history of Alexander the Great and also on tactics and philosophy. Somewhat later, probably in the mid-second century, another Greek writer, Appian from Alexandria in Egypt, wrote an extensive history of the rise of Rome that he finished writing in the 160s. It treated the history of Rome as a series of victorious wars against foreign peoples. Each major war received separate treatment.[8] The work covers wars from the origin of Rome to those of the emperor Trajan, including the civil wars that marked the transition from the Roman Republic to the Empire in the last century BC. Unlike Florus, who covers many of the same wars, Appian's work is detailed and extensive.

History writing continued in the Greek east, but what is striking is the general absence of contemporary history focusing on developments in the eastern provinces of the empire. There is some evidence for writing about the mid-second century conflict with the Parthians, but nothing has survived. At best these would narrate a single conflict. However, the surviving historians like Appian and Arrian treat of Rome's past not her present. This may reflect the effect of contemporary trends in Greek culture that seem to have become focused on a more glorious past than the Roman present. But at least large-scale history survived.

Florus's history of Rome's wars points to a future of abbreviated sketches of Roman history that was to last until almost the end of the fourth century. Shortened versions of works like Livy's massive history of Rome were epitomized or short imperial biographies with one major exception (see below) were written. The reasons for the absence of history written in Latin is not clear. Part of the answer may be changes in the circumstances of those who wrote history and in those who read it.[9]

Most authors of histories of Rome were senators. As mentioned earlier, the membership of the senate had changed since the end of the first century. Men from the East and North Africa often preferred to read and write in Greek. They had to have at least a basic knowledge of Latin, but they would have felt more at home in Greek. Secondly, the position of senators had changed. Whereas they had been able to exercise independent influence and command, with the absolute power of the emperor all of that had changed. It is significant that the period when Tacitus was writing saw the last discussions among senators of restoring the Republic. The period was also marked by the rising position of men outside the senate. Often, they ended their careers as senators, but they came, like the Emperor Pertinax, from classes that did not share the literary culture of the traditional senatorial class. This was especially true in the west. In addition, it was the emperor not the senatorial class that now mattered. His personality, abilities and relations with the senate were what interested readers and authors alike. The turn to biography was a natural outcome of these developments in the west.

In the east, which was more prosperous and urbanized than the west, traditional education and a highly developed literary life served to keep alive earlier literary traditions both in history and in other genres of literature. Literary culture in antiquity was urban and the presence and strength of eastern cities also helped to preserve traditional cultural pursuits. Both halves of the Empire suffered in the course of the third century when the Empire was pressed hard in the north, and by a revived Persian Empire in the east. This was especially true of the period from 235 until the empire's revival in a different form after 284. We still have evidence for historical works in the east but even short biographical summaries in Latin only reappear in the mid-fourth century.[10]

Cassius Dio was a contemporary of Septimius Severus. He knew the emperor personally, served as a member of his council of advisors, and later continued as an advisor for Severus's son Caracalla. After Severus's seizure of power in April 193, Dio, who had a strong personal belief in the truth of dreams and omens, wrote a pamphlet describing the dreams and portents that motivated Severus's coup and signalled divine approval for it. He sent a copy to Severus who in return sent a complimentary acknowledgment of the work. Dio claims that the acknowledgement arrived late at night. He notes that he soon fell asleep and in a dream a divine spirit came to him and commanded him to write a history of Severus's civil wars, which he did.[11] Dio does not date the work but it seems likely that it was written in or soon after 197, which marked the conclusion of the wars that had brought Severus to power. Like the pamphlet on dreams, it too received the approval of Severus. Dio claims that encouraged by the approval of the emperor as well as others, he was prompted to produce a full-scale history of Rome from its beginning until his own day, incorporating his work on the civil wars. In this too he was supported by the divine spirit who had approved and supported his earlier work.

Dio claims that he spent ten years collecting material for his history, which initially ended with the death of Severus (211). He then states that it took him another twelve years to write it down. He adds that he will continue to research and write as long as possible. The dates of Dio's research and this composition of his history have been the subject of much discussion. Following T.D. Barnes, I would place the research from 211 to 220 and the composition 220 to 231.[12] The work was exceptional. As far as we know it was the first comprehensive history of Rome written since that of Livy at the beginning of the first century AD.

Much of the text of Dio's work has been lost. The only substantial parts of the text preserved are unfortunately from the books covering the last century BC and parts of the first century AD. The rest is preserved only by epitomators, except for a short section covering 217–220 after Severus's death. The work ends with Book 80 in the year of Dio's consulate, 229 during the reign of the emperor Alexander Severus. The relevant section for Septimius Severus is preserved in an epitome by the monk Johannes

Xiphilinus writing in the second half of the tenth century, covering books 36–80. It is not so much an epitome as a selection of material chosen at the personal whim of Xiphilinus. But there are compensations: he generally preserves Dio's material in order and tends to quote his text literally. There is some other supplemental material, but Xiphilinus is our key source.

Dio's use of his sources is not clear nor is his dependence upon them. For Severus's reign, the only written source mentioned is Severus's auto-biography.[13] There is another known written source: Aelius Antipater, from Hieropolis in north-central Asia Minor. He was an important figure in Septimius Severus's court. He acted as tutor to the emperor's sons, served on his advisory council and was in charge of Severus's correspondence. He wrote a history of Severus's exploits, but Dio never mentions him as a source. There is no evidence for the use of the Latin biographies dealing with the reign of Severus by Marius Maximus, who was also a contemporary.[14]

Most of Dio's information must have come through personal obser-vation and experience, the emperor's reports to the Senate, and other documents and friends and acquaintances. As far as events in Rome are concerned, it seems most likely that either Dio was an eyewitness or relied upon information from his friends. As a member of the emperor's council, he would have had access to important individuals and documents.

It is not clear how he obtained his material for his original treatment of civil and foreign wars. At this point, Dio had not yet established a relationship with the emperor and was still a relatively junior senator. There is no evidence that he was present on any of Severus's campaigns. It is probable he used the emperor's dispatches to the Senate and information from personal friends who did participate in the campaigns. It is even possible that he used Aelius Antipater's account, whom he would later have known as a fellow member of the advisory council, but there is no proof of it.[15]

In assessing the value of Dio's text, there are severe difficulties, due its fragmentary state. In the text that we have, major events are omitted. There is no mention of the trip of Severus and his family to Africa nor of the massive building programme he undertook in his hometown of Lepcis Magna.[16] He also omits the games held on Severus's tenth anniversary as emperor. It seems to me that the omissions are the result of a faulty text and not carelessness or intentional exclusion. Dio is often explicit in his judgments on various personalities. He is very positive in his evaluation of Helvius Pertinax, who was assassinated after a short reign of almost three months. In this Dio seems to have followed the Senate's majority opinion.

This is no doubt why Severus during his seizure of the throne posed as an avenger of Pertinax.[17] On the other hand, Dio is extremely negative about his successor Didius Julianus.[18]

His attitude towards Severus has been the subject of debate. Some have seen a positive or neutral attitude towards the emperor. There is no doubt that he criticizes his wars in the East and his cruelty towards the followers of his defeated enemies during the civil wars.[19] In his obituary for Severus, his summing up of the man and his career is not particularly hostile.[20] It is best to see Dio as not especially well-disposed to Severus, but who, given the circumstances of the time, saw him as adequate. He states what must have been the common view among the elite that the death of Marcus Aurelius represented a deterioration in the government of the empire. As Dio describes developments after Marcus's death, he characterizes the period as a descent from a kingdom of gold to one of iron and rust.[21]

Herodian, whose history was also written in Greek, shares this attitude with Dio, as does our other major source, the *Historia Augusta*.[22] One scholar has suggested that Herodian saw the era after the death of Marcus Aurelius as an era of chaos when the comforting rules of the previous period no longer applied.[23]

Unlike Dio, Herodian did not come from the senatorial elite and little is known about his life. His history begins with the death of Marcus Aurelius in 180 and ends in 238 with the accession of the child emperor Gordian III. He was probably born sometime in the late 170s and died perhaps around 250.[24] The dates are an inference from a claim by Herodian that he wrote of events that he had either seen or heard of during his own lifetime.[25] His place of origin is also unknown, although some scholars have inferred that he came from Asia Minor. He mentions that he participated in these events through service both at the local level and as a member of the imperial civil service.[26] The general view is that his imperial post was a minor one.[27]

From his comments he seems to have been in Rome for some of the events he describes. C.R. Whittaker infers that he was present during the years 180–193 and then again in 238.[28] However, given his relatively low status and his youth, if he was born in the late 170s it is hard to assess what his presence contributed to his history in the absence of explicit evidence. He is less forthcoming about himself than Dio. We can only conjecture about whatever direct sources he had.

As far as written sources are concerned, only two are directly cited. The first is a reference to Marcus Aurelius's writings,[29] the second is to Severus's autobiography. He cites the latter for the details of the dreams and prophecies that persuaded him to pursue his plans to become emperor.[30] Aside from the two sources just mentioned, the rest remain anonymous. Aelius Antipater's work on Severus might have been used but as in the case of Dio there is no specific reference to him.

The most pressing source question is the relationship of Herodian to his slightly older contemporary Dio and to the biographies of Severus and his rivals in the civil war in the *Historia Augusta*.[31] There is no explicit mention of Dio. Perhaps the most striking instance of the difference between them is the omission by Herodian of the first Parthian campaign in 195. Herodian claims that Severus put off a campaign against Parthia until he dealt with Albinus, his last rival for the imperial throne.[32] Herodian also conflates the first and second sieges of the city of Hatra into one.[33] However, Herodian's differences from Dio and from the *Historia Augusta* may simply be the result of his own defects as a historian. The judgments on his value as a source have varied widely. A.R. Birley, in his now standard biography in English, characterizes him as being careless, ignorant and deceitful; more interested in spinning an appealing story than in accuracy.[34] C.R. Whittaker is less critical, stating that he is not to be ignored as a source.[35] Certainly, where Dio is unavailable or differs from Herodian, the latter is not simply to be dismissed, but must be evaluated on the basis of other available sources. What makes this so difficult is the scantiness of other evidence.

The third major source is the *Historia Augusta*. It is a series of biographies written in Latin that cover the years 117 to 284 with a gap from 244 to 260. The biographies include the lives of twenty emperors, five heirs who never succeeded to the throne and forty unsuccessful pretenders who are labelled as tyrants in the work. The biographies are attributed to a collection of six authors. There are cross references in which one author mentions another, but none of them is cited by any other source. These authors claim they are writing at the beginning of the fourth century in the reigns of Diocletian and Constantine. Since the late nineteenth century, it has been recognized that the date of composition is, in fact, at the end of the fourth, perhaps even the beginning of the fifth century. Secondly, it is now generally acknowledged that the work is the product of a single author. In the later lives, the work is filled with fictious documents and bogus individuals. Over two hundred of the latter are mentioned in the work, none of whom appear in any other source.

Thus we have a work purporting to be a set of accurate biographies that, in fact, contains a great deal of bogus information, written by a single individual. The work claims to be written at the beginning of the fourth century, but in fact was written towards its end. All of this subterfuge raises the question of why it was written. Some scholars have argued that it is pro-pagan propaganda directed against the growing power of Christianity. It seems more likely that Ronald Syme's portrayal of the author as a rogue grammarian is closer to the truth.[36] I think Syme is right, but that still does not answer the question as to purpose. There is a possible solution. Surprisingly, at the end of the fourth century a great Roman historian, Ammianus Marcellinus, emerged. Although a Syrian Greek, he wrote in Latin. He was not well-disposed towards the contemporary Roman aristocracy. He claims they are intellectually frivolous and devote themselves to trivial pursuits such as reading the satirist Juvenal and the biographies of Marius Maximus.[37] Seen in the context of Ammianus's strictures, the *Historia Augusta* was possibly written as competition to Ammianus. It began with a series of basically reliable biographies and later turned to fabrication to produce a work that was entertaining and could compete with both Juvenal and Marius Maximus by offering a single work that combined biography and satire.

The biographies important for the reign of Septimius Severus consist of a life of Severus himself and one each of his rivals in the civil wars, Didius Julianus, Pescennius Niger and Clodius Albinus. Also important are the biographies of Helvius Pertinax and of Severus's two sons, Caracalla and Geta. In general the biographies of emperors down to and including Caracalla contain much useful material but their quality declines sharply after his reign. The lives of pretenders are generally of lower quality with much fabrication.

The biographer is much more explicit about the written sources he used. This difference is the result of the different rules that applied to biography versus history writing. This is in line with the practice of earlier biographers like Suetonius who are much more forthcoming about their sources and quote directly from documents. The biographer cites Severus's own autobiography as do Herodian and Dio. He does so several times and like Dio and Herodian criticizes it.[38] It is not clear if the biographer cited it directly or indirectly. A.R. Birley suggests he used Marius Maximus for these passages.[39]

Marius Maximus is also significant in understanding the sources that the author of the *HA* used. He is probably to be identified with Lucius Marcus Maximus Perpetuus Aurelianus.[40] Maximus was probably born about 160 and had a primarily military career that lasted from c.180 and continued to his second consulship in 223. Senator and praetor in 193, he joined Severus in the latter's bid for the throne, commanding various military forces against Pescennius Niger and then Clodius Albinus.[41] He was rewarded with the governorships of prestigious provinces, and the prefecture of Rome under Severus's son and successor Caracalla, and finally he received a second consulship (an important honour) under the last of the Severans, Alexander Severus. He is also mentioned in a number of inscriptions.[42] He composed a series of lives in imitation of Suetonius. He is unusual in being a biographer of senatorial status.

The lives probably began with the Emperor Nerva but how far the work went is uncertain.[43] Attempts have been made to establish an endpoint for Maximus's biographies on the basis of the lives in the *Historia Augusta*. The quality of the *Historia Augusta* lives decrease dramatically after Caracalla. This may or may not signal the end of Maximus's work. We have no way of knowing. Nor is there a way to know when Maximus began writing nor when he completed his work. The work has not survived, all we have are quotes and references in other authors. The *Historia Augusta* cites him on a number of occasions and is a principal source for such citations.[44]

Any estimation of the value of his work depends on this very meagre evidence. Ammianus Marcellinus seems to consider him a frivolous source. The other references to him are in the *Historia Augusta*. It claims that Maximus was an accurate writer.[45] But earlier in the same work he is branded excessively wordy and is criticized for indulging in mythical history.[46]

He seems the most likely candidate to be the source of the lives of Severus and Pertinax which contain valuable material. On the other hand, the lives of Julianus, Niger and Albinus are mostly farragoes of fiction and misinformation, most probably the compositions of the author of the *Historia Augusta* himself based on a small factual core. Maximus, like Severus, came from Africa and this may have played a role in his success under Severus and his son. Given his position, he would have had excellent access to information about the civil wars. The continuation of his successful career after the end of the civil wars implies that he continued to enjoy high favour with Severus. Problems remain about how far he was used by the *Historia Augusta* and what material in the lives was drawn from other sources. We simply do not know, nor has there ever been any solid proof, that either Dio or Herodian ever used Maximus.

Later writers, including the Latin epitomators of the fourth century and the Greek historian Zosimus in the late fifth or early sixth century, add little to our main sources. One further literary source is a work of Flavius Philostratus, a contemporary of Dio and Severus. Philostratus personally knew Severus's empress Julia Domna and shared cultural interests with her.[47] Two major works by him, one of the lives of eminent teachers and orators from the Greek east called the *Lives of the Sophists* and a life of a first century AD wonderworker, Apollonius of Tyana, supply some information about contemporary events. The *Apollonius* was written at the instigation of Julia and so provides some insight into the intellectual interests of Severus's wife and the court. Philostratus supplies the only reference we have to the trip of Severus and his family to his native Africa in 203.[48]

Besides the literary sources, we also have inscriptions and coins that offer information on Severus's reign. There is an old, but useful collection of inscriptions relating to the reign of Severus.[49] Luckily, his reign represents a high point in the number of inscriptions produced with a steady decline after its end to reach a nadir in the late third century. The images and legends on the reverse of Roman coins can be important sources of information. For instance, the gold and silver coinage of Severus indicates that in his bid for the throne he was supported by all but one of the fifteen legions in the provinces stretching along the northern tier of the empire from the Black Sea to the Germanies.[50] From this we can deduce that substantial planning and plotting preceded his bid for power.

Archaeology as well as coinage and inscriptions contribute to our knowledge of those propaganda themes that the government wanted to project and what groups they thought worth trying to convince. Severus built extensively in Rome, in his home city of Lepcis Magna, and in Byzantium after his siege and capture of the city in the war against Pescennius Niger.

In Rome, he undertook a number of building projects. The two most important ones were the Septizodium and the Arch of Severus. The Septizodium, dedicated in 203, stood at the southeastern corner of the Palatine Hill. It was dedicated to the seven planetary deities with a central statue of the sun, which is likely to have been made in the image of the emperor. The purpose of the building can only be guessed at. The statues of the planets suggest a connection with astrology and perhaps the idea that Severus was predestined to rule according to astrological signs.[51] The location of the structure at the base of the Palatine Hill and the imperial palace serves to reinforce this theme. The Septizodium stood on the route used to stage triumphs. This location served to link it to the crucially important theme of success in war.[52]

Another example of the use of a monumental structure for propaganda is the Arch of Severus in the Roman Forum. There was also a companion arch erected in Severus's hometown of Lepcis Magna. The arch in the Forum was voted by the Senate and dedicated in late 202 or early 203. It was located at the base of the Capitoline Hill. It memorialized Severus's victorious wars in the East as well as advertising his sons Caracalla and Geta. The arch bore friezes illustrating the triumphal parade that Severus may have celebrated for his victories over Rome's main eastern enemy, the Parthian Kingdom, as well as other eastern victories.[53] The combination of the arch as well as a large equestrian statue in the Forum presented him as a great military leader.[54] The effect of such propaganda is visible in the text of Herodian who in his characterization of Severus calls him the most successful military leader of all emperors. It must also have served as propaganda directed at the army which had come to play an increasingly important political role.

The literary sources for Severus's rise to power and his reign are comparatively abundant, although it is not clear why this should be. Chance certainly played a part. It may also be the result of the civil wars that provided the impetus for this writing. The dramatic circumstances and events must have made this period an attractive subject for a writer. This seems to have been the case for Dio and perhaps Marius Maximus, who were contemporaries of the events and involved in them. Herodian, writing later, may equally have been attracted by the same qualities of the period. Part of the attraction may also have been based on the idea that after reaching an apogee under Marcus Aurelius, the empire had suddenly and inexplicably precipitously declined. The idea of Roman decline had long appealed to Roman writers. Writing of these events may have been a way of trying to explain and understand what had happened.

Chapter 2

Prelude

The future emperor was born at Lepcis Magna in Tripolitania on 11 April 145[1] while Antoninus Pius was on the throne and a revolt was in progress at the other end of Roman Africa in Mauretania Tingitana.[2]

The city of his birth was among the largest in Roman Africa, with a population of perhaps 50,000 to 60,000.[3] The city had been founded by Phoenicians from Tyre in the mid-seventh century BC.[4] It had started life as a trading port dominated by Carthage. Although occasionally at war with its rivals Oea and Sabratha, it had become the dominant city of Tripolitania, which made up the extreme eastern portion of Africa Proconsularis. As has been pointed out by Birley, the area extended along the coast between the Gulf of Gabès in the west and the Gulf of Sidra on its east.[5] It consisted of a narrow, relatively fertile coast bordering the Mediterranean and inland of an extensive desert area extending into the Sahara. As mentioned earlier, its primary source of wealth was the cultivation of the olive and the export of olive oil. Its proximity to some of the best agricultural land in the region may have played a role in its growth. Trans-Saharan trade played a part as well, but the city's wealth rested on the olive.[6] The immense productivity of the land of Lepcis is evidenced by the fine Julius Caesar levied on the city. He imposed a fine of three million pounds of olive oil for having chosen the wrong side in the civil war.[7]

Unlike areas that lay further west where Roman and Italian colonists played a central role, its expansion and its growth in wealth had been accomplished by an aristocracy composed of Libyphoenican families, that is Phoenician settlers who had intermarried with the local Libyans. It may have been the relative remoteness of the city from other population centres and the absence of good cereal growing land which deterred the settlement of immigrants from Italy.[8] The governor of Proconsularis resided in faraway Utica in modern Tunisia and the city and the region were for the most part only disturbed by raids from desert tribes and occasional inter-city conflicts which also were frequent in many parts of the empire where the central government was weak.[9]

Despite the financial penalty imposed by Caesar, the Libyphoenican aristocracy of the city continued to dominate. The culture of the Lepcis reflected the small impact of Italian settlement. Elsewhere in Africa, despite Roman domination local cultures persisted, but their persistence was more noticeable in Tripolitania given the absence of Italians. The local culture was a compound of Punic and Libyan elements. Punic language endured after the Roman conquest. The language survived into the Roman period not only in Tripolitania but also in much of Roman Africa. Literary evidence confirms this. In the middle of the second century the writer Apuleius of Madura claims in a lawsuit that his stepson had regressed to speaking nothing but Punic despite the family wealth which implies that Latin fluency was normal among the upper classes.[10] Severus is said by the *Historia Augusta* to have been fully competent in Latin and Greek, but his sister who came to Rome could hardly speak Latin, and after giving her son the right to stand for senatorial office and many presents, sent her back to Africa.[11] Punic persisted in the countryside into Late Antiquity.

At Lepcis a number of bilingual Punic/Latin inscriptions appear, starting in 8 BC.[12] Inscriptions in Punic alone occur rarely on public or private monuments until the end of the first century AD, the last one at Lepcis is dated to the reign of Domitian which ended in AD 96. In the second century Punic appears only in traditional formulas.

The other native language in Roman Africa is best called Libyan.[13] It was used all across North Africa as far as the Atlantic coast. It is probably represented in the archeological record by a number of inscriptions in Latin lettering but are not in Latin. There was also a Libyan script in use.

The wealth of Lepcis Magana allowed the local aristocracy to engage in extensive building projects as early as the last decade BC. The projects continued until the last third of the first century AD. They included the forum or city centre begun in the first century BC and continued during the first century AD. In the first century AD, six temples, a senate house, a market building, a theatre and a basilica were constructed in or near the forum. The aristocracy's attempt to identify with Rome is evident in the dedication of the monumental porch of the basilica to the numen (spirit) of the dead Augustus.[14] Beyond the city walls an amphitheatre was constructed. It is of special importance because it is a clear marker of the increasing romanization of the city. Under Nero a large portico was built near the harbour and dedicated in 62. The imperial government constructed roads that improved Lepcis' communications with the south, presumably to facilitate trade with the interior and to provide for the movement of troops needed to control the tribes of the interior.

As elsewhere, these building projects were paid for by the local elite, although publicly dedicated by the central government in the emperor's name. Such munificence is characteristic of Greco-Roman culture and has a long history both in Greece and in Rome. The provision of money for civic projects was a long-established practice of the elite. It enabled it to publicize and to memorialize itself.[15]

Building continued in the second century which was a time of remarkable prosperity in Roman Africa. This prosperity was visible in the major cities of Tripolitania including Lepcis' rivals Oea and Sabratha. At Lepcis there was significant building under the emperors Trajan, Hadrian and Antoninus Pius. During Trajan's reign, a triumphal arch was built near the harbour to commemorate the emperor's benefactions to the city. It was later modified under Septimius Severus. The most noteworthy building project before Severus were the luxurious baths constructed by Hadrian and dedicated in 127. A triumphal arch as well was constructed to honour Pius.[16]

From the beginning of Roman control, Lepcis, along with its two neighbours Oea and Sabratha, was allowed a large measure of autonomy. However their exact status is uncertain.[17] They could have been treated as autonomous allies or what the Romans described as free cities, that is cities which were considered part of the province but were freed, in theory at least, from the provincial governor's direct control. Whether Lepcis was awarded freedom from taxation (a status the Romans called *immunis*) is even less clear.[18] As was the case with Greek and Roman cities, it had a citizen body, a council and magistrates as well as a set of procedures which usually was highly influenced by Roman and local law.

The status of Lepcis was raised by AD 77 to that of a city with what the Romans called Latin rights. The most important aspect of this grant was that it allowed municipal magistrates to receive Roman citizenship at the end of their year in office.[19] This was an important step for wealthy families like that of Severus. The possession of citizenship now gave them access to positions in the central government and to the wealth and status that offered. Thirty years later in 109 the city received colonial status and universal Roman citizenship. Given its wealth and connections it seems to have outpaced other Tripolitanian cities in achieving this.[20] It also meant that the city had assimilated Roman culture and administrative procedures as well as Roman law, which now became the law of Lepcis.

This change facilitated the entry of men from Lepcis into senatorial and equestrian administrative posts.[21] By the end of the second century senators and equestrians from Lepcis are on record. Their growing importance is visible at Lepcis. Until the middle of the second century some members of the local senate were honoured in the city's forum in the first and second centuries. However, from the middle second century on, it is senatorial and equestrian families that are so honoured in inscriptions and dedications.[22] The change is visible about a generation and a half after the awarding of colonial status at the beginning of the second century. Among these families, the most eminent of which supplied senators or equestrian officials, were the Fulvii, Granii, Cornelii, the Silii Plautii and the Septimii, the family of the future emperor. As was normal, the leading families of Lepcis were connected to each other by marriage and other ties of friendship and family. A good example of the interconnection was Lucius Silius Plautius Haterianus who served as a quaestor in the combined province of Crete and Cyrenaica in 165. From the mid-second century and continuing into the third, members of this family are attested in the Roman senate.[23] It is in this context of increasing romanization and the entry of the local elite in the central government that the family and career of Septimius Severus must be set.

The future emperor was the son of Publius Septimius Geta and Fulvia Pia. His mother's family was descended from Italian settlers who probably came as merchants.[24] There is some dispute as to the origin of the father's family; at issue is whether he too, like his mother, was descended from Italian colonists or was native to Lepcis. A.R. Birley in his biography of Severus leans towards an origin in Lepcis, while T.D. Barnes thinks that the ultimate origin of the family was in Italy.[25] The question is further muddied by a Septimius Severus who is mentioned by the poet Statius writing under the Emperor Domitian at the end of the first century.[26] The argument about whether this Septimius was a relation of the emperor hinges on the possession of property at Veii across the Tiber from Rome. The evidence is too uncertain to provide a definitive answer.[27]

Severus was named after his paternal grandfather whose status is obscure, although he no doubt belonged to one of the great families of Lepcis and probably had held local office in the city. According to the *Historia Augusta* Severus's ancestors held equestrian status before the city became a colony in 109.[28]

Severus's father probably did not hold office in the imperial adminis-tration. He certainly held Roman citizenship, and given the status of the family it is likely it was a personal choice that lay behind his failure to seek office in the central administration. It seems all the more likely because Severus's father's cousins were already senators at the time of his son's birth. One cousin, Publius Septimius Aper, was to attain the consulship in 153, and the second, his brother Gaius Septimius Severus, in 160. The couple had two other children, a daughter and Severus's elder brother Publius Septimius Geta, probably born a few years before Severus.[29]

We are informed that as a boy Severus received an excellent education in both Latin and Greek literature that formed the cultural prerequisites for any sort of political career in Rome.[30] Dio claims that he was eager for more education than he received, and that as a result he became a man of few words. This would seem to imply that his knowledge of Latin and Greek was not at a level that he found acceptable and might have been a problem for him.[31] A writer of the late fourth century also from Africa claims that he was fluent in Punic.[32] Given the culture of Lepcis this would not be surprising.

Soon after he had turned 18, Severus came to Rome to start his career, as was the usual practice, under the patronage of a relative, Gaius Septimius Severus, who had already held the consulship.[33] His uncle attained the *latus clavus* or broad purple stripe for his protégé from the emperor Marcus Aurelius. It conferred senatorial rank and the right to hold offices open to members of the Senate. It took its name from the fact that senators would wear togas bordered by a large purple stripe as a mark of their status. This was necessary since Severus's father had not held senatorial office. In addition, his family owned land in Italy at Veii about seventeen miles north of Rome. Such ownership was crucial to the pursuit of a senatorial career as Trajan had made it a requirement that senators had to invest a third of their capital in Italian land. Marcus Aurelius had reduced the amount to a quarter.

Usually the first step in pursuing a senatorial career would either be serving as a military tribune in a legion or as commander (*praefectus*) of an allied cavalry unit.[34] Another possibility was serving on one of the boards of minor magistrates (*vigintivirate*). A.R. Birley thinks that it was likely that he served in one of the posts of the vigintivirate, although there is no evidence to support this hypothesis. But it would be highly unusual for a man beginning his career to omit both of these posts. It seems likely that our source, *Historia Augusta*, simply omitted the civilian post.[35] Interestingly, his brother Geta did see service as a tribune in one of the legions in Britain, the II Augusta, perhaps in the early 160s.[36]

For the next few years the record is a blank. The *Historia Augusta* states that at this period of his life he acted foolishly and on one occasion he was accused of adultery but acquitted.[37] This hiatus in Severus's public career came to an end with election to the quaestorship. At 25 he could hold one of the twenty annual quaestorships. He probably stood for election in 169 when still 24 for a quaestorship for 170 and was elected. He seems to have served his year in office in Rome and for the following year he was assigned to Hispania Baetica to serve as proquaestor.

The twenty annual quaestors served either in Rome or under the command of governors in provinces, not under the emperor's direct control. Of these the two most important were Africa Proconsularis and Asia. Their duties were primarily financial, but they could be assigned any tasks at the discretion of their superiors. It was also not unusual that the term of service would be extended for a second year and that would be as proquaestor in one of the senatorial provinces. In this period the Iberian Peninsula was divided into three provinces. Baetica was the southeastern one with a long coastline on the Mediterranean and was easily accessible from Africa.

Before he could take up his proquaestorship Severus heard of his father's death and returned to Africa to settle his family's affairs there. After he had finished, he was prevented from taking up his post in Spain by an invasion of Baetica by a group of Moors sailing from Mauretania. Their raid was serious enough that Baetica was temporarily transferred to imperial control and necessitated the use of a substantial military force to reestablish order.[38]

Given the situation, Severus was reassigned to Sardinia. Soon after, he served as legate to his uncle and patron Gaius Septimius Severus who was proconsul of Africa in 173/4. This is known from an arch the proconsul erected at Lepcis to commemorate his governorship.[39]

Severus then served as one of the ten tribunes of the plebs. Interestingly, he received imperial commendation which guaranteed his election to the office. He probably served in 175 when he was 30.[40] There is no other evidence in his career for such direct imperial favour.

Around this time, perhaps also in 175 at the age of 30, he married his first wife, Paccia Marciana. This was the normal age of marriage for elite men; their wives were usually at least ten years younger. Her family came from Lepcis and had probably held citizenship from the first century when Lepcis still possessed only Latin rights so that the chief magistrates alone were granted Roman citizenship. So, as one would expect she must have come from a prominent and wealthy local family.[41] She died in or before 187.[42] The marriage despite its length remained childless. It is striking that Severus did nothing about his childless marriage. Interestingly, as opposed to the silence about her in the autobiography, he did erect statues to her at Lepcis when he was emperor. His autobiography, which omitted Paccia, was written soon after his victory in the civil wars with the intention of justifying his conduct and his victory. At that time, he would have been concerned to stress his second marriage and his sons by his second wife Julia Domna as his potential heirs. That might explain his silence in the autobiography and, once he was firmly established in power, his readiness to set up statues of Paccia in Lepcis which would only be of interest to a local audience.

The next stage in the normal senatorial career was the praetorship. Eighteen praetors were appointed each year, primarily for legal duties in Rome and in the provinces. In 177 Severus was one of the candidates in a contested election for the following year. Elected in 178 he was sent back to Spain to serve as a judicial legate to the governor of Hispania Taraconensis. In contrast to Baetica, it was a wilder and far less romanized area, and supplied recruits to the army. The use of men recruited in less urbanized areas was a continuing phenomenon in Roman recruitment. The same pattern is visible in Greek mercenary recruitment as well, where mercenaries came from marginal areas with few economic opportunities.[43]

His departure from Rome for service abroad may have interfered with his fulfillment of the customary giving of games by a praetor. They were put on in his absence. Normally praetors gave games during their year in office, which enhanced their popularity and probably made it somewhat easier for them to advance to the next stage of their career. It was about this time that the expenses of putting on games had risen substantially. However, providing wild animals would have been easier for him than for most, with his connections in Africa.[44]

After his year in office an ex-praetor would normally hold a propraetorship. Various posts were open to an ex-praetor. He could govern a small imperial province or a senatorial province or command a legion in an imperial province. At this time, Syria had three legions, although its garrison had varied over the years. It represented the largest concentration of military force on the eastern frontier. In 162–65 there had been a major war with the Parthians in Syria and Mesopotamia from which the Romans emerged victorious.[45] The conflict had resulted in a period of quiet on the eastern frontier which continued into the time of Severus's service in Syria.

As legate, he was put in command of IV Scythica probably in 182–183, which was stationed probably at Zeugma (modern Gaziantep) on the Euphrates, about ninety miles from the provincial capital at Antioch.[46] The province also contained two other legions, III Gallica at Samosata[47] and XVI Flavia Firma near Antioch.[48] The province was peaceful during the period of his tenure. Its exact length is unknown but anywhere from one to three years is possible.[49]

In 180, Marcus Aurelius died, and his son Commodus succeeded him. Marcus had had other sons, but Commodus was the only survivor. He was born in 161. In an attempt to stabilize the succession, often a problem in imperial Rome, Commodus was named Caesar at the age of 5 in 166.[50] In 177 he was made co-Augustus or co-emperor with his father. The last part of Marcus's reign was taken up by a series of difficult wars against the Germanic tribes of the Quadi and Marcomanni on the Danube. In fact, by the end of Marcus's reign the major concentration of Rome's military forces now guarded the Rhine-Danube frontier. There was almost continuous warfare against the tribes from 167 until Marcus's death.[51] From 177, Commodus accompanied his father on his military campaigns. While the situation on the frontier was still uncertain, Marcus died at Sirmium (modern Sremska Mitrovica) on the Danube on 17 March 180.

All three of the major sources portray the succession of Marcus's son as the beginning of a radical change for the worse. The idea is most memorably put by Dio, who as both a contemporary and senator, could speak with personal experience of the reigns he had lived through:

> *Just one thing prevented him (Marcus) from being completely happy, namely, that after rearing and educating his son in the best possible way he was vastly disappointed in him. This matter must be our next topic; for our history now descends from a kingdom of gold to one of iron and rust, as affairs did for the Romans of that day.*[52]

The new emperor was the first to have been born in the imperial purple. He was only 18 at his succession, and his father could not deny him succession, even if he had wanted to. As a counterforce to his youth Marcus had surrounded him with a group of advisors drawn from his closest friends and counsellors.

The historical tradition on the character of Commodus is uniformly negative. Dio is probably the most positive. He claims that Commodus was not naturally evil, but a simpleton and a coward. Because of these traits, he was easily corrupted by his companions and led into lustful and cruel habits. Under their influence and his own laziness, he rejected his father's counsellors' proposal to continue the war, many of whom were the best men in the Senate, and left for Rome as soon as he could.[53] The *Historia Augusta*'s evaluation of Commodus is even more negative. Rather than an easily corrupted simpleton, it portrays Commodus as inherently cruel, lewd and debauched.[54] Given his alienation of the Senate, there was probably a temptation to portray him more negatively then his behaviour warranted.

But what does seem clear is that in the course of his reign he displayed little interest in governing the empire and delegated governance to others, which led to his falling under the influence of one advisor after another. It was they who directed policy and determined the course of the reign. This allowed the emperor to pursue a reign governed by pleasure and by his own whims.[55]

Probably in the spring or early summer of 180, the emperor and his advisors made peace with the German tribes. It seems it was concluded against the advice of at least some of his father's advisors. The sources claim that Commodus had concluded this unfavourable peace with the German tribes because he was anxious to return to the delights of the capital.[56] Despite what could be seen by some as an absence of a decisive victory, Commodus returned to Rome and entered it in triumph on 22 October 180.[57] He was never to leave Rome again, despite flareups in the Balkan area in the middle and late 180s.

Accompanying Commodus at his triumphal entry and later in his triumph was his close friend and confidant Saoterus, who served as his *cubicularius* or chamberlain.[58] His duties included personal attendance on the emperor as well as screening of visitors. Such a position allowed the *cubicularius* to develop personal ties with his master and to directly influence him, but the chamberlain's standing and future were determined exclusively by his employer.[59] While Saoterus maintained his relationship with Commodus, Marcus's advisors and others among the aristocracy were excluded from the councils of the emperor and were no longer called to attend court. The most important group congregated around Lucilla, Commodus's older sister. She had been widowed early, but as an Augusta (empress) she was a standing danger to the emperor if left unmarried, as a marriage to her would give a potential usurper a claim to the throne. The usual solution was to marry her off to a safe man who would be no threat to the emperor. Marcus's choice was Titus Claudius Pompeianus, the elderly son of a Roman knight from Syria. He did not possess the prestige or the following necessary to pose a threat. He became a close advisor and an effective soldier during the German wars of Marcus. Despite his age, Pompeianus and Lucilla produced a son.[60]

The discontent with Commodus matured into a conspiracy which burst out in 182. It was centred on Lucilla and consisted of a few of her family members, a nephew of her husband and several non-family members. Importantly, it seems that Publius Tarrutenius Paternus, one of the two praetorian prefects who had been appointed by Marcus, was involved.[61] The precise details are disputed, but it seems that Lucilla's stepson, Claudius Pompeianus Quintianus, tried to kill Commodus in or near the Colosseum, but the imperial bodyguard overcame him before he could carry out his plan. Saoterus was executed by order of Paternus.[62] There is no doubt that Saoterus had been a major reason for the alienation of much of the aristocracy from the emperor who now legitimately feared plots against himself. Lucilla's plot also precipitated the removal of many of Marcus's advisors. Paternus seemed for the time being to be free of suspicion and was in fact promoted to the Senate, but the promotion did have the effect of removing him from command of the praetorians and so left him seriously weakened. This was followed by his execution. Clearly the promotion had been a deliberate manoeuvre to separate him from any military support before the emperor struck.

Interestingly, Paternus is portrayed in diametrically opposite ways by Dio and the *Historia Augusta*. Dio claims he had no part in the conspiracy as he could easily have murdered the emperor if he had wanted to.[63] The life of Commodus in the *Historia Augusta* claims that his execution was the result of his part in killing Saoterus and possible participation in Lucilla's plot.[64]

The conspiracy naturally inflamed Commodus's suspicions about other possible conspirators against him. The two Quintilii brothers, who had been consuls as long ago as 151 as well as important in Marcus's reign, were executed for plotting. One of their sons happened to be in Syria and an extensive manhunt was carried out, presumably by the governor and Severus the legate of IV Scythica. The failure to find the fugitive must not have sat well with the emperor and in late 182 the governor P. Helvius Pertinax was removed as well as the legate of IV Scythica.

The dismissal seems to have been linked to the rise to favour of the remaining prefect, Tigidius Perennis, who now became the sole commander of the praetorians. Given the character of the emperor, both military and civilian affairs were thrust into his hands. He had the misfortune to assume power when the empire faced a series of military challenges of which the most serious occurred in Britain. In the north, the Roman province was attacked by a tribal coalition, and initially disaster ensued with a Roman governor killed in the fighting. Perennis appointed a new commander, Ulpius Marcellus, in place of the dead governor. Marcellus was an effective but unpopular commander, a harsh disciplinarian who alienated his troops. There seems to have been an attempt by the troops to set up as a rival emperor a legionary legate named Priscus, but it came to nothing.[65]

The accounts of Perennis's ruin are discordant. Herodian connects his fall to a conspiracy to place Perennis's own son on the throne in place of Commodus but it came to nothing.[66] The *Historia Augusta* and Dio both attribute his fall to repercussions from the war in Britain. The *Historia Augusta* attributes it to disgruntled senators and commanders in Britain.[67] Dio has a rather remarkable account of a deputation of 1,500 soldiers chosen by the troops to be sent to Rome to lodge their complaints against Perennis to Commodus in person.[68] The soldiers claimed that Perennis was plotting to replace Commodus with his own son. The deputation has been accepted by scholars, but it still represents a puzzle. How did these troops travel from Britain to Rome without being stopped or opposed?[69] There is a further problem: why did Commodus listen to these troops at all? It may be that the answer lies with the next individual to control Commodus and his government, Cleander.

Marcus Aurelius Cleander came from Phrygia in north central Asia Minor.[70] He was initially a slave, and later became an imperial freedman.[71] After Saoterus's death Cleander replaced him as *cubicularius*. He is assigned a major role by Dio in the destruction of Perennis as persuading Commodus to hand his prefect over to the soldiers who killed him.[72] Dio claims that there had been incessant conflict between the freedman and the prefect. It may have been Cleander and his confederates in Britain who organized and facilitated the journey of the soldiers to Rome.

The sources present divergent opinions of Perennis. Dio praises him for his personal and political conduct. His only negative comment is on Perennis's doing away with Paternus.[73] The *Historia Augusta* renders a totally opposite verdict portraying him as violent and corrupted.[74] Herodian shares the latter's view.[75] There is no way to resolve the discordant views of the prefect. But it may be that the combination of Perennis's policies on Britain, especially the selection of the widely disliked Ulpius Marcellus, the alienation of certain senators and the ambitions of Cleander, lay at the heart of his troubles and eventual death.

Severus, in apparent disfavour, withdrew from public employment and, as so many Romans had done before, retreated to Athens for tourism and study. Given what Dio characterizes as his eagerness for study, it was hardly a surprising choice. Perhaps the best evidence for such a sojourn is provided by his contemporary Dio:

As far as education was concerned, he was eager for more than he obtained, and for this reason was a man of few words, though of many ideas.[76]

According to the *Historia Augusta*, he suffered wrongs at the hands of the Athenians and bore them a grudge which would result in the curtailment of their civic rights after he became emperor.[77]

It seems clear that the temporary hiatus in Severus's career was linked to the removal from office of the governor he was serving under in Syria, Publius Helvius Pertinax. Pertinax, who was to play an important role in events after the fall of Commodus, had enjoyed a very unusual career. His father was a freedman from northwestern Italy. For a man who was to rise to the consulship and higher, this was an extraordinary origin that would have normally excluded him from senatorial office, much less the highest office of them all.

His road to advancement came through the army. It was the wars of Marcus Aurelius's reign that provided the opportunity for his advancement. He served in Britain as an equestrian tribune of VI Valeria Victrix at York and then held other posts in Britain in the early 160s. This was also when Severus's brother Geta was there and it may well be that he met Pertinax in Britain. A relationship of his brother with Pertinax might explain Severus's later post in Syria under him. After the trouble in Britain ended, Pertinax was sent to the most important of the empire's frontiers, the Danube. There he commanded an auxiliary cavalry regiment or *ala*. The military part of his career allowed him to form connections that would be useful for the future. He now served in civilian posts as he had reached the end of the three different posts which normally made up an equestrian army career. With the German invasion of Italy in 170, his career experienced a temporary halt for unknown reasons. However, his patron Claudius Pompeianus took on Pertinax as an aide in compensation. The war against the Germans proved costly, so there was an urgent need to provide senators of praetorian rank and above to command the legions. The talents of Pertinax, and perhaps the influence of his patron, resulted in his promotion to senatorial status to command I Adiutrix. He was successful in driving the Germans out of Raetia and Noricum. Raetia covered much of central and eastern Switzerland, while Noricum extended over much of Austria and Slovenia. His success was such that he held one of the consulships of 175. He then governed a series of provinces along the Danube before being appointed to Syria where Severus joined him as one of his legates.[78] With Perennis's death his career was restarted. He was sent to Britain to try to reimpose discipline in 185–7 and although he was successful, he was nearly killed by his mutinous troops.[79] The cause of the mutiny was his imposition of strict discipline, a practice that was later to have fatal consequences for him.

After his service in Britain, he was given a civilian appointment in Italy. Most likely it was a function of his age: in 188 he was 62. But trouble flared up in Africa and Pertinax was sent as its governor in the summer of 188 to deal with the problem, as he had earlier been sent to Britain. On his return he was named prefect of the city in 189. And as a mark of high favour from Commodus he was appointed to a second consulship with the emperor as his colleague. His links to Severus were probably still active and may have played an important role in the latter's career.

As was the case with others whose closeness to Commodus allowed them to dominate public affairs, Cleander had also been a close friend of the emperor while they were both young. Probably in consequence he had been appointed *cubicularius* and eventually also joined the two praetorian perfects, probably in 188, with the unusual title of *a pugione* or dagger bearer which allowed him to exercise authority over the Praetorians. He formed an alliance with the emperor's influential and powerful concubine, Marcia, to run the government. Commodus had begun occupying himself more and more with fighting in the arena, which generated a great deal of negative comment in the sources. The corruption of Cleander and Marcia had become so excessive that twenty-five consuls were appointed for the single year of 190. One of them was Septimius Severus.

Finally, in 190 Cleander followed the path of his predecessors and was executed. He was the victim of a plot by the man in charge of the capital's grain supply, Papirius Dionysius, and by Marcia. The machinations and manoeuvring in the palace before his murder are not clear, but it may in some way have been connected to the execution of Commodus's empress Bruttia Crispina on a charge of adultery.[80] The year of her death was also marked by a number of other executions and it may be that Cleander was involved in some form of dynastic crisis.

The issue that precipitated events was a grain shortage in Rome. It is likely that it was an artificially engineered crisis designed to destroy Cleander. A crowd was attending horse races at the Circus Maximus. It began blaming Cleander for the grain shortage. This was followed by a full-scale riot accompanied by demands for his execution. Cleander sent troops against them, but the crowd was too strong for the force he sent. The crowd had the assistance of at least some of the Praetorians. Marcia informed Commodus of the situation. In fear and to enhance his popularity he ordered the execution of Cleander and his young son. Hekster points out that given the alienation of the Senate, Commodus was especially dependent on popular favour and could not risk its alienation.[81]

The accusations against him in Dio are the standard ones of greed, corruption and murder, especially of senators.[82] It has been suggested that at least part of the animus against Cleander was the result of the fact that as an individual of low status his power posed a threat to the elite.[83] But it was not so much a threat as an inversion of the social hierarchy, the idea of an inferior wielding power over a superior that must have been offensive. The same negative reaction is prominently on display over one hundred years before in the reactions to the power wielded by imperial freedmen secretaries.[84]

Perennis's death in 185 had marked an upturn in the careers of Pertinax and Severus. The latter's first post was an appointment as governor of Gallia Lugdunensis. The capital of the province was located at Lugdunum (modern Lyons). It was probably the most romanized of the provinces in western Europe. Aside from a cohort of troops guarding the imperial mint at the capital there were no military forces under the governor's command. The chronology of the governorship is not securely established, but most likely his term ran from 185–188.[85]

While he was serving in Gaul, probably in 187, Paccia Marciana died after a decade of marriage that had produced no heir. Severus was now 42 and the need for both a wife and an heir must have pressed heavily on him. Soon after, he married again, this time to a wife from Syria, Julia Domna, who was to play an important role as his empress.[86]

Julia Domna came from the small state of Emesa (modern Homs) which was situated on the Orontes River to the north of Antioch. It was one of the more important cities of the Roman East. It served as an agricultural centre and had excellent connections to Antioch, the provincial capital, and to Beroea, the modern Aleppo. Both were major trading centres.[87]

The city was ruled by a local dynasty when the Romans first came into contact with it who were not only kings but also high priests. In 63 BC Pompey had brought Syria under Roman control. The area had previously been under the control of the collapsing Seleucid Empire, established by one of Alexander's generals after his death. Emesa along with other Syrian cities in the area had been subject to intensive influence from Greek culture. This is evidenced by the fact that Emesa's remains yield only inscriptions in Greek.[88]

At the time of the Roman conquest Emesa and its territory were under the control of a local dynasty of Arab origins. The Romans left the dynasty in power and it became a client kingdom under Roman control. There were a number of other small to middling size kingdoms like Emesa, especially in the highly urbanized eastern half of the empire. Normally these kingdoms were located at the frontiers of the empire. Their internal administration was left to the local dynasty. This was of crucial importance since the empire had a very small cadre of officials. The kingdoms served as buffers against invasions and would supply troops for Roman military operations when requested. For instance, Emesa contributed 4,000 troops to aid the Roman suppression of the Jewish revolt of 66–73.[89] The dynasty ended around AD 75 and the kingdom was annexed.[90] The annexation seems to be in line with the Emperor Vespasian's general policy of annexing client kingdoms in the east, and placing them under regular provincial government; this is particularly evident in Asia Minor.

The granting of citizenship to individuals from Emesa and elsewhere in Syria began under Augustus, as the use by many Emesa nobles of the family name of Julius or Julia indicates. Grants of citizenship to members of the elite continued after Augustus and romanization continued, but there is little evidence about the history of the city until Severus's reign.

Presumably Severus met his future wife when he was serving as legate of IV Scythica at its base at Zeugma. The base is relatively close to Emesa. It lies approximately 160 miles to the southwest of Zeugma. Since Roman officials relied on the cooperation of local elites, it is likely that Severus as commander of the closest legion to Emesa had visited the city and had had contact with local leaders. The *Historia Augusta* has a story that after the death of his first wife, Severus examined the horoscopes of a number of women and found that Julia's horoscope indicated that she would marry a king.[91] There may be a kernel of truth in this, as Severus was a devoted adherent of astrology as were many of his contemporaries. The pamphlet that first brought Dio to Severus's attention and ultimately friendship with him was on the dreams and portents that predicted the emperor's victory in the civil wars and the success of his reign.[92] In 187 there was no reason for Severus to think that he had a chance at supreme power. It is more likely that, as Levick has suggested, the anecdote was invented after the fact to glorify the marriage and to make Severus's rise to supreme power seem inevitable.[93] It is probable that the original source of the story was Severus's autobiography.

Julia's family was prominent at Emesa. It may have been but cannot be proved that it was related to the defunct dynasty that had ruled the city. But her family did have a definite connection to a central institution at Emesa, the cult of its chief deity Elagabal who was worshipped in the form of a conical black stone that was said to have come down from heaven. The stone or betyl had an important role in divination; it was thought to be a living object. This way of worship was widespread among the Phoenician colonies in North Africa, and at Emesa may have formed a link between Severus and Julia's family.

When Severus arrived in Emesa, Julia's family was deeply involved in the cult of Elagabalus. Her father Julius Bassianus was the priest of the god. His name makes clear that he was a Roman citizen and the family name of Julius points to the fact that his family had been given it either at the end of the first century BC or in the early first century AD.[94] Julia had a younger sister, Julia Maesa, who was to play an important role in the politics of the imperial house after Severus and Domna's deaths. She was already married to Gaius Julius Avitus Alexianus from another important Near-Eastern city, Petra, in modern Jordan. He had begun his career as an equestrian official. Later he profited handsomely from Severus's rise to power, becoming consul in c.200. He experienced a temporary check because of Severus's praetorian prefect Plautianus, but with the prefect's fall his career continued under Severus and his son Caracalla until Avitus' death in 217.[95] The important position of Julia's family in the local elite evidenced by her father's position as priest of the main deity and its probable wealth must have been crucial considerations for Severus. In addition, Julia was admired for her beauty and for her mind. She was also young and so must have appealed to the middle-aged Severus who would certainly want an heir.[96] Her future husband brought a great deal to the match. He was the product of a very wealthy family with property in Africa and Italy. In 187 he had had a successful senatorial career with the prospect of a consulship in the offing. Advantages accrued to both sides. The marriage took place in 187 and, unlike Severus's first marriage, yielded offspring. Their first son Lucius Septimius Bassianus (Caracalla) was born on 4 April of the following year (188) at Lugdunum during his father's governorship.

At the end of his governorship Severus returned to Rome where in normal sequence he was waiting for the drawing of the lots to yield an appointment as a proconsul. Before that a second son, P. Septimius Geta, was born.

Severus received the proconsulship of Sicily.[97] He was named consul for 190, a year which saw a record twenty-five consuls appointed. It was not a particularly prestigious appointment. Two things stand out about Severus's career so far. First, it was not a particularly distinguished one to this point, in fact it was quite ordinary. Second, it was unmilitary. The only military command he had received, IV Scythica, had come in a province at peace and was not an independent command.

Interestingly, there is a marked contrast with his brother Geta's career. Geta began his career in one of the twenty junior senatorial posts (the vigintivirate); he then moved on to serve as a military tribune in II Augusta stationed in Britain. Unlike Syria during Severus's service with IV Augusta, there was warfare in Britain and so Geta obtained some military experience.[98] He then served as a questor in the peaceful province of Crete and Cyrene, and then was put in charge of the finances of Ancona. After serving as praetor, he went on to command I Italica, probably in 185, which had originally been raised by Nero in 66.[99] It was stationed at Novae (modern Svishtov in Bulgaria). The command gave Geta his first experience of the Balkan armies which would be useful later. He then served as proconsul in Sicily, perhaps in 187/8, anticipating his brother's later service. He went on to govern the province of Lusitania which was located in the far west of Spain and Portugal with its capital at Augusta Emerita (modern Mérida), most likely in 188 to 189. This was followed by a consulship probably in 190, the same year as his younger brother. He then governed the imperial province of Moesia Inferior, probably in 191.[100] In 193 his brother's presence in a Danubian province was a decided advantage for Severus. Perhaps the most interesting aspect of Severus's brother's career is that it was like his brother's, a good but not spectacular career; and he had acquired so much more military experience than Severus had. It may be that when things fell apart in 193 Severus's lack of military experience proved a source of strength, not weakness.

Such an outcome had much to do with the situation in Rome, especially of the imperial court. Changes are visible in the court after the fall of Cleander. A new praetorian prefect emerged: Quintus Aemilius Laetus, an African, who appears at least initially to have had no colleague. Cleander was replaced in 191 by a new *cubicularius*, Eclectus, who had previously served in the imperial court. Importantly, Eclectus formed a liaison with Marcia.

Meanwhile, Commodus seems to have become increasingly interested in courting popular favour, while neglecting the Senate. He seems, at least at times, to have shown deliberate hostility to senators. Dio recounts an incident which seems to be illustrative of the enmity between Commodus and the Senate:

> *This fear was shared by all, by us senators as well as by the rest. And here is another thing that he did to us senators which gave us every reason to look for our death. Having killed an ostrich and cut off his head, he came up to where we were sitting, holding the head in his left hand and in his right hand raising aloft his bloody sword; and though he spoke not a word, yet he wagged his head with a grin, indicating that he would treat us in the same way.*

According to the *Historia Augusta*, the murders of senators continued. It provides an extensive list of those executed in the last years of the reign.[101]

As a counterweight to his alienation from the elite, Commodus turned even more strongly to the army and the people. The city had recently been devastated by a fire and the recurrence of the plague. According to Herodian, the fire and plague had weakened popular support for the emperor, who had been well liked by the populace.[102] Popular support needed to be sought and cultivated. The importance of the people's good will had been demonstrated by the fall of Cleander.

It may have been in an attempt to win favour with the military and the populace that Commodus began to identify himself with Hercules, whose cult was extremely popular in the Roman world.[103] What is striking about his identification are the extreme measures Commodus took to associate himself with the god. Earlier emperors such as Caligula had tried to connect themselves closely with Hercules, particularly as he represented the transition from the mortal to the divine through extraordinary feats while still human. But it was the intensity of the identification that makes Commodus unique. Although it has been argued he acted with a deliberate plan, the extravagance of his measures raises some doubt about such an interpretation. It may be that there was a generalized attempt to create a countervailing weight to his opponents, but that it was fuelled and guided by an overwhelming need to assert himself after being directed and controlled by others.[104]

Commodus declared himself the new Hercules and as a second founder of the city he renamed it in his own honour 'Colonia Commodiana'.[105] He renamed all of the months of the year in his own honour. His name was added to a number of institutions including military units. Other extravagant acts followed. Most strikingly, he fought as a gladiator in the arena. Gladiators were normally of lower-class origin and fighting as one was an unheard of loss of status for an emperor. This linked up with his identification with Hercules and with other actions that emphasized his role as protector and as a military figure.[106]

The situation seems to have become untenable as 192 drew to a close. A plot was formed to assassinate this Roman Hercules. His behaviour had become too extreme and threatening to members of his immediate entourage. Several motives are alleged by the sources, but it seems best to see the main conspirators' fear for their own safety as the situation became more menacing as the most important one. The key members of the plot were the praetorian prefect Laetus, the chamberlain Eclectus and Commodus's active and enterprising concubine Marcia. Others were involved as well including perhaps Pertinax.[107]

Dio's version has Eclectus and Laetus as the main movers in the plot. He says they were upset about his actions as well as fearful for their lives. He claims that they had learned that Commodus was going to kill both of the new consuls and replace them as sole consul for 193. He was to enter upon his office from the gladiatorial barracks.[108] The two men decided to proceed, drawing Marcia into the conspiracy. Herodian offers a similar but far more circumstantial story.[109]

Marcia administered poison to Commodus when he returned from his bath. Evidently, the dose was not strong enough and the conspirators had to hurriedly call on the services of the athlete Narcissus who strangled the emperor. The Senate and other members of the elite may have been overjoyed if the acclamations that took place in the Senate after Commodus are given accurately by the *Historia Augusta*.[110] A momentous step had been taken. The Antonine dynasty was no more and it might prove extremely difficult to replace it.

Chapter 3

Things Fall Apart

The first day of 193 was crucial for those who had killed Commodus and for the Roman state. The assassins needed an immediate replacement for the dead emperor who was acceptable to them and would guarantee their safety. The state was also in peril. The end of a dynasty, in this case the Antonine Dynasty,[1] had in the past been a time of danger and potential violence. The end of the Julio-Claudians had led to a year and half of violence and civil war that lasted until a new dynasty, the Flavians, had been established in power.[2]

The second break in dynastic continuity came in 96 with the assassination of Domitian, the last of the Flavian emperors.[3] Interestingly, the assassination of Domitian has many resemblances to the murder of Commodus. It also came after a period of increasing alienation from the Senate and was engineered and carried out by members of the imperial household. Given the proximity and contact between the emperor and his members of the imperial staff, it hardly surprising that they would succeed in carrying out an assassination.[4] In fact, only one senatorial plot succeeded in murdering a monarchical ruler, that against Caesar in 44 when the boundaries between the imperial court and the Senate had not yet become as rigid as they later would be. Civil war did not break out, but the new emperor Nerva, the choice of the Senate, had a difficult time dealing with the praetorian guard and his problems were only resolved by adopting as his successor a military man, Trajan, who controlled the Rhine frontier which had the highest number of legions of any imperial border.

The Antonine Dynasty was not a dynasty in the normal sense. The emperors of the dynasty were linked to each other not by blood but by adoption and marriage. The only exception was Commodus who was the natural son of Marcus Aurelius.[5] But at the death of Commodus there was no obvious successor in view. Several senators were anxious to replace the dead emperor but did not command sufficient support. The conspirators were thus left free to make their own decision. Their choice fell on Publius Helvetius Pertinax, then serving as prefect of the city.[6] Behind their choice must have lain a calculation of how successful he would be in dealing with the Praetorian Guard. They were the largest military force in the city and, at the time of Commodus's assassination, consisted of ten cohorts of 500 men. Another unit of the garrison was formed by the imperial horse guard, the *equites singulares,* who had been reformed by Trajan at the beginning of the second century. They constituted the emperor's horse guard and numbered 1,000 troopers. There were also two other sizeable armed units in the city, the *vigiles* who served as a nighttime police force and as fire fighters. They were probably 7,000 strong, and the urban cohorts, which likely numbered 1,500 men, who like the Praetorians were heavily armed infantry. They stood under the direct control of the emperor, so their situation on the emperor's death is unclear.[7] The importance of these troops is clear. They were the key factor for gaining control of power. A figure with a military reputation offered the most likely candidate to successfully surmount the crisis and become emperor.

Laetus and Eclectus approached Pertinax, a sensible choice given his military experience and his apparent acceptability to the Senate. At this point the sources diverge on Pertinax's relation to the plotters. The *Historia Augusta* claims that he was a part of the conspiracy from the beginning and that the approach to him was already part of the plan.[8] Dio and Herodian claim the opposite, that Pertinax was taken by surprise and had no part in the assassination. Dio, who had a high opinion of Pertinax, claims that he was taken unawares and would not give way to the requests of Laetus and Eclectus until he had sent a trusted friend to view Commodus's body.[9] Herodian is a little less positive. Despite his praise for Pertinax, he points out the problems raised by Pertinax's father's status as a freedman and the probable reaction of aristocrats in the Senate.[10] Herodian claims he was not reassured about Commodus's death until the conspirators showed him a tablet in Commodus's hand with their own names listed among those who were to be murdered.[11]

The choice between the two versions of Pertinax's role is not easy and various scholars have supported one version or the other. Several points can be made in favour of Pertinax having had advance notice of the plot and what his role was to be. First, it would seem to have been extremely dangerous for the conspirators to move without some advance planning, especially as the Pretorians were strong supporters of the dead emperor and would be looking for a way to strike back at his assassins.[12] Pertinax would have been attractive, not only because he had previous military experience, but as governor in Britain had recently put down a serious mutiny which had almost cost him his life.[13] In addition, as urban prefect he probably controlled the urban cohorts.

A further argument has been made that certain provincial appointments imply the existence of a wider conspiracy and advance planning. There was the appointment of Septimius Severus, a junior consular to the important province of Pannonia Superior with its garrison of three legions. What is especially striking is the fact that an important province with a strong garrison and close to Italy was given to a man with no military experience. Decimus Clodius Albinus was assigned to Britain, another province with a large legionary force, also of three legions. Finally, there was the appointment of Septimius Severus's brother Publius Septimius Geta to the province of Moesia Inferior also with three legions. All three of these men came from Africa and they held provinces with stronger military forces than was the norm for consular governors. Consular provinces normally had two legions. Given Laetus' control of military appointments, he was probably responsible for the appointment of these men to their posts, because of their shared African background.

In my view, the argument against a carefully worked out plot involving Pertinax seems more convincing. There is no other evidence for this supposed African tie in operation and an examination of Septimius Severus's later appointments shows no evidence for it.[14] If these appointments by Laetus were designed to provide military support for his coup, why would he put the man with the least military experience, Septimius Severus, closest to Italy?[15] It is more likely that no plot existed when Septimius Severus was appointed, and as evidenced in many other appointments under Commodus, it was the lack of a potential military threat from the provincial governor that was the most important criterion in many appointments. Septimius Severus was chosen because he seemed to offer no threat because of his lack of military experience.

Further, it seems strange that Pertinax asked to view the body (in Dio's account) if he had already been a member of the plot. Laetus' later lukewarm support for Pertinax when he was under threat from the Praetorians seems to indicate that there was no prior arrangement between them. With no prior agreement between them, it makes Pertinax's concern to view the body understandable. Herodian's account also supports Pertinax's innocence. His fear that he might be being tricked was not an unrealistic fear. According to Dio, the people of Rome and some of the provincial governors were also suspicious and were afraid that the story had been put about to test their loyalty to Commodus.[16] If there had been an elaborate plan including

Laetus, his behaviour is hard to explain. He seems to have done nothing to prepare the guard, who were attached to the emperor, for the murder and was more than willing to abandon the new emperor when the guard turned murderous.[17]

The choice of Pertinax is also not as straightforward as it might seem. Despite Dio's praise for him he was not necessarily an obvious choice. His career had suffered a setback under Perennis, but with the prefect's death and the ascendancy of Cleander he had again been entrusted with important posts. As mentioned earlier, in 185 he was made governor of Britain where he served until 187. His harsh discipline brought about a mutiny which almost resulted in his death. He succeeded in restoring order, but then asked to be relieved of his post because of the hatred the troops felt for him.[18] On his return to Rome after a long interval, he went as proconsul to Africa in 188 to put down disturbances there. Upon his return he was appointed prefect of the city in 189. Finally, in 191 he was given the important honour of a second consulship opening 192 as a colleague of the emperor.

In addition, his relationship with the Senate was complicated by his low birth and his having attacked some of Marcus Aurelius's former advisors. Two of them, Antistius Burrus and Arrius Antoninus, were charged with conspiring to rule, probably in 189.[19] These men had been opponents of Cleander who had revived Pertinax's career.[20]

It seems more likely that the assassination was at first the reaction of the three conspirators to Commodus's increasingly bizarre actions which turned in the end to fear for their personal safety, and that they reacted spontaneously to what they perceived to be an immediate threat. Pertinax was an obvious, although flawed, choice. He was 67 in 193 and, given his low status, unlikely to be able to establish a dynasty. Therefore he might, if necessary, act as a place holder until other arrangements could been made. This echoes the appointment of the senator Cocceius Marcus Nerva after the assassination of Domitian in 96. He too was a senatorial choice and, like Pertinax, old.[21] Interestingly, he too had trouble with the praetorians. The other problem was his reputation with the troops as a harsh disciplinarian. He would represent a sharp and unwelcome contrast with his predecessor. At this point Laetus and Eclectus had no obvious alternative.

After persuading Pertinax that Commodus was dead, Laetus and Eclectus, along with a group of followers, accompanied him to the Praetorian camp in the early hours of the morning of 1 January. They were uncertain of what their reception would be. Pertinax addressed the troops claiming that power had been thrust upon him by Laetus and Eclectus. He told the troops that

Commodus had died a natural death brought on by overeating. The lie was prompted by the known partiality of the troops for the dead Commodus. The attachment to Commodus remained very strong. After Pertinax's death the new emperor chosen by the guards, Didius Julianus, had to give written promises that he would restore Commodus's good name. Their allegiance was made even clearer when they accompanied the new emperor to the Senate House acclaiming him as Commodus.[22]

Enthusiasm was raised when Pertinax offered them a donative or cash gift of 12,000 sesterces per man, the equivalent of three-years' pay.[23] He then spoke to them stressing that he intended to make changes. He also issued a watchword: 'Let us now be soldiers'. The soldiers took the statement and the watchword as pointing to the abolition of the privileges they now enjoyed.[24] The *Historia Augusta* adds the detail that the troops were hardly enthusiastic. At first only a few acclaimed him as emperor, although later the rest followed.[25] Herodian seems to have embellished the people's enthusiasm for Pertinax. He portrays them as rushing to the Guard's camp to demand that they submit to Pertinax.[26] Dio also claims that there was substantial support among the people for Pertinax's accession.[27]

Pertinax's next step was to seek formal approval from the Senate. A special meeting was called, as it was still dark when he arrived at the Senate House. According to Dio who was present, Pertinax pleaded age and ill-health and asked to be excused from his new office. This seems to have been the standard rhetoric used on such occasions. The Senate voted its approval, which after the action of the guard, was a formality.[28] After the investiture, the Senate launched into a series of ritual denunciations of the dead emperor.[29] So with the approval of the guard, which was the only approval that really mattered, and that of the Senate, Pertinax became emperor on 1 January 193.

Pertinax made a great show of deference to the Senate. He received all of the customary titles and in addition that of *princeps senatus* (leading man of the Senate) which went back over the centuries to the days of the Republic. He was then immediately given the title of 'Father of his Country' which was unprecedented. Previously the title was assumed sometime after accession. Its immediate bestowal was probably a compliment to his age. He sat eminent senators on his imperial bench in the Senate. In general he acted in an accessible and affable manner. There no reason to doubt that he did so because he desired to conduct a government in which the Senate would play a larger role and by doing so would strengthen his ties to the aristocracy at a time when his power was not yet fully secure.[30] After the formalities had been concluded, he went to the Capitoline Hill to pay his respects and make his vows to the chief god of the state, Jupiter Optimus Maximus (Best and Greatest).

Pertinax faced a very unstable and threatening situation. On 2 January, the statues of Commodus were overthrown.[31] The reaction among the troops was not encouraging; some of them groaned aloud.[32] A more serious expression of discontent came on the next day, 3 January, which was the date when all of the empire's soldiers renewed their personal oath to the emperor. An attempt was made by some of the praetorians to replace Pertinax. They dragged a senator, Triarius Maternus, into camp to replace Pertinax. He was an unwilling candidate and fled. He went to Pertinax who was then in the palace to explain that the action had been taken against his will and was then allowed to leave Rome in safety.[33]

The key to Pertinax's problems was the attitude of the Guard and the other troops in the city. That problem was complicated by the empty state of the treasury and the accession donative he had promised the soldiers. Pertinax resorted to the sale of the contents of Commodus's palace including concubines and other palace staff. It was an expedient that Marcus Aurelius had used when his treasury was drained by the costs of war.[34] The sale brought enough for him to give the promised donative to the Praetorians and to distribute an accession gift of 400 denarii per man to the populace.

He also accepted the title of Caesar for his son, which marked him out to be his father's successor. But he qualified the grant by stating that his son would be given the title if he 'earned it'. He refused the title of Augusta or empress for his wife. Whatever senatorial support he gained by these actions, he forfeited by ruling that those who had been given praetorian rank but had not served as praetor would rank below those who had actually served. Many of the latter would have been associated with the old regime, but it was foolish to create gratuitous enmity simply on formal grounds.[35]

As well as paying off these huge debts, he restored normal financial functions, allowing the government to meet its normal expenses.[36] Herodian lists a series of financial measures he took whose results were not beneficial for long and earned him further unpopularity.[37]

Pertinax had not mollified those who wanted him gone. The palace attendants, like the soldiers, missed the freedom and lifestyle that Commodus had allowed them and were unhappy with Pertinax's careful stewardship of public money. In addition, and probably more importantly, there was still a strong level of hostility against him among the Praetorians.[38] Dio claims that it was only the lack of weapons that restrained the palace staff from moving against the emperor. The praetorians had both the equipment and the will to act. His stinginess and his enforcement of strict discipline finally proved too much.

According to Dio, a conspiracy by Laetus and the Guard tried to replace Pertinax with one of the consuls of the year, Sosius Falco.[39] He was chosen, according to Dio, for his wealth and family connections. He is also quoted in the *Historia Augusta* as making an insulting remark to Pertinax.[40] The plot was set in motion while Pertinax was on the coast at Ostia inspecting the grain supply of the city. At the news, he hurried back and with his return the plot fell apart. Pertinax ostentatiously spared Falco, who wisely went into retirement.

The plot's failure changed nothing. Laetus and his men remained disaffected and the prefect continued to plot. He seems to have been disappointed in his choice for emperor. His behaviour indicates that he was never strongly committed to Pertinax and the subsequent behaviour of Eclectus seems to indicate that it was he who persuaded Laetus to accept Pertinax.[41] This would further support the idea that the plot against Commodus was a sudden decision taken by conspirators caught in a threatening situation. The aspects of Pertinax's behaviour that caused the difficulties were well-known and it could have easily been foreseen that at the least some of them would cause trouble with the Guard. The strict discipline and the stinginess of the emperor must have irked Laetus as well as his men. As a result, it must have been difficult to control them and substituting a more compliant emperor would have seemed attractive both to the prefect and to his men.

The Falco incident, according to Dio, allowed Laetus to further inflame the guard against the emperor. According to Dio, who is hostile to Laetus, he killed a number of soldiers and so drove the others to mutiny. Around two hundred of them advanced on the palace with their swords at the ready.[42] The attendants and guards, overwhelmed by the show of force, abandoned their posts and the emperor. Dio thinks he could have saved himself with the forces he had, or he could have escaped harm. Instead of doing either, he advanced on the mutineers to overawe them with his appearance and to try to convince them to stop their threatening behaviour. His surprise appearance initially quieted the soldiers. Suddenly, one of the soldiers, spurred on by anger and a grievance. attacked and wounded him. The action spurred the others on and a general attack on the aged emperor ensued. His only defender was his chamberlain Eclectus, who died with the emperor. The dead emperor's head was cut off and fixed to a spear.[43]

The *Historia Augusta* offers a slightly different version of his death. It adds that the palace attendants supposedly urged the soldiers on. It claims that the initial assailant was a Tausius, a Tungrian from northeastern Gaul, who threw a spear at Pertinax, who veiled his head in preparation for death and then died under a hail of blows from the soldiers.[44] Dio also notes the bravery of Eclectus in defence of his emperor and adds that other chamberlains fought for their master and likewise perished.[45] It claims that his death was greatly regretted by the people as Pertinax had issued orders to control the soldiers' conduct in the city. They had to stop insulting behaviour towards the populace, were forbidden to assault those they encountered and were forbidden to seize civilian property.[46]

Pertinax died on 28 March 193 after a reign of eighty-seven days at the age of 66.[47] The *Historia Augusta* offers a less appealing portrait of Pertinax stressing his stinginess and greed.[48] Dio offers a critical assessment of the reign. Despite his experience and his good character, Pertinax failed because he tried to effect change too quickly and not in the most effective manner.[49] These strictures are to some extent true, but the real failure of the emperor was his inability to win over the praetorians and the other troops in the city.

He had started with a significant disadvantage. Whatever the defects of Commodus as a ruler, he was young and engaged in activities, such as fighting in the arena, which were popular among the troops, and he had allowed them unrestrained license. Further, he was the son of a popular father and an heir to a dynasty that had more or less lasted for the past century. Pertinax's age must also have told against him. More importantly, his reputation as a strict disciplinarian and his curtailment of the troops' privileges, justified or not, must have heightened their enmity to him. Their disaffection may have been further increased by his ostentatious deference to the Senate. As Dio points out, his reforms, although apparently well-meaning, alienated much support. His crucial failure was his assumption that he could command the Guard's allegiance without taking the steps necessary to win it. He also failed to recognize the importance of Laetus, who seems to have retained control over the Guard. It may be that they personally did not like Pertinax.[50] Once he lost Laetus' support, Pertinax lost the troops and with that loss there was probably no possibility that he could survive. His rise and fall gave further evidence that it was the military and not the Senate who chose emperors.

The removal of Pertinax had created a serious problem: there was no suitable replacement immediately available. This presented Laetus and his allies with a dangerous quandary.

Before his murder, Pertinax had sent his father-in-law Tiberius Flavius Sulpicianus, whom he had appointed city prefect after he had vacated the office to become emperor, to the praetorian camp to try to calm the soldiers and re-establish order. The absence of any immediate obstacle persuaded Sulpicianus, who was inside the camp, to attempt to persuade the troops to accept himself as their new emperor. While this was going on, Marcus Didius Severus Julianus, a senior consular, was approached by two tribunes who according to the *Historia Augusta* almost dragged him to the Guards' camp.[51] The reluctance to compete for the empire implied in this account is unlikely. There is no hint that Julianus showed any hesitation or doubt in his subsequent actions. The two men then competed against each other for the Praetorians' favour. Eventually the bidding reached 20,000 sesterces per man; however Julianus clinched the nomination by offering 5,000 more. 25,000 sesterces per man was a huge amount: it represented the equivalent of five years' pay. Pertinax had promised the Guard the large donative given by Marcus Aurelius and in the end failed to fully deliver it.[52] The sum worked out at 20,000 sesterces per man. Julianus's offer was the highest on record and the *Historia Augusta* claims that he later added a further 5,000 sesterces to bring the grand total to 30,000 sesterces.[53] Dio compares the competitive bids to an auction and notes how shameless it was that the empire was to be sold to the highest bidder.[54] But in fact donatives given to the Guards at the time of accession date back to Claudius in 41 and had become the norm by this time. What was new was the idea of competing donatives.

Julianus prevailed over Sulpicianus for two reasons. Firstly, Sulpicianus could not match his bid and secondly, and perhaps as important, he was the father-in-law of the man the Guard had done away with and therefore a potential danger to them.[55] Despite his failure to gain the throne, Sulpicianus seems to have survived Julianus and to have been put to death in 197 by Severus for his support of Clodius Albinus, one of Severus's opponents during the civil war.

Of all the men who contended for the throne in 193, Julianus had the most impressive background. His father came from Milan and his mother from Hadrumentum in Africa. He was brought up in the household of Domitia Lucilla, mother of Marcus Aurelius, and Marcus had helped him at various stages of his senatorial career.[56] After his praetorship he served as a legate in several provinces. He gained military experience in Gaul and the Balkans. He held the consulship as colleague of Pertinax in 175. He was forced to retire to his estates early in the reign of Commodus but then was brought back. He may have been hindered in his career by Perennis but allowed back by Cleander as Severus and Pertinax were. He had also followed Pertinax in the prestigious position of the proconsul of Africa.

Dio paints Julianus as greedy and a glutton. The historian claims that while he was acting as an advocate in the courts he had proven Julianus guilty of various offences and had prosecuted Julianus for some unknown offences. He also seems to have automatically assumed that Julianus was implicated in Pertinax's death and feared a reprisal for the favours he had received from the dead emperor.[57]

The negative picture of Julianus also dominates the accounts of the *Historia Augusta* and Herodian.[58] The *Historia Augusta* may be echoing Marius Maximus, like Dio a contemporary of the incidents, but little is certain. Herodian may also have been influenced by Maximus, but his description of these happenings has so many implausible elements that his account may depend upon later elaboration of these events. It is probably impossible to reach an objective assessment of Julianus or of his reign. Julianus was subject to a great deal of negative propaganda by Severus and his supporters. He became the foil of Pertinax, the 'good emperor'.

The recognition by the Guard entailed support for the rehabilitation of Commodus, that is, restoring his inscriptions and statues. Julianus had supposedly tried to influence the soldiers by promising them that he would do so and Dio reports that as he went from the Praetorian camp to the Senate building in the evening he was accompanied by a larger than normal group of Praetorians who in extolling him called him Commodus. It was no accident that he then executed Marcia and Laetus as Commodus's assassins.[59] His dependence on the Guard was evident in his appointment of two new praetorian prefects, Flavius Genialis and Tullius Crispinus, on the recommendation of the soldiers.

In the presence of many of the Guard who must have been seen as an implied threat, Julianus's imperial status was confirmed by the usual decrees of the Senate. He, as Pertinax had done, appointed a relative, Cornelius Repentinus, his son-in-law, as city prefect to replace Sulpicianus. His wife and daughter were voted the titles of Augusta.

From the Senate House he proceeded to the palace. At this point in his narrative Dio has an anecdote. He claims that Julianus, finding a dinner prepared for Pertinax, made fun of it and sent out for expensive food with which he gorged himself while gambling.[60] The *Historia Augusta* has a similar anecdote, that as an insult to Pertinax's simple eating habits he held an extravagant banquet. The author reports this story was generally agreed to be false, claiming that Julianus was frugal and restrained in his eating habits.[61]

The Senate was for the moment cowed, but the people were unrestrained in expressing their opposition to the new emperor. The crowds heaped abuse upon him and tried to interfere with a sacrifice that he was performing before he entered the Senate House. Julianus tried to placate the crowd, even offering a cash distribution. His attempt failed and fighting broke out between the Guard and the crowd, in which some were wounded and killed. Further infuriated, the throng seized arms, rushed into the Circus Maximus and stayed there overnight and through the next day. The Circus was the most important place where the masses of people could express their opinions to the emperor. It had played a role in the fall of Cleander a few years before. It was the one place where the people could directly confront the emperor and yet remain anonymous. The *Historia Augusta* insists he restored measures of Commodus to quiet the people, but we are not told what these were.[62] The *Historia Augusta* may have mistaken measures in favour of the soldiers for those designed to calm the populace. Dio is studiously vague. Given the antipathy between the Guard and the crowd it seems unlikely that resuscitating Commodus's measures would have found favour with the people. Many of these were ones that Pertinax had abolished and been applauded by the people for doing away with them.

The people charged Julianus with the crime of parricide, that is of having murdered Pertinax and calling him a usurper. The charge has no basis in fact. It is hard to escape the conclusion that the Praetorians acted on their own, out of resentment and anger at the way Pertinax was behaving. It may be that seeing Julianus surrounded by the Guard, being hailed as Commodus, and his action to restore the measures of Commodus, convinced the people that he was part of a plot to remove Pertinax. More surprising is the report of Dio that the populace kept calling on Pescennius Niger the governor of Syria to rescue them.[63] It is hard to understand the reason for the appeal to Niger without assuming some sort of agitation by either Niger's own agents or supporters, although we hear nothing about them. It is odd that Severus was not mentioned by the crowd as well, but it may well be that his career so far had not garnered enough interest to attract the crowd's attention.[64]

Julianus's actions as emperor are not described in any detail. The best that can be said is that he attempted to conciliate his opponents and failed. As Dio notes: 'Julianus managed affairs in a servile fashion, paying court to the senate as well as to all the men of any influence. He would sometimes make promises, sometimes bestow favours, and he laughed and jested with anybody and everybody.'[65] As was the case with Pertinax, he had financial problems because of the poor state of Rome's finances.[66]

The death of Pertinax and the succession of Julianus set the stage for a re-enactment of the events of 68 after Nero's suicide in June. The historian Cornelius Tacitus' comment that the secret was revealed that an emperor could be made elsewhere than Rome was once again proved true.[67] The strength of the army lay in the provinces and the Praetorians had not fought in the field for over thirty years.

There was no formal procedure to regulate the succession or any individual in the capital who could command enough support to secure the throne. The way was now open for ambitious provincial governors to act on their own behalf. Three governors emerged as contenders: Septimius Severus in Pannonia Superior, Pescennius Niger in Syria and Clodius Albinus in Britain. They all controlled provinces with substantial legionary garrisons. In Pannonia Superior, the province closest to Rome, Lucius Septimius Severus commanded a force of three legions and auxiliary formations. He could also count on his brother Septimius Geta who governed the nearby province of Lower Moesia with a force of two legions and further auxiliary units.[68] He must have entered into communications with other governors of the northern provinces soon after he heard of the death of Pertinax, probably by 1 April. There is no record of any of the governors putting up resistance to his plans to march on Rome and seize the throne. The five legions under the command of Severus and his brother probably went some way to inhibit competition. At the same time, he must have begun to work on his men to win them over. Finally, on 9 April at Carnuntum, probably by prearrangement, Severus was saluted as imperator (emperor) by his troops.[69] We know from numismatic evidence that the legions in Upper Pannonia, Upper and Lower Moesia, in Dacia, Noricum and Raetia and Upper and Lower Germany went over to him. Most came over quickly, but several governors hesitated, perhaps waiting to see which way things would turn out.[70] April 9 remained the anniversary date of Severus's accession to power, despite a later formal vote by the Senate, probably on 1 June.[71] The support of all of these legions and the acquiescence of their commanders in his seizure of power is not easy to explain, especially in the light of his limited military experience. Whatever his lack of military expertise, it is clear that he was an extremely skilled politician and an excellent administrator. He must have heard of the difficulties of both Pertinax and Julianus at Rome and decided that Julianus's weakness offered him a valuable opportunity to seize power, especially given the weakness of Julianus's military support. His most difficult task was convincing his officers to follow him. However, his skill in dangling future appointments yielding power and profit must brought them over.[72]

He marshalled his forces, mostly Danubian troops, and began to deal with possible threats before beginning his march. It seems that at this point he was most concerned by Decimus Clodius Albinus, the governor of Britain.[73] Albinus's family, like that of Severus, came from Africa, in his case from Hadrumentum (modern Sousse) in eastern Tunisia. It was a fair-sized city, grown prosperous because of the fertility of its fields and whose grain found its way to the capital.[74] He is also said to have come from an aristocratic family of Italian origin. Probably becoming consul in the mid-180s, he had a successful military career. He campaigned successfully in Dacia and on the Rhine.[75] By 191/2 he was governor of Britain with a formidable force of three legions and numerous auxiliary units. His appointment seems synchronized with that of Severus and Niger and may all be due to Laetus. In parallel with Severus, the appointments of Albinus and Niger were made to make sure that their provinces with their large garrisons were in the hands of men Laetus thought would not be a threat.

Severus seems to have worried that Albinus would also try to seize power in Rome. His forces could form a threat to Severus's right flank as he turned south to march on the city. He decided to try to buy him off by offering him the position of Caesar which signalled that the recipient would in due course follow the current emperor on the throne. It is true that in 193 Severus had children. The elder son Bassianus was born on 4 April 188 and the younger Geta on 7 March 189. The crucial act of adoption of Albinus by Severus was at first postponed and then never carried out. The adoption would have made Albinus Severus direct successor. However, at least for the time being, Albinus's agreement to the arrangement meant Severus's northern flank was secure.

At the same time Severus produced propaganda to justify his cause. He emphasized his claim to legitimacy by stressing his connection to Pertinax and posing as his avenger. He added the dead emperor's name to his own, styling himself Imperator Caesar Lucius Septimius Severus Pertinax Augustus after assuming the office of emperor.[76] After his successful march on Rome he held a funeral for the dead emperor, had him deified and punished the Praetorian Guard for its killing of Pertinax.[77]

A third candidate emerged, Gaius Pescennius Niger, the governor of Syria with its three legions and twenty auxiliary infantry cohorts and cavalry *alae*, in all about 30,000 troops. In addition, he assembled an army of ten legions by drawing on the garrisons of Thrace, Cappadocia, Judaea Arabia and Egypt. All of these provinces also included auxiliary cavalry and infantry units. Such units could be of crucial importance. By the mid-second century, there is evidence for 257 units of infantry and cavalry totalling 227,000 men, almost 70,000 more than then filled the legions. In addition to his military strength Niger's possession of Egypt was a potential threat to Rome's grain supply.

Of Italian background, Niger began his career as an equestrian official and saw extensive military service. In the early 180s he served in Dacia and in Gaul.[78] He became consul probably in 190 or 191. Dio claims that he was appointed to Syria because he was a nonentity who presented no threat.[79] Like Severus's appointment, his appointment would not be a threat to the emperor.[80] Dio paints a picture of a mediocre man neither deserving praise nor blame.[81] The *Historia Augusta*'s portrait is more positive, stressing his enforcement of military discipline and his personal restraint.[82] Herodian's portrait is also more favourable than Dio's. His comments on Niger's character are not as explicit as Dio's and often presented indirectly. He notes his reputation for fairness and military skill.[83] Julianus stressed his own reputation for fairness by later adopting Iustus (the just man) as part of his name.[84]

Soon after Julianus took the throne, the crowds in Rome began to call on Niger to save them from him. Niger was also popular with the Senate. The combined popularity made him a serious threat to Julianus.[85] It is not hard to surmise that Niger's partisans in Rome had been working on the crowds to support him. It was probably the news of Septimius Severus's proclamation that pushed Niger to take the final step and have his troops salute him as emperor. This was probably towards the end of April.[86] In response Julianus dispatched assassins to do away with Niger as he was later to do against Severus. Neither attempt was successful.[87]

By late April or early May, there were these two rivals, Severus and Niger, to replace Julianus. From the start he had little hope of survival. Of the three politically important groups in Rome he was strongly rejected by two, the people and the Senate. The third, the military including the Praetorian Guard and other troops stationed in the city, appears to have been mostly indifferent. Their loyalty depended on the money that Julianus could provide and the state of the treasury limited his ability to provide it. Perhaps more threatening was the fact that even if all the troops in the city supported him, they could not prevail against the might of the provincial armies, especially that of Severus which was rapidly approaching Rome.

Julianus was quickly informed of Severus's proclamation and as a first step he had the Senate declare him a public enemy.[88] He also sent a deputation of senior legates of consular rank to try to win the soldiers away from their allegiance to Severus.[89] Among them was Vespronius Candidus, a former governor of Dacia, who must have been known to the troops stationed along the Danube. A more practical step was the assignment of a former centurion in the imperial secret service to assassinate Severus. Instead of doing so, he went over to Severus's side and later found employment with him.[90] The senatorial deputation also failed. Bribes persuaded the envoys to join Severus and address the soldiers in his favour.[91]

The failure of his assassination attempt and also of the senatorial legation forced Julianus to turn to military preparations to thwart Severus. His main force consisted of the Praetorians who probably numbered approximately 4,500 men, plus the urban cohorts who numbered 1,500 men and several other units. In total they numbered perhaps 11–12,000 men, most with little or no battle experience, while Severus was on the march with his own three legions and probably others and so could muster at least 15–20,000 men who had fighting experience. He decided to try to confront Severus outside the city. He ordered the Praetorians to construct a fortification outside the city and fight Severus there. Dio paints a picture of colossal ineptitude in Julianus's preparations. He describes a city turned into an encampment, filled with troops drilling and training. He also began training elephants for war. Dio claims all of these measures were in vain. The Praetorians, softened by luxurious living, were of little worth and the elephants were less than useless.[92] He now executed Laetus and Marcia for their involvement in the assassination of Commodus and had Narcissus torn to prices by ferocious animals.[93] No doubt this was a way to show the soldiers his commitment to the memory of Marcus Aurelius's son. In his further panic, he asked the senate to authorize another deputation, this time including the Vestal Virgins and priests as well as senators, but his weakening authority and the threatening approach of Severus led to a refusal.

He was advised to block the passes into northern Italy from the Julian Alps, but he could not do so fast enough, given the speed of Severus's march. He also sent Tullius Crispinus, one of the praetorian prefects, north to try to stop Severus. But once Severus was through the passes, there was little he could do. Crispinus managed to gain control of the fleet stationed at Ravenna, but his resistance was futile. Severus moved south through Emona

(Ljubljana) and then Aquileia rendering Crispinus' further attempt to stop the enemy's advance pointless. Severus easily took Ravenna. Crispinus fled and resistance in northern Italy collapsed. In addition to these measures other minor operations are mentioned in the sources, but none of them had any impact on the course of events.[94]

With Severus close to the city, in desperation Julianus passed a decree making Severus his joint ruler. He also began to stress a relationship to Severus by adding Severus, one of the names of his grandfather and great grandfather, to his official name.[95] He then appointed a new guard prefect who had already been given the post by Severus, presumably to try to placate his co-emperor, and sent Crispinus to announce to Severus his new appointment as co-emperor.[96] Severus explicitly and insultingly rejected the proposal and Crispinus was executed for his pains. To facilitate his entry in the city, Severus dispatched parties of soldiers to infiltrate it, reconnoitre and post up placards with pro-Severan propaganda. He also began to contact senators whom he knew favoured his side. Among the most important of his partisans was Lucius Fabius Cilo who was to play an important role during the reign of Severus and that of his son Caracalla. With Severus he fought against Niger in the east, then went on to become the tutor of Caracalla, and eventually held the office of city prefect before his murder by his former pupil during Caracalla's reign.

By this time most senators were ready to abandon Julianus. The Senate had been alienated from him from the beginning of his reign and the chances of his prevailing against Severus's forces were nil.

In the absence of more tangible alternatives Julianus turned to magic to avert his impending fate. Magicians sacrificed certain animals according to non-Roman rites, chanted and sang sacrilegious songs before a mirror. After that, specially selected boys had bandages removed from their eyes so they could see the future.[97] Dio adds that the boys were sacrificed, but this may be a reflection of his hatred for Julianus.[98] The practice of magic rites was dangerous when they concerned the emperor's fate.[99]

In 205 during Severus's reign a proconsul of Asia named Apronianus was charged with treason. The charge was that his nurse had dreamed that Apronianus would become emperor and then the proconsul had used magic rites to make sure this happened. Apronianus was condemned *in absentia*, while still serving at his post. The proceedings were, as usual at this level, conducted in the Senate. Dio describes the frightening procedure in the Senate at which he was present, which resulted in the death of another senator who was said to have overheard the dream and not reported it.

Severus seems to have paid particular attention to dreams and also to astrological predictions and oracular reposes. It was a royal horoscope that supposedly led Severus to choose Julia Domna as his second wife.[100] It will be remembered that it was Dio's account of the dreams and portents that heralded Severus's reign that first introduced him to Severus and after its favourable reception to Dio's historical work.[101] The use of magic and faith in dreams and the use of horoscopes were a common phenomenon that could have important effects in personal and political life.

Finally the last support of Julianus's throne collapsed. Encouraged by letters of Severus, the Praetorians decided to throw in their lot with him. Severus informed them that they would come to no harm if they arrested the killers of Pertinax and turned them over to him and did nothing to oppose him. That is exactly what they did.[102] They informed one of the consuls, Silius Messalla, of what they had done. Messalla assembled the Senate and it pronounced the sentence of death on Julianus and also named Severus as emperor. Dio claims Julianus was found sitting in the palace at his wit's end. There the soldiers killed him. Dio claims his last words were 'What evil have I done? Whom have I killed?' The *Historia Augusta* presents a slightly different version which has Julianus begging Severus for his life.[103]

Dio assigns him a reign of sixty-six days, the *Historia Augusta* gives him a reign of two months and five days. Dio's figure is usually preferred. On that calculation Julianus was killed on 1 June 193.[104] The reign of his successor would give particular poignancy to Julianus's claim of having executed no one. His successor had no such scruples.

Chapter 4

The Civil Wars: Act I

A rriving at Rome in early June, Severus carried out two measures before entering the city. First, he executed the murderers of Pertinax. It was a symbolic gesture. From the first he had linked himself to Pertinax. At the time of his proclamation he added the dead emperor's name to his own to become Lucius Septimius Severus Pertinax Augustus. It appears on his early coinage and after his formal assumption of power Pertinax became part of his official name. It must have been a potent symbol for the troops and governors he courted before he openly proclaimed his revolt. The effects are hard to assess. Pertinax's reputation with the troops was not uniformly positive. His problems as governor in Britain must have been known and given at least some of the soldiers pause. It may be that the main value of Pertinax with the troops was to threaten the position of the Praetorians and, given Severus's later actions, it may have formed part of a promise that the Praetorians would be punished and, more importantly, replaced.[1]

The Praetorians were only one of the units on guard in the capital, however they were the most important because of their numbers. They originated in the bodyguards of military commanders during the Republic and like the rest of the army they were institutionalized and professionalized under the first emperor, Augustus. At first they were organized in nine cohorts. Their initial size has been a subject of dispute. Some scholars have supported a cohort size of 500 and others of 1,000. The evidence seems to point to a unit size of 500 men.[2] The number of cohorts fluctuated over various reigns. Finally the number of cohorts was fixed at ten by the Emperor Domitian at the end of the first century. It remained at that number until the guard was disbanded by Constantine in 312.

The recruiting grounds of the Guard differed from those of the legions. Initially areas close to Rome such as Etruria, Umbria, Latium Vetus and the Latin colonies were used. Gradually the area from which the guard was drawn widened to include the more romanized and urbanized western provinces such as Gallia Narbonensis, Noricum, Spain and Macedonia. Despite the wider area for recruitment, Italians remained the dominant group down to the end of the second century. They were paid at a substantially higher rate than the legions and received a bonus over one and a half times larger than that of the legionaries on discharge. In addition, the cash donatives or gifts that were distributed to the troops on various occasions were always higher for Praetorians. Their service in the metropolis was far easier than that of the legions strung along the imperial frontiers. Dio, commenting on Julianus's preparations to face Severus, notes how the Guard was useless as a fighting force, undone by their easy living in Rome.[3] From 2 BC they were commanded by the two praetorian prefects who had direct access to the emperor and could on occasions, as under Commodus, become the political masters of the state.

The Pretorian Guard and their commanders had acted as an important political force almost from their foundation. Their proximity to the emperor and the fact that they formed the main strength of the garrison of Rome gave them a political importance out of proportion to their numbers. By the middle of the of the first century, they were instrumental in placing the Emperor Claudius on the throne. They were again important at the outbreak of the civil war of 68–70. Their significance was made clear by one of the unsuccessful contenders for the throne in 69, Vitellius, who disbanded them and replaced them by a guard, now enlarged to sixteen cohorts, assembled from his own army.[4]

Severus summoned the Praetorians to assemble unarmed in a large open space outside the city. Once they had gathered, he made a speech harshly critical of their conduct. He then ordered his own troops to surround them and required them to hand over their weapons and equipment, disbanded them and exiled them from Rome. They were forced to live at least one hundred miles from the city on pain of death. He then formed a new Guard manned by his own troops.[5] Although now generally excluded from the Guard, Italians could serve in the other military units within the city. The change was not to everyone's liking, but his claim to be Pertinax's avenger had already made this move a foregone conclusion. In addition, their half-hearted support of Julianus only emphasized how untrustworthy they were. Given Severus's attitude, it is likely that as part of his inducements to the Danubian army to march to support his bid for the throne, Severus had held out service in a new Praetorian Guard. It was used in battle outside the city at Lugdunum in 197 and was severely handled by Albinus's British legions.

Besides his reconstitution of the Guard, the new emperor also enlarged other units stationed in Rome. Herodian exaggerates his enlargement of the garrison, claiming that he quadrupled the number of troops.[6] Their number had probably been increased from about 11,500 to 25,000.

After these actions Severus changed into civilian clothes and entered the city on foot, probably on 9 June. However, the entire army, both cavalry and infantry, followed him in full equipment. Dio describes an ecstatic populace eager to hear what the new emperor had to say, and a city festooned with festive decorations. The *Historia Augusta* offers a much more hostile portrayal of the entry with a populace trembling in fear and Severus's men stealing civilian property without hindrance. Herodian is in general agreement with the *Historia Augusta* in its stress on general fear and agitation at Severus's entrance.[7] As F. Millar points out, the highly positive tone of this description contrasts with the generally negative account of the early part of Severus's reign. He suggests it may have been taken from an earlier work written while Severus was still alive which must have been laudatory in tone.[8]

The crowd and decorations formed a backdrop to Septimius' ascent of the Capitoline Hill to sacrifice to Jupiter Optimus Maximus, the chief god of the Roman state. The new emperor now proceeded to the Senate House to address the assembled members. He spoke in a conciliatory tone, promising that during his reign no senators would be put to death. He requested the senate to combine with him for a joint decree which ordered that Julianus and anyone assisting him should be considered public enemies if they violated this decree.[9] He was following the precedent of over a hundred years standing. The promise not to execute senators had first been made by the Emperor Nerva a century before. It had been repeated by successive emperors and had become merely formulaic, sometimes implemented and sometimes ignored. As Dio indicates, Severus's promise in the end meant nothing. But at the time it must have helped solidify his senatorial support in the face of the impending conflict with Niger.

At his own request Severus was officially given the name of Pertinax by the Senate. He also added the dead emperor's name to oaths and prayers and established a shrine to him. The most dramatic step he took was to stage a lavish public funeral for the assassinated emperor. Julianus had done nothing to honour his predecessor.[10] Dio has left us an elaborate description of the funeral in which he himself took part. It included a eulogy delivered by the new emperor. There is no doubt that Dio's obituary of Pertinax is highly favourable on the whole. He ends his account with the observation that it was in this way that Pertinax was made immortal. By this he means that Pertinax was deified, as many of the previous emperors had been, and became part of the state cult. But it is hard not to suspect a certain irony in his closing statement. Given what was to come, it has ironic echoes.[11]

During his short stay in Rome the emperor gave a cash distribution to the populace, which was a customary measure for a new emperor, and gave games to celebrate his succession. Also of crucial importance was a distribution of a promised donative to his troops. The promise had caused some trouble, as Severus appears to have postponed its distribution. While Severus was in the Senate House, the soldiers began to clamour for it. It is probable it had been promised at Carnuntum. They demanded the huge sum of 2,500 denarii each, which was equivalent to approximately eight times the yearly pay of a legionary. According to Dio, Severus was able to bargain the troops down to 250 denarii.[12] How he managed to pay even this, given the low state of the treasury, is a mystery. It is probable that Severus took steps to recover at least some of the large sums that Julianus had lavished on the praetorians to pay the distribution.

He appointed a new city prefect, Domitius Dexter, and more importantly he sent troops to Africa to hold the province, which was a mainstay of the capital's food supply. All told, Severus's stay in Rome was short: according to the *Historia Augusta* it lasted only thirty days.[13]

Severus had already taken steps to confront Pescennius Niger. Once he had learned that Niger's agents were arriving in the city with proclamations to be posted and with letters addressed to the Senate, Severus took immediate steps to intercept them. He must have been especially worried after the demonstrations by the people in favour of Niger during Julianus's reign. He had taken the children of Niger as well those of Asellius Aemilianus, the proconsul of Asia and commander of Niger's forces, presumably to use them as hostages.

There was one other important matter still to be resolved that would have to await the elimination of Niger: how to deal with Clodius Albinus, the governor of Britain. As mentioned earlier, Albinus was offered the position of Caesar or heir by Severus and accepted it. It seems he did so in expectation that the extremely young children of Severus would not survive to contest his position.[14] But what was going to happen if Severus and his sons survived?

Severus and his army marched out of Rome probably in early July, heading northeast along the Via Flaminia to link up with the Via Egnatia, the main military road from Italy to Byzantium. He also assembled the imperial fleets, supplemented by naval contingents drawn from the Italian cities, and used them to transport troops straight to the Thracian coast.[15] The march was interrupted by a mutiny at Saxa Rubra about nine miles north of Rome on the Via Flaminia (modern Grottarossa). The mutiny was supposedly over the choice of a campsite.[16] The uprising was quickly resolved. Unfortunately we are not informed how Severus ended it. Birley suggests that a quick distribution of cash did the trick.[17] It is a reasonable suggestion, given how frequently cash was used to win military loyalty.

With the advance of the main army under Severus and his numerical superiority, Niger tried to use the same bargaining tactics that Julianus had tried, with the same result. He offered Severus half of the empire, which of course he refused. Declared a public enemy by a man who would brook no rivals, there was little that Niger could offer that would have had any effect. The best concession he could get from Septimius was an offer to spare his life if he surrendered unconditionally and then went into exile. One wonders how genuine an offer this was. It was in Severus's interest to completely eliminate Niger. Niger refused what might have looked like a death sentence.[18]

Niger's army under the command of Asellius Aemilianus defeated Fabius Cilo, who was attempting to seize Perinthus, in a bloody battle with heavy casualties somewhere to the west of Byzantium. This was the only victory that Niger's forces achieved in the course of the war. It may have been in part due to the generalship of Aemilianus, who had been governor of Syria under Commodus. This allowed Niger to occupy Byzantium. Meanwhile, Severus had dispatched another army drawn from the two legions of Moesia Inferior under the command of Marius Maximus, who was then serving as legate of I Italica, to lay siege to Byzantium.[19] Later Maximus was to profit handsomely from his early support of Severus. More importantly a large army drawn from the forces garrisoning the Pannonian provinces under the command of Claudius Candidus also moved against Aemilianus.[20] The combined strength of these two army groups forced Aemilianus to abandon his campaign in Thrace as well as his base at Byzantium and withdraw back over the Dardanelles to Asia. Tiberius Claudius Candidus, also of African background, began his career as an equestrian commander of a cohort of auxiliary infantry. This was a career path shared by many of the senators commanding military forces in the late second century. He later was in the quartermaster corps under Marcus Aurelius. During the reign of Commodus, he was raised to the rank of praetorian senator and served in various positions involving finance. He, like Severus, had not had an impressive military career until Severus's seizure of power.[21] Marius Maximus also came from an equestrian family, but his father had secured his admission to the Senate before the son had begun his career.

Severus did not join Maximus in the siege of Byzantium, which turned out to be a long and costly business, but went in pursuit of Niger. He must have used his fleet to ferry his troops over the Dardanelles. It is not clear whether the landing was opposed, although we hear of several early encounters. Aemilianus was defeated by Claudius Candidus and then captured and killed near Cyzicus. It was a serious setback for Niger's cause.[22] The defeat isolated Niger at his base at Byzantium and forced him to retreat back to Asia Minor. It also gave Severus an excellent landing point for his troops. Niger's army now moved east along the coast into Bithynia in northwestern Turkey.

The arrival of Severus's forces awakened local rivalries among the cities in Bithynia. This was an old problem in the Empire. During the civil war of 68–70 an intense rivalry broke out between Vienne and Lyons in Gaul in which each city supported opposing sides. For instance, in the opening struggle in which Vindex, the governor of Gallia Lugdunensis, rebelled against Nero, the citizens of Lyons remained loyal to Nero, while Vienne came out in support of Vindex. The final winner of the civil war, Vespasian punished Lyons for their loyalty to the dead emperor.[23] The reason for their being on opposite sides was the fierce rivalry between the two cities for primacy in the province. City rivalries were a chronic problem in Bithynia as well, where almost a century before Severus's war with Niger competitive spending had to be suppressed by the central government.[24] In the case of Bithynia, it was the longstanding rivalry between the two major cities of the province, Nicomedia and Nicaea (modern Iznik). Nicomedia lay just over the Bosporus so Severus would have encountered it first before he arrived at Nicaea which lay south of it. Nicomedia supported Severus while Nicaea supported Niger who had managed to return to Asia Minor to take up command of his troops there.

Niger took his stand in the rocky defiles between Nicaea and Cius, Nicaea's port, probably to the south of Lake Ascania where there was a road that joined the two cities. On the Severan side the commander was Claudius Candidus; Severus himself was not present. Dio offers the fullest description of the battle which probably occurred in the winter of 193, perhaps in December or January. The victory was known at Rome by the end of January. An immediate consequence of the battle, and an especially welcome one, was the defection of Egypt from Niger. Dio's account of the battle is of higher quality than the rest of his narrative of the war against

Niger and that may be the result of his local knowledge. It is likely that Severus's army was based at Cius as it would have offered a port for his fleet. Niger was based on Nicaea. Herodian describes the cities as virtual armed camps.[25] Dio's description is worth quoting:

> *Some fought in close order on the plain, others occupied the hills and hurled stones and javelins at their opponents from the higher ground, and still others got into boats and discharged their arrows at the enemy from the lake. At first the followers of Severus, commanded by Candidus, were victorious, for they had an advantage in fighting from the higher ground; but later, when Niger himself appeared, the pursuers became the pursued, and victory rested with Niger's men. Then Candidus seized hold of the standard-bearers and forced them to turn round facing the enemy, at the same time upbraiding the soldiers for their flight; at this his men were ashamed, turned back, and once more got the upper hand of their opponents. Indeed, they would have utterly destroyed them, had not the city been near, and had not a dark night come on.*[26]

It was Candidus who saved the day for Severus's forces. As Dio's account makes clear, the battle took a heavy toll of Niger's forces and he now had no choice but to retreat east back to his base at Antioch in Syria. Most of the army fled through the Cilician Gates (the modern Gülek Pass) near Iskenderun in Turkey, the only practical pass from upland Anatolia through the Taurus Mountains to lowland Cilicia and then into Syria. It formed part of the main commercial highway and was an invasion route from Turkey into Syria from antiquity to modern times. Alexander the Great used it to invade Syria and it was later used by the knights of the First Crusade for the same purpose. Niger fortified the pass and left behind troops to man them and block Severus's route into Syria while he continued on to Antioch to collect money and to raise troops.

Meanwhile, Severus seems to have remained at Perinthus occupied in administrative matters. Dio praises his attention to detail and his capacity for hard work.[27] He summoned a new supreme commander for the pursuit of Niger. This man was Cornelius Anullinus.

Anullinus came from southern Spain and was about a decade older than Severus. It may be that they met in Rome in the early 160s when Severus was beginning his senatorial career. Severus served under Anullinus when he was quaestor in Hispania Baetica in 170–172. Birley has suggested that his second year of service was at Anullinus' express request.[28] He was suffect consul under Marcus Aurelius, probably before 176. When he was called to lead Severus's forces against Niger he was serving as proconsul of Africa.[29] He seems to have been an early supporter of Severus and this probably played a role in his new appointment. We do not know enough to assess his military competence at this point: he had served as legate of Upper Germany and may have acquired military experience there. The fact that he was a senior senator with a successful career may have been a factor in his appointment. His selection was perhaps meant to stress Severus's readiness to cooperate with the Senate. Fabius Cilo was installed as the new governor of Bithynia. His defeat at Perinthus may have played a role in his loss of command. But there is no doubt that given the troubles among Bithynian cities, it may have been his administrative talents that really account for the appointment.

Anullinus's line of march into eastern Anatolia was not the most direct route to take in pursuit of Niger. Our knowledge of the situation in eastern Asia Minor is minimal and there may well have been disturbances that needed his attention.[30] He then marched to the Cilician Gates. Once on the Cappadocian side of the pass he prepared to force it. Despite being a main route, it was a difficult pass. It was only about 300 feet long, but its sides were formed by overhanging cliffs that rose to 500 feet and its maximum width was only fifty feet. At its highest elevation it rises to about 3,000 feet. To make matters worse, a stream flowed through it which further narrowed the road. At various points he had to widen the road or construct bridges of wooden planks. The pass ran from the ancient city of Tyana (modern Kemerhisar) on the Cappadocian side to the Cilician plain along the Mediterranean coast terminating near Tarsus, the most important city of lowland Cilicia.[31]

Forcing the pass was a difficult undertaking. Narrow winding tracks formed the approaches to Niger's fortifications, which were constructed on the heights of the pass as well as across it. They were well-sited with a high, overhanging mountain on one side and a cliff with creek channels that ran into the valley below on the other. This forced the Severans to attack uphill. Their opponents on top of their fortifications threw down stones and bombarded the attackers with other weapons.

According to Herodian, the attempt to force the pass did not go well. The attackers were exhausted by their struggle. Herodian claims that the repeated failures of their enemy led to Niger's forces relaxing their efforts in their belief that their position was secure.[32] At this point nature and chance intervened. One night, a heavy mixture of rain and snow fell.

Its waters formed a stream that came pouring down the hillside and swept the fortifications away. The troops manning the fortifications hurriedly retreated in fear that they would be surrounded and attacked both front and rear. According to Herodian, Severus's troops saw the flood as the work of divine providence and made their way through the pass, thinking that the gods favoured their enterprise.[33]

The forcing of the pass by Anullinus' army meant that the road to Niger's capital, Antioch in Syria, was now open. It left Niger no choice but to hasten his preparations to meet Severus's forces. The road from Tarsus to Antioch runs east to the edge of Cilicia where it crosses the Pyramus River (modern Ceyhan Nehri) and then leads into a line of hills. These hills form part of another mountain chain, the ancient Mount Amanus (modern Nur Mountains) which ran north and south and divided Cilicia from Syria.

The route from the Cicilian Gates followed the coastal plain past the Gulf of Issus (the modern Gulf of Alexandretta) where the eponymous village lay. The narrow coastal plain is bounded on its west by the gulf and by the mountains to its east. It forms a funnel and is the logical place to confront an army coming from the north. It is crossed by the Pinarus river which could be used as a defensive barrier to further movement south. It was on the northern bank of the river that Persian King Darius positioned his army awaiting Alexander's attack from the south at the decisive battle of Issus in the autumn of 333, which ended in a crucial victory for the Macedonian conqueror.[34]

In May 194, Niger moved north to engage the Severan force under Anullinus and his commander of cavalry Lucius Valerius Valerianus.[35] Birley suggests a Pannonian origin for Valerianus. He was of equestrian status and seems to have been a trusted supporter of Septimius. He may have held a cavalry command before his command in the war against Niger.[36] The two armies arrived at the battlefield in the evening and pitched camp. Niger set up his camp on a hill and fortified it. Dio gives the best account of the battle, although there are some problems with it. He describes an unusual formation for Niger's troops. He states that Niger stationed his heavily armed men, no doubt legionaries, in the front of the battle line. To their rear were placed light-armed javelin men, slingers, and then in his rearmost line he placed his archers, the idea being that the heavy-armed troops would fix the enemy while the lighter-armed troops would bombard them with missiles. Since Niger was encamped on a hill, it probably makes sense to assume that the light-armed were echeloned up the hill.[37] He then placed his baggage carriers to the rear to hinder the flight of his own troops. His flanks were protected by forest and cliffs.[38] In response Anullinus adopted a similar formation with his heavies in front and his light-armed behind. According to Dio, the formation was used to counter the difficulties of having to attack uphill. The light-armed would keep Niger's heavy-armed back to allow his own heavies to ascend the hill while facing less resistance. More importantly, he sent his cavalry under Valerianus to advance through the woods on Niger's right and then attacked Niger's troops from the rear.

The battle opened with the advance of Anullinus' men who formed a *testudo* or tortoise. This was a formation in which the front ranks of advancing infantry held their shields in the usual position to protect the front of the formation while the rear ranks raised their shields above their heads to protect against missile weapons. It was a formation normally employed in sieges where there was a serious threat from missiles launched from above. The battle went on for a long time. Niger's troops proved superior and the battle was turning in their favour. They were probably helped by being able to fight from higher ground. Finally, it looked as if they were going to defeat Anullinus' army when according to Dio two developments turned the tide and resulted in their opponents' victory. The first was a heavy storm which appeared out of a clear sky with high winds, thunder, lightning and a violent rainstorm which blew in the faces of the defending troops. Doubts have been expressed about the reality of this storm. It mirrors a famous storm which took place under Marcus Aurelius. It too turned possible disaster into victory and is shown on the Marcus Aurelius column in Rome.[39] It also seems to be a doublet of Herodian's narrative of the defeat of Niger at the Cilician Gates.[40] The fact that Dio does not mention the earlier battle seems to indicate a conflation of the two. The decisive action was Valentinus' successful attack from behind which caught Niger's forces in a pincer. Already giving ground, Niger's army dissolved in panic.[41]

Dio reports a casualty figure for Niger's army of 20,000 dead.[42] He fails to report a figure for Severan losses. Niger realized that resistance was no longer possible and sought safety in flight. There was little he could now do. The seizure of the children of various commanders and other officials on Niger's side had seriously weakened Niger's army and boded badly for the future. It seems likely that two legions had already defected.[43] His men had fought well at the Cilician Gates and then at Issus. It was a standard view evident in Roman and Greek writers that the armies of the east, especially the Syrians, were poor and cowardly fighters. It is a view that extends back to the early Empire. Niger's men had shown the falsity of it.

Despite the negative judgments of Dio, who saw him as a man of mediocre talents and limited intelligence whose real strength lay in his choice of Aemilianus as his commander, and Herodian who criticized him as slothful and addicted to luxury,[44] Niger put up a more than credible defence.[45] The effect of his presence and his ability to inspire his men were in evidence at Issus. In the end, Valerianus' cavalry attack doomed him. Niger's only remaining hope was flight and to seek sanctuary in the east.

His flight back to Antioch destroyed much of Niger's remaining support. Anullinus soon followed and occupied the city. Niger then fled east with a few companions, perhaps to seek refuge with the Parthians, but was overtaken and beheaded. His head was mounted on a pole and displayed at Byzantium to dishearten the inhabitants who were still holding out against Marius Maximus' siege.[46] Cities that had supported Niger developed second thoughts in their anxiety about what the victor would do to them. It is likely, as Southern has suggested, that Laodicea quickly abandoned its allegiance to Niger as Nicomedia had at an earlier stage of the war. It was the main rival of Antioch, Niger's capital, for prominence in Syria.[47] Its rivalry with Antioch naturally inclined it to favour Severus. It benefitted handsomely for choosing the right side. Severus bestowed Antioch's revenues on Laodicea and in addition gave it a grant of tax exemption and gifts of money. It was also rewarded with the title of metropolis or first city of the province. As a further humiliation, Antioch was reduced to the status of a subordinate village of Laodicea.[48] Other cities also suffered for their allegiance to Niger. The *Historia Augusta* mentions that the citizens of Neapolis (modern Nablus) in Palestine were deprived of their civic rights for fighting on Niger's side.[49] Like Laodicea, other cities benefitted from supporting Severus. For instance, Tyre, in Phoenicia, received tax exemption, and added the title Septimia to their city name to honour Severus in turn. Some cities received grants of tax exemption, while others were given the title of metropolis.[50]

Cities who had supported his opponent were not the only sufferers in the aftermath of the war. Severus treated many individuals harshly. They suffered fines and loss of status. Others were executed. Soldiers who had fought on Niger's side were particularly pursued, so much so that, according to Herodian, a number managed to reach and cross the Tigris River and find refuge among the Parthians. Herodian claims that many of these men were technicians and aided the Parthians to develop more effective weapons.[51] Severus also used the opportunity to remorselessly exact funds from the defeated cities and individuals. According to Dio he fined them four times the amount of funds they had given to Niger, whether they had done so voluntarily or under compulsion.[52]

In accordance with his oath he condemned no senator to death for his support of Niger but confiscated their property and imprisoned them on various islands. Such treatment of senators was lenient compared to what he did after Albinus was defeated in 197. It may be that at this point, with Albinus still a potential rival, he felt that he needed as much senatorial support as possible.

The victorious end to the campaign against Niger, probably in May 194, was signalled by the assumption by Severus of the title Imperator IV.[53] It is not certain when Severus arrived in Rome after the defeat of Niger, but it was probably in the autumn or winter of 194.

Severus now replaced Niger's governors with his own and undertook an administrative step of great importance which he was later to repeat in Africa and in Britain in the far west. He divided Syria into two provinces, Syria Phoenice and Syria Coele.[54] The northern province, Coele or Hollow Syria, was garrisoned by two legions under a consular governor, while the southern portion of the old province of Syria, Syria Phoenice, was placed under an ex-praetor with its capital at Tyre with one legion. The award of capital status was no doubt part of the reward for supporting Severus. Despite the name, it covered an area far larger than Phoenicia, including all of coastal Syria. Its border with the northern province extended from the Mediterranean coast to the Euphrates.[55] Syria Coele extended from the Amanus Mountains to the Euphrates. The obvious purpose of the reform was to lessen the power of the most important governorship in the East.

Twice within a generation Syria had served as a base for an attempt to seize the imperial throne. Under Marcus Aurelius, its governor had rebelled against the emperor and made a bid for power. That governor, Gaius Avidius Cassius, was himself of Syrian background. He had had an impressive record as a commander during Marcus's war with the Parthians between 162 and 165. As a reward he served as consul in 166 and as governor of Syria from 166. The outbreak of a major rebellion in 171 in Egypt led to Cassius being given the task of suppressing it and since Marcus was embroiled in a war with Germanic tribes, he gave Cassius general oversight of the eastern provinces as *Rector Orientis*.

In 175 Cassius rebelled. The origins of the attempted usurpation are difficult to untangle. A story found in the main sources (Dio and the *Historia Augusta*) claims that he was moved to revolt by news of Marcus' death sent by Marcus' wife Faustina. But despite learning the truth,

Cassius persisted until he was assassinated by a centurion, probably in July 175. The incident pointed out the potential threat of Syria and its three legions.[56] The Parthians on Rome's Euphrates frontier were a serious threat and a sizeable force was needed to contain them. The case of Syria pointed to a difficulty experienced by all ancient imperial states. They needed their border defences to be powerful enough to confront an immediate threat. But that force posed a threat to the central government, if a local commander decided to use it for his own purposes.

The defeat of Niger did not bring an end to the fighting. Some client states in Mesopotamia lying beyond the Roman frontier had aided Niger. The civil war had loosened Roman control and there were rebellions against it in Osrhoene, Adiabene and among the Scenite Arabs.

Osrhoene in northern Mesopotamia was a kingdom with its centre at Edessa (modern Urfa in southeastern Turkey). The king of Edessa and of Osrhoene was Abgar VIII. He owed his throne to the Romans who had re-established his father as king there after Parthian attacks in the 160s. It appears that Roman power was only weakly established in the region in Edessa and further east at the important city of Nisibis. Abgar, as was often the case with client kings, especially one who was sandwiched between two great states, manoeuvred to retain as much independence as he could. The disturbances caused by the Roman civil war gave him an opportunity to weaken Roman control.[57]

Adiabene was another small client kingdom in northern Mesopotamia. Its main territory lay east of the Tigris River, although there was some territory to the west of the river as well. It had mostly been a client state of the Parthians and they had granted the two strategically important cities of Singara and Nisibis to the kingdom. It too was manoeuvring to better its position and to take advantage of Roman troubles. There was also trouble with the Scenite or nomad Arabs who allied themselves with the two kingdoms.[58] They had placed Nisibis under siege, claiming they were besieging Niger's troops on behalf of Severus, despite having attacked and expelled Roman garrisons in northern Mesopotamia. The threat of his approach led these states and the tent dwelling Arabs to send an embassy to him. They brought gifts and promised to hand over to him the captives and whatever spoils would be left after the conclusion of the siege. Yet they were unwilling either to abandon the forts they had captured or to receive garrisons, but actually demanded the removal from their territories of such Roman garrisons as still remained. It was this that led to the present war.[59]

Just as important as the reassertion of Roman power in the area was the need for Severus to enhance his standing with the eastern armies. For the most part, they had fought loyally for Niger. Severus needed to redirect their loyalty to himself. The ravages that the fighting produced in Asia Minor and Syria would not have endeared him to them. There is no reason to doubt Herodian's picture of the people of Antioch bewailing the fate of their sons and brothers who had died in the fight on Niger's side.[60] The flight of soldiers to the Parthians is some indication of the feelings of at least some of the troops who had supported Niger. The purge Severus undertook after his victory must have further estranged the elite. There was another consideration as well. Severus's victories had been won by others. Given his lack of military experience, this was the most effective course of action for him, but it did little to enhance his reputation as a commander with the troops. The troops' attitude was in the last instance the most important factor in gaining a throne and, in Severus's present situation, keeping it. There was still the threat of Albinus in the west to deal with. A campaign in Mesopotamia under his overall command would enhance his standing with the troops and back in Rome. The disparity in resources between Severus and his enemies meant that his victory was never in doubt and that made the expedition even more attractive. Dio's description of the campaign as a quest for glory is not wrong, but the glory had a political dimension as well as a personal one, and given all of the other reasons to campaign it was a sensible response to the situation Severus found himself in after Niger's defeat.[61] A further factor is revealed by a Syriac source, *The Chronicle of Arbela*, which indicates that the Parthian king had fomented the revolt by the Osrhoeni and Adiabeni against Rome; there is also some evidence that he encouraged Niger. Given the relations between Rome and Parthia, this would be a natural step in an attempt to weaken Roman control in the east. However, the Parthian king failed to support the revolts because he was distracted by unrest in the eastern provinces of his empire.[62]

In addition to these two kingdoms, the important city of Hatra had sent a unit of archers to Niger's aid, and Severus intended to punish Hatra as an example to deter such actions in the future. Of the three recalcitrant kingdoms, Hatra was the most important. It was located in northern Mesopotamia about 180 miles northwest of Baghdad,[63] an important caravan city and well-fortified. It also was an important pilgrim centre for its cult of the sun god, which added to its wealth in addition to its commercial activities. It had become a very wealthy city and so was a tempting target. It had survived a siege by the Emperor Trajan in 116/17. As Dio notes, the region lacked water, timber and forage as well as the other resources needed to support a large besieging army.[64] The situation had not changed by the time of Severus. For the present, action against Hatra was deferred, but other Mesopotamian targets were not so lucky.[65]

Severus began his campaign in the spring of 195. He decided to make Nisibis his base for the war. The heavily fortified city was part of Adiabene and had earlier belonged to Osrhoene. Like the other Mesopotamian cities, it had prospered from trade. Crucially, it stood on the main road link between northern Mesopotamia and Syria. Like much of the area it had been a client state of the Parthians. During the Roman-Parthian war of the early 160s it had been captured by the Romans and a Roman client-king was installed, as well as a garrison of Roman troops.

The march from Syria to Nisibis, modern Nusaybin in Turkey, at high summer was a difficult one, as must have been foreseen. The lack of resources and the privation of the troops intensified once they left the Euphrates valley as they marched east. The intense heat and the lack of water caused immense suffering among the troops. To add to their misery, a violent dust storm blew up, temporarily blinding the troops and intensifying their thirst. At last, water was found, but at first the troops were put off by its strangeness according to Dio. What constituted its strangeness is not specified, but perhaps a mixture of minerals and even some run-off from petroleum would have been possible. Severus, in a theatrical gesture, had a cup filled with the water and then proceeded to drain it in full view of the troops. This ended their reluctance to drink and quieted their thirst. The anecdote recalls one associated with Alexander the Great in which the Macedonian king refuses water which is brought to him in a helmet to show his unity with his troops since they had none to drink.[66]

Despite these difficulties the army reached Nisibis and lifted the siege. It seems that the city remained loyal to Rome despite its difficulties. It was placed under the command of an equestrian prefect and awarded various honours.[67]

Severus, setting up his headquarters there, divided his army into three sections. One was commanded by Sextius Magius Lateranus,[68] who came from a noble Roman family. As a reward for his services, he was made consul in 197. Another section was formed of troops drawn from the Illyrian legions which formed part of the Pannonian army. This was led by Claudius Candidus; the last column was under the command of a Laetus. This Laetus is probably Julius Laetus, the same man who had accompanied Severus on his march to Rome as well as defeating Julianus's praetorian prefect Tullius Crispinus near Ravenna and after having captured him persuaded Severus to execute him. It seems that the plan was to lay waste the territories of the rebellious kingdoms and the territory of the Scenite Arabs.[69]

It seems that Severus's first attempt to defeat these peoples was not totally successful. A second tripartite expedition was mounted, this time with two different commanders. Laetus was retained, but Anullinus and Probus were appointed to replace Candidus and Lateranus.[70] There is no reliable account of the campaign. Herodian confuses it with Severus's second eastern war and the *Historia Augusta* has nothing of value to say. One additional piece of information is provided by the career inscription of Valerius Valerianus.[71] He may have served once again as Anullinus's deputy, but it seems that in the later part of the campaign after Severus' departure he was placed in command of the expedition and finished off the war.[72]

One immediate result of the war was the creation of a small new province formed from land confiscated from Abgar of Edessa. An equestrian procurator was installed as governor, Gaius Julius Pacatianus. Interestingly, Abgar was neither executed nor deposed. His kingdom lost a fair amount of territory, but the king retained his capital of Edessa as well as other territory. He was able to repair his relationship with Severus. He retained his right to coin, which was a positive sign in itself. His coins have Abgar on one side and Severus on the other. He was later invited to Rome by Severus. The visit was marked by elaborate displays and ceremonies.[73] To show his loyalty Abgar offered Severus a unit of archers. Given Severus's general hardheadedness and reliance on calculation, it is best to assume that he saw the maintenance of Abgar as a way of stabilizing that part of the eastern frontier. Not powerful enough to challenge Rome with its losses of territory, the kingdom might prove useful in controlling the desert Arabs and serve as a buffer.[74]

The campaigns against Adiabene and the Scenite Arabs were successful as well. To celebrate his victories, he took the imperial titles of Adiabenicus and Arabicus. The original titles were Parthicus Arabicus and Parthicus Adiabenicus. The title of Parthicus was later dropped to avoid offending the Parthian king.[75] In 195, Severus received three more imperial acclamations, numbered V, VI and VII. Given the lack of a coherent narrative of the campaign, it is not clear to which of the campaigns each imperial acclamation belonged.

One problem remained unfinished; that was the siege of Byzantium. It did not succumb to Severus's forces until the end of 195. It took the army under Marius Maximus a full two years to capture the city. The length of the siege was partly due to the city's impressive fortifications and its difficult topography which made its conquest challenging. Later as Constantinople it was to survive a number of sieges until its fall to the Turks in 1453.[76]

In the end, it was starvation that defeated the Byzantines. The city had sent out a naval foraging expedition, but it was defeated. That ended any hope that it could hold out any longer.[77] All military personnel and the civilian magistrates were executed, but surprisingly the rest of the population was spared. Their property was confiscated and the city was demoted, as Antioch had been, to the status of a dependent village, tributary to nearby Perinthus, long jealous of Byzantium's prominence.[78] Once the siege had ended, Severus had its fortifications destroyed. With Niger's defeat Byzantium was in a hopeless situation. Help was nowhere to be found. It was only fear of the consequences of defeat that caused the citizens to resist for so long. Severus received the news of the city's fall while he was still in Mesopotamia, so he returned to Rome in the winter of 195/6. He took his eighth imperial acclamation for its fall. Dio emphasizes his delight at the fall of the city.[79]

As a further measure to both celebrate his victory and to bind the troops to himself and his family, Severus bestowed the title of *mater castrorum* (mother of military camps) on his wife Julia Domna on 14 April 195. The title was ratified by the Senate and the occasion was celebrated annually. There was a precedent for this title. Faustina the Younger, the wife of Marcus Aurelius and mother of Commodus, had been given the title, probably in the 170s.[80] As Mary Boatright has stressed in her article on the award of the title to Faustina, it was an extremely unusual title since the propaganda centring on imperial women normally stressed their fecundity and their association with home and family.[81] She suggests that the title was an attempt to help ease the succession of Commodus to the throne, especially given his youth. As the daughter of the previous emperor Antoninus Pius, she had also played a crucial role in establishing Marcus Aurelius's legitimacy as emperor. For Severus, the attempt to link his family to the army was even more important.

He was emperor because of military success. He had no prior connections to the imperial family that might have enhanced his claim to empire. His fictitious link to Pertinax could be seen as problematic and in fact was later dropped from his titulature.[82] Whatever qualities Pertinax may have had, he was linked to the assassination of Commodus and the end of his dynasty and was especially unpopular with the military. Despite his commitment to

Clodius Albinus, Severus was intent on founding his own dynasty. His two sons, Bassianus (Caracalla was a nickname) and Geta, stood waiting in the wings and could not simply be disinherited. If they did not succeed, their chances of survival would be slim. They would be a potential threat to a successor from outside the family and so were likely to be eliminated.

To bolster his own dynastic pretensions Severus formally adopted himself into the family of the revered Marcus Aurelius. This made him Commodus's brother and linked him directly to the Antonine dynasty, implying continuity and legitimacy. Bassianus adopted the name of Marcus Aurelius Antoninus and was made Caesar on the march home from the east at Viminacium in Moesia Superior in late 195.[83] All of these considerations form the context for the adoption of the title *mater castrorum* by Julia. It served as another link to the preceding dynasty. Just as Marcus Aurelius's wife had held the title, so also did Severus's wife. As Barbara Levick stresses, the title also placed the troops under the protection of the empress and linked dynasty and army.[84] The renaming of Bassianus and his receiving the title of Caesar were obvious signs of the trouble ahead for Clodius Albinus.

On his way back to Rome Severus was clearly preparing for the coming conflict with Albinus. New legions and other formations were raised. The war against Niger and the desert campaign must have taken a heavy toll. He placed trusted men in charge of crucial provinces. There was not yet an open break with Albinus, but Herodian and the *Historia Augusta* claim that Severus had dispatched assassins to kill him. Given Severus's previous conduct Albinus had reason to fear him. The assassins pretended that they had an important message for Albinus that they wanted to deliver to him in person. Albinus had them seized and tortured. They revealed their true mission and were executed.[85] Although such stories could easily be propaganda fabrications, it is more likely that some truth lay behind this one. It seems odd that despite Severus's victory such a story would survive his propaganda. Herodian is hostile to Severus, the *Historia Augusta* is not, yet both repeat the story. There is no way to decide on its truthfulness. According to Herodian, Albinus, because of his senatorial ancestry, was favoured by some senators who were in correspondence with him. The letters supposedly urged him to leave Britain and come to Rome to take over the government.[86] It is unclear if their request had any effect.

There could no longer be any doubt about what would come next. Another round of civil war was now unavoidable. At the end of 195 Albinus was declared a public enemy. Both sides now prepared for the inevitable conflict that was soon to follow.

Chapter 5

The Civil Wars: Act 2

In Rome, the prospect of another civil war was a harsh blow to the populace and provoked open protest against continued fighting. Dio reports a demonstration during the chariot races at the Circus Maximus before the holiday of the Saturnalia, which took place on 17 December 195.[1] He notes that he was present when the protest took place.

At the end of the races the crowd silenced each other, then clapped their hands, and at the same time prayed to Rome. They addressed the city as a goddess, Roma, and asked her how long the war and their suffering would continue. Dio thinks the demonstration was divinely inspired because of the unanimity of the actions and cries of the people. It is more likely that the inspiration was human. What is less clear is who mobilized the protest and set it in motion. The races and gladiatorial combats were favourite venues for popular protest in the imperial period. The emperor was usually present and the crowd large enough for individuals to remain anonymous. It could also be effective. A popular demonstration had brought about the fall of Commodus's favourite Cleander only five years before.[2]

The exact chronology of events is uncertain, but it is likely that Severus heard of Albinus's proclamation as Augustus before he reached Rome, before the end of 195, as the anecdote on popular protests in Dio in December 195 makes clear. It is somewhat of a mystery why Albinus hesitated for so long before being forced into a civil war by Severus's actions. His coinage gives no hint of his plans besides echoing the normal slogans of the loyalty of the legions and celebrating Jupiter as the bringer of victory. He even retained the title of Caesar. As Birley notes there is no obvious explanation. The mercilessness of Severus's struggle for power had long been evident. His treatment of Niger's wife and children must have increased his reputation for cruelty: as soon as the conflict with Albinus broke out, Niger's family was murdered, presumably to make sure they would not be a rallying point for any opposition.[3] Still, it is hard to believe given the Roman preference for hereditary heirs that Severus would have allowed Albinus to succeed him, unless none of Severus's sons survived. Emperors who were not sons of the previous emperor were the results of a lack of heirs. Perhaps Albinus's apparent passivity during the previous two years can be explained by the following considerations. First, Albinus may have thought that the war with Niger would so weaken Severus's and Niger's forces that in a confrontation with either man he would have a good chance of success. Second, Albinus needed time to ready and strengthen his own forces. He had most likely become governor in 192. The three legions of the garrison province had been unstable in their loyalties since the mid-180s. Their loyalty to the central government was uncertain. There had been fierce fighting along the northern border of the Roman province in the late 170s and early 180s. Perhaps as a result of the turmoil of this period, there was a mutiny under the governor Ulpius Marcellus at an unknown date, probably as the result of his harsh discipline.[4] The legate Priscus was selected as a new emperor but declined the dangerous honour. Dio quotes him as saying: 'I am no more an emperor than you are soldiers.'[5] The unrest among the legions continued to 185. In that year the soldiers chose 1,500 of their number and sent them as a deputation to Commodus. He met them outside Rome and listened to their accusations against his influential praetorian prefect Perennis. In Dio's version this led to his fall, although there are alternative stories.[6]

Unrest continued until the arrival of Pertinax as governor in 185. He assumed the governorship with what seems the special task of suppressing dissent among the troops there. It was a dangerous task. The troops were still looking for another emperor, perhaps Pertinax himself. He suppressed the mutiny but almost lost his life in the process. Finally, in 187 he requested permission to return to Rome and was granted it. We do not have enough evidence to explain the situation in Britain, but it should be pointed out that the distance of Britain from the political centre and the frequent warfare there may have helped convince the army that their interest would be better served by an emperor chosen by them.

The dissatisfaction of the soldiers of the British legions was probably still a factor, though of less intensity when Albinus arrived in 192. Unfortunately we know almost nothing about the history of the island between the governorships of Pertinax and Albinus. It may have taken time for Albinus to establish his authority in the chaotic conditions that followed Commodus's assassination. Severus's grant to him of the rank of Caesar shows that he had re-established control by mid-193 at the latest. The province's troubles must have slowed his recruiting and the formation of a fleet took time. But Severus's decision to make his son his successor now left Albinus no choice but to fight.

and chaos in the province. Albinus would probably have taken all the men he could have, even to the point of seriously weakening the defence of the turbulent province. If he lost his fight with Severus, his life would be forfeit. He had to risk everything if he was to survive. So, with recruiting in Gaul, he probably had 50–60,000 men. Despite the reduced size of the British garrison there does not seem to be any evidence of a major disturbance in Britain.[16]

Dio remarks, this was the first major battle that Severus was present at. It appears that initially Albinus's left wing was defeated and driven back to his camp. The Severans proceeded to slaughter the fugitives and sack the camp. On Albinus's right wing the battle developed very differently. Albinus's troops had prepared the ground in advance. They had constructed trenches and pits and then covered them to hide them from the enemy. They advanced as far as the pits and then hurled their javelins at the enemy as it approached the hidden pits and trenches. Then at a prearranged signal they began to fall back. The feigned retreat worked. The troops at the front of Severus's battle line hurried in pursuit and fell into the pits and trenches. This broke the forward impetus of the Severan line and threw the troops following the front line into confusion. Maintaining cohesion and formation was crucial to ancient massed fighting units. Their loss could be fatal. The Severans were caught with a ravine behind and trenches to their front. Their enemy deluged them with showers of missiles which caused very heavy casualties. Seeing the continuing difficulties of his left-wing, Severus came up with the Praetorians in support. They fared no better and Severus endangered his own life when he lost his horse. He tried to stem the flight of the fugitives. Some halted but created even more chaos when they turned around and were cut down by the men behind them who mistook them for the enemy. The Severans were rescued by the arrival of their cavalry under the command of Laetus. It had not yet intervened in the battle; it now attacked Albinus's men in the flank and, just as at Issus, the cavalry determined the result of the battle, which ended in a bloody Severan victory.[17] Dio mentions that the losses in this battle were severe but gives no figures. Herodian mentions that various historians gave different figures, depending on their political allegiances.

The end of battle did not end the carnage. Severus's troops pursued the fleeing enemy back to Lugdunum where they sought refuge. It was probably at this point that most of the casualties were inflicted. In mass battle before the use of gunpowder, it was when one side broke and fled, rendering themselves defenceless, that the bulk of the killing occurred.[18]

The city was quickly taken, then sacked and burned. Albinus, rightly thinking that capture meant death, hid in a house near the Rhône. According to Dio, his hiding place was discovered and surrounded by Severus's men. Knowing that the situation was hopeless, he committed suicide.[19] Dio mentions that his version of Albinus's death is the authentic one and not the one Severus gave in his biography. In Herodian, it is his pursuers who kill him and then send the body to Severus. The *Historia Augusta* has a particularly brutal account of Severus's actions after the body of Albinus was brought to him.[20] Common to all versions is decapitation of the corpse and the sending of Albinus's head to Rome to advertise Severus's victory. He had done the same after Niger's defeat.

The victory had disposed of Albinus, but unrest and fighting on a much smaller scale persisted. In Spain, Novius Rufus continued to resist. Claudius Candidus was now dispatched to become governor of the province of Novius, Hispania Tarraconensis, and end resistance there. Rufus, who could expect no other fate than death, was captured by Candidus and executed.[21] Reprisals were taken against Albinus's supporters in Gaul by Severus and Marius Maximus. Vallius Maximianus was also sent to suppress opposition in Hispania Baetica (south central Spain) and in Mauretania Tingitana (Morocco). In the province of Arabia, the garrison of the province, III Cyrenaica had declared for Albinus and after his fall set up their own candidate. His name is unknown and he soon disappeared. It is not impossible that the persecution of Niger's partisans in the area by Severus had created this resistance to the victorious emperor.[22]

Severus's treatment of the Senate contrasted with his handling of it after Niger's defeat. According to the *Historia Augusta,* after his defeat of Niger, he refrained from punishing senators, except for one man. Dio also seems to indicate a relatively mild handing of the senatorial opposition.[23] His defeat of Albinus had allowed Severus to capture his correspondence. Among the letters were those from senators who had supported him. He would be merciless towards them.

Severus returned to Rome by 9 June 197. The people welcomed him with full honours. To further ingratiate himself with them and the army, he made a money distribution to both after he had performed the customary sacrifices to Jupiter.

He instituted a number of military reforms to make military service more attractive.[24] These would further strengthen the loyalty of the troops to himself. He then turned his attention to the Senate and made his animus against it clear in a speech he read to the assembled senators. Dio, an eyewitness, reports that he praised Marius, Sulla and Augustus, who had instituted proscriptions against their political opponents. He claimed that the clemency exercised by Pompey and Caesar had led to their downfall. He even read out excerpts from the letters of Albinus's supporters among the senators.[25] He then praised Commodus and conferred divine honours on him. This had followed his adoption of Marcus Aurelius as his father and Commodus as his brother. Whatever positive feelings there were about Commodus, especially in the army, this sent a clear message to the Senate that he identified himself with an emperor who had often been actively hostile towards it and had executed a number of its members. Severus launched a purge of the Senate. Eventually sixty-four senators were arrested; of these, twenty-nine were executed and thirty-five released.[26] The *Historia Augusta* claims he executed many others below senatorial rank.[27] The purge of supporters of both Niger and Albinus continued. After the defeat of Albinus we hear of action taken against his supporters in Gaul, Spain, Noricum and perhaps Africa, which as Albinus's homeland had probably given him some support.[28]

His speech to the Senate provides evidence about the reasons for his conduct towards it. After two civil wars, Severus was determined to firmly establish his rule so that no future threats could destabilize it. The wars had cost him and his supporters a great deal of blood and treasure. Purges and confiscations were speedy ways to fill empty coffers. The methodical thoroughness of his actions in the provinces evoked fear and mistrust at home. The purges also guaranteed that he would have time to rebuild the army unmolested. In a moving passage, Dio describes the scene of destruction and carnage in the wake of the battle at Lugdunum:

> *Thus, Severus conquered; but Roman power suffered a severe blow, inasmuch as countless numbers had fallen on both sides. Many even of the victors deplored the disaster, for the entire plain was seen to be covered with the bodies of men and horses; some of them lay there mutilated by many wounds, as if hacked in pieces, and others, though unwounded, were piled up in heaps, weapons were scattered about, and blood flowed in streams, even pouring into the rivers.*[29]

His animosity against the Senate was fuelled by an additional factor. Albinus's family, unlike that of Severus, had originated among the Roman nobility. His background had led to a far readier acceptance for him among the elite.[30] This had also been the case with Niger. These rejections must have heightened Severus' sense of exclusion and increased his animosity to the Senate. Dio presents a picture of the fear that Severus's actions inspired:

> *All pretended to be on the side of Severus, but their pretence of support fell away as often as any sudden tidings arrived, being unable to conceal the feelings hidden in their hearts. For when off their guard they recoiled at reports that came without warning, and in such ways, as well as by their countenances and behaviour, the feelings of every one of them became manifest. Some also by pretending overmuch were recognized all the more readily.*[31]

Severus had now cowed opposition in the provinces and in Rome and Italy. He had installed his own men as governors in crucial provinces. His finances were now sound. They remained so for the rest of his reign. Whatever his military talents were, he was a more than competent administrator and manager. He appointed equestrian procurators to administer the property of those caught in the purge.

He also used his new wealth to stage elaborate games and made further cash distributions to boost his popularity and erase the memories of the carnage.[32] Finally, he took steps to strengthen the claim of his eldest son to the succession.

Chapter 6

Encore: War in the East and Sightseeing in Egypt

After another short stay in Rome, Severus set out for the East, probably in the summer of 197.[1] While he had been fighting Albinus in Gaul with the main weight of Roman forces, the Parthian king Vologaeses V (191–208) had crossed the Tigris and attacked the strategically important town of Nisibis in Mesopotamia with its Roman garrison. Despite the attack, the garrison held out under the command of Julius Laetus, who was to play an important role in the new war in the East.[2]

This is not the first time the Parthian king had engaged in hostile moves against Rome. During Severus's war against Niger, he had shown his sympathy for Niger.[3] The Romans and Parthians had engaged in sporadic war with each other since the middle of the first century BC. It was the one enemy that Rome faced until its fall in the early third century that was an organized state and a formidable military power.

The Parni (Parthians) were an Iranian tribe living in northeastern Iran. They appear in the historical record from the mid-third century, but the foundation of the kingdom and its rise to power took place under Mithridates I who ruled from 171 to 132 BC. At its greatest extent the empire that Mithridates built and his successors enlarged stretched from the Indus to the Euphrates Rivers, including the modern states of Iraq, Iran and Afghanistan, as well as portions of Armenia and the Syrian desert. To the north, Rome and Parthia disputed control of Armenia. It was of strategic importance offering invasion and trade routes into Roman Asia Minor and into northern Parthia.[4] Control of Armenia alternated between them. More often than not it was controlled by Parthia, and the Parthian crown prince sat on its throne before he succeeded to the rule. In fact, Severus's adversary Vologaeses V had ruled Armenia from 180 to 191 until he acceded to the Parthian throne.

The kingdom had two centres: the first was Ctesiphon. It lay on the eastern bank of the Tigris, about twenty-two miles southeast of Baghdad. No modern city has replaced it. It was located on two important trade routes, one from Central Asia and the other from the Persian Gulf. It sat across the Tigris from the Greek city of Seleucia-on-the-Tigris.[5] Seleucia on the river's west bank served as a twin to Ctesiphon and also grew immensely rich on trade. The fortunes of both cities were intertwined and also uncertain throughout the period of Parthian rule. The wars with Rome had led to several sackings and destructions of both cities. In 116 Trajan captured Ctesiphon without resistance.[6] In the war with Parthia in the early 160s under Marcus Aurelius and his co-emperor Lucius Verus, who served as a figurehead commander of the expedition, Seleucia was stormed and burnt.[7] Despite the intermittent destruction the cities continued as the centre of Parthian administration and Ctesiphon remained the main residence of the Parthian king.

The Parthian Empire possessed a very different structure from Rome's. The monarchy was hereditary within the Arsacid family but was unstable. Pretenders arose both within and outside the royal family. This was the case with Septimius Severus's opponent Vologaeses V, whose succession to the throne was contested by an Osroes, who had already established a kingdom in northeastern Iran in Media. He was quickly done away with. A further indication of the same problem is evident from the fact that when Septimius Severus invaded Parthia, a brother of Vologaeses accompanied the invading army. Later when he died, his son Vologaeses VI's accession to the throne was again contested. Despite this institutional instability several of the Parthian kings managed to stay on the throne for extended periods.

Beneath the king and the royal family, the empire possessed a large and powerful noble class which played a central role in administration. They, along with members of royal family, sat on the councils that advised the king. At the apex of the nobility were the great territorial magnates over whom the king often exercised only a weak control. They governed the provinces of the empire essentially as feudatories of the king and provided the nucleus of the royal armies. Alongside the provinces ruled by territorial magnates, there were a number of client kingdoms, often loosely controlled. Armenia was the most important, but there were many others such as Hatra, Elymais and Gordyene.[8] In accordance with the general weakness of the central administration, cities often enjoyed a great deal of autonomy.[9]

The loose structure of the kingdom was reflected in its mix of languages and cultures. Despite the Iranian language of the dominant Parthians, there were two other languages common in the empire. The first was Greek; it was the language of the cities which were often Greek foundations. It was in widespread use and was adopted as the language of the central administration. The second of the major languages was Aramaic. Its long history in Mesopotamia as well as its broad spread led to the adoption of its script for official purposes.[10]

Parthian armies differed greatly from their Greek and later Roman adversaries. The main strength of both Greek and Roman armies lay in their heavy infantry. This emphasis seems to have been partly linked to the importance of the city and peasant farming in their economies and culture. For instance, it is noticeable that classical Greek fighting forces in non-urban areas of Greece relied on light-armed infantry and cavalry as their most effective arms. Another factor was that the northern shore of the Mediterranean did not produce year-round grasslands capable of sustaining large herds of horses. The Macedonian cavalry of Alexander the Great's army was as good or better than any force it met in Asia. However, Macedonia differed from much of the southern Balkans in its climate and topography. It had areas of sufficient rainfall as well as plains suitable for the grazing of horses. It also had few cities. It shared another feature with other cavalry armies in the Mediterranean basin and the Near East of the period and that was rule by a horse-breeding aristocracy over a subordinate peasantry who provided labour and support for the great lords. There was a traditional tie between cavalry and aristocracy in the ancient world which persisted in Europe into the nineteenth century.

The Parthian army consisted mostly of the retainers and followers of the great nobles. In addition there was probably a small standing army used by the central government for police and garrison duty. The way the army was constituted was a serious limitation. Since it was raised as occasion demanded, it had little time to train as a cohesive body. Also, the power of the nobles leading their separate contingents could create problems of conflict over command decisions, as they later did in the Western European armies of the Middle Ages. They were largely cavalry armies consisting of two separate types of troopers. The great majority were lightly armed horse archers, using a composite bow of great strength. They were excellent horsemen who were skilled enough to employ the so-called Parthian shot. Their light equipment and agility enabled them to feign a retreat in the face of enemy cavalry and, while retreating, to twist around in the saddle and fire backwards over their shoulders at their pursuers. It was a tactic that demanded exceptional horsemanship. The 'Parthian shot' was used extensively in Central Asia from where the Parthians originated.[11] The other major arm of the army was formed by heavily armoured lancers, the cataphracts. Both man and horse were protected by either scale or chain mail armour. The lance (*kontos*) they wielded was about twelve feet long and they also carried a secondary armament of either a sword or axe. Infantry, mostly archers, existed, but seems to have been of little importance.

Our most detailed description of the army in action are the accounts of the battle of Carrhae in 53 BC in which a Roman army commanded by Marcus Crassus was completely destroyed by the Parthians.[12] In this case the Roman cavalry was drawn off by a feigned retreat which employed the Parthian shot and finally led to the loss of perhaps one-third of their cavalry. The Roman infantry formation was fixed in place by the threat of the cataphracts' lances and then worn down by showers of arrows so that it eventually disintegrated.

The cataphracts seem to have been particularly effective in battle. By the second century, the Romans countered their effectiveness in two ways. First, they adopted a version of the long two-handed lance used by Iranian cataphracts and used it in phalanx-like formation to prevent charges by Iranian cataphracts. Horses will not charge a solid wall of pikes.[13] Second, as they encountered not only Iranian cataphracts but also those of other enemies who were armed in a similar way, they adopted the cataphract and increasingly used units of archers to counter their eastern enemies.[14]

Such an army would be most effective in the flat, open spaces in much of the northern Near East. As has been pointed out in sieges or in confined battlefields, they would be far less effective than Roman heavy infantry.[15] Even in the field, as Goldsworthy has indicated, the Parthians could be defeated by contemporary Roman armies. The defeat of Crassus was the result of his army being deficient in archers and cavalry. Foot archers, despite their comparative lack of mobility, could outrange bowmen on horseback and keep them out of range. If the archers were ineffective, there was little or no chance of a successful charge by the cataphracts who were useful against infantry, but ineffective against more mobile enemy cavalry.[16] After Crassus, there were several Parthian victories against Roman forces, but for the most part large-scale battles did not go well for the Parthians.

Although there were successful Parthian invasions of Roman territory, they were not particularly aggressive towards Rome and mainly fought the Romans because of Roman aggression against their territory. This was certainly true at the end of the first century BC and in the first half of the first century AD. Once the de facto border between the two empires had been established on the Euphrates, conflict between Rome and Parthia diminished. The one great exception was the Parthian invasion of the 160s. Armenia remained the most dangerous problem for both empires. Its strategic location at the borders of the two states could and did invite conflict. In the second century it was mostly Roman aggression that led to fighting. For the Parthians it was the more serious problems on their eastern frontiers that preoccupied them. When the Parthian kingdom fell in the first third of the third century, the agent of their fall was another Iranian people on their southeastern frontier, the Sasanians.

While Severus was occupied fighting Albinus in the West, in 197 Vologaeses V took the opportunity to invade Roman Mesopotamia. He had attacked Nisibis, which was the main Roman base in northern Mesopotamia. It had been attacked by the Parthians in the first war with Severus. The city was saved by the energetic action of Julius Laetus, who had also played a crucial role at Lugdunum. It highlighted a continuing problem for the Parthians: their inability to successfully pursue sieges.[17] The other sources are not particularly informative; most of our information comes from Dio. It is likely that Armenia was taken by Vologaeses as well.[18] Adiabene was also invaded, as the allegiance of its king to Parthia seems to have been wavering. Vologaeses destroyed several cities in the kingdom and drowned its king Narses in the Great Zab.[19] But Vologaeses, like Severus, was preoccupied elsewhere. The Medes and Persians in his rear revolted and were only defeated after difficult fighting.

The news of the Parthian attack must have reached Rome quickly. Probably in late autumn 197, Severus set out for the east. In his army were two new legions, I and III Parthica. It is likely that these legions were raised as early as 195 after the war with Niger, and likely used to garrison the new province of Mesopotamia when Severus departed for the west.[20] The third Parthian legion, II Parthica, was probably recruited in Italy and located at Albanum about sixteen miles south of Rome at Alba. This was a major departure from earlier practice. Before the establishment of this legion no legions had been quartered in Italy. The only troops had been the garrison of Rome and marines from the fleet at Ravenna.[21] This also meant that with the Praetorian Guard he had a mobile force of legionaries with their attendant formations to deal with problems in Rome and Italy or as a strike force for overseas expeditions. Probably Severus now had a force of 30,000 troops or the equivalent of six legions immediately available for use in Italy and Rome.

Both the *Historia Augusta* and Herodian claim that Severus's motivation for renewing hostilities with the Parthians was a personal one.

The *Historia Augusta* states that Severus was seeking glory and was not facing a serious threat.[22] Herodian notes that Severus claimed that he was setting out to punish supporters of Niger, in particular Barsemius the king of Hatra, but that personal aggrandizement was his real purpose.[23] Dio in his description of the campaign claims that it was a response to Parthian aggression. He criticizes not Severus's motives but rather the wastefulness of his wars against the Parthians. He debunks Severus's claim that his wars in the east and his annexations there greatly strengthened the defences of Syria.[24] In general he seems hostile to expansionary wars in the east. He has the same attitude towards Trajan's eastern campaign.[25] It has been suggested that there is some truth in Dio's negative judgment about Severus's conquest. The permanent occupation of northern Mesopotamia had important consequences. The border between Parthia and Roman Syria now lay closer to the Parthian capital at Ctesiphon than to the capital of Syria at Antioch. Therefore the Roman lines of communication were significantly extended and those of the Parthians shortened. With the extension of Roman control, the border now ran through territory that had been under nominal Parthian hegemony and so remained less secure.[26] Rome's eastern border now lay on the Tigris with Nisibis as her major base for invasions of Parthian territory. Along with Nisibis, Singara and Rhesaina also seem likely garrison towns in Mesopotamia for I and II Parthica which made up the garrison for the province of Mesopotamia.[27] The use of these cities for bases is not unusual in the eastern provinces.

Severus embarked, along with his family, for the east at Brundisium, the usual port for sailing to the east. His wife Julia with her Syrian connections at Emesa probably proved to be a substantial asset in Severus's dealing with local Syrian princes. This must have been especially useful in the area where Severus would be operating.[28] Also on the expedition was his praetorian prefect Gaius Fulvius Plautianus. Like Severus he came from Leptis Magna and was related to him through Severus's mother's family. An inscription claims he accompanied Severus on all the expeditions in which the emperor took part.[29] No doubt a portion of the Guard as well as II Parthica accompanied him. His ship made its final stop at the port of Aegae in southeastern Asia Minor.[30]

At the news of Severus's arrival in the East, Vologaeses, already facing threats in the east and rivals within his own family (his brother was with Severus), withdrew before the Roman advance and the siege of Nisibis was abandoned. He probably thought that if he had to face Severus's army, he would be better off fighting in the Mesopotamian plains which offered ideal cavalry country. If worse came to worst, he could retreat and trade land for time to strengthen his forces.

After his arrival in Syria, Severus assembled his forces at Antioch and then crossed the Euphrates, the old boundary between the Parthian and Roman empires. It was probably at this point that he removed the disabilities he had imposed on Antioch after the victory over Niger. Severus marched on to Edessa. Its king Abgar VIII placated the emperor, giving his children as hostages and the offer of a unit of Edessa's famed archers. These were permanently incorporated into the Roman army. They were to play an important role in future campaigns. They were probably a positive factor in the eventual promotion of Edessa to colonial status.[31] The military contribution may also have been behind Severus's relatively lenient treatment of Edessa in both his first and second Parthian campaigns. The king of Armenia followed Abgar's example, and by offering gifts, hostages and a treaty forestalled an attack.[32] It may be at this time that Severus took his tenth imperial acclamation.[33] He established his base at Nisibis in preparation for his invasion of Parthia.

Severus now began to move against the Parthian heartland. He had boats constructed on the Euphrates and began to move downriver by boat and by land.[34] The river offered an easy entry into Parthian territory and many of the major Mesopotamian communities which could provide supplies lay along the Euphrates or the Tigris. In addition it has been pointed out that the river route favoured the Romans. It did not offer the open areas of the Mesopotamian plain that suited cavalry fighting.[35] Severus detached a column which captured an undefended Babylon, and captured Seleucia and Ctesiphon, both also undefended.[36] If there was resistance, it was minimal. As a reward for the rigours of the campaign, Severus allowed his troops to plunder Ctesiphon. During the sack there was a wholesale slaughter of the inhabitants. Dio claims he took 100,000 captives, probably for sale as slaves. In addition, the royal treasury was captured.[37] The capture of the city probably occurred at the end of 197, for in January 198 Severus took the title of Parthicus Maximus to emphasize his triumph over the Parthians and to make clear that he could defeat foreign enemies as well as domestic ones. Just over three decades before, Marcus Aurelius's co-emperor Lucius Verus had sacked Ctesiphon. It was an added propaganda bonus that his Parthian expedition and its success also emphasized this link to his adopted father Marcus Aurelius. It was certainly a connection worth having. Among the contemporary literate classes, which filled the imperial administration, a laudatory tradition about Marcus is apparent. Severus proclaimed his older son Antoninus (Caracalla) Augustus and his younger son Geta Caesar.

Less clear is what exactly he intended to do with his new conquests. Although the results of the war were disparaged by Dio as a plundering expedition, it led to the establishment of a new province of Roman Mesopotamia. The new province had Nisibis as its capital. It lay to the east of Osrhoene extending to the upper Tigris. In parallel with Osrhoene it was given an equestrian governor Tiberius Claudius Subatianus Aquila. The province's garrison consisted of two legions, I and II Parthica.[38] They were stationed at Singara in northern Mesopotamia near the Tigris, which formed an important nodal point on the province's road system, and at Rhesaina which also was an important communication node. Rhesaina controlled the route that ran from the Euphrates to the Tigris and was close to Nisibis. The organization of his new province and other matters probably consumed the best part of the spring of 198. The army, now laden with booty acquired on the campaign as well as prisoners, also needed to be reorganized for the trip up the Euphrates, especially the booty taken from Ctesiphon, as well as prisoners captured there.

It seems to have been Severus's original intention to return along the Euphrates. But his army's journey south had left that route so denuded of supplies that it was no longer usable. Severus now turned north and proceeded up the Tigris instead in conjunction with his fleet. As Platnauer long ago pointed out, the sources are so fragmented that after Ctesiphon there is no way of deciding what the emperor's ultimate goal was. It is likely that by deciding on a route that followed the Tigris he could attack Hatra, which lay about fifty miles southwest of Mosul.

Hatra, a caravan city, lay on an important route connecting Seleucia and Nisibis. Its strategic position later led to its being used as a Roman garrison point. Economically and militarily it was important, but there were other factors that probably influenced Severus's decision to try to capture it. Taking it offered important advantages. First, it would complete the Roman capture of all the major fortress cities between the Euphrates and Tigris. Second, its strong economy had made it into a very wealthy city and that wealth would offset the enormous expenses of the war with the Parthians. But there were also compelling intangible factors. He had duplicated the successes against the Parthians that Rome had enjoyed under Marcus. However, the achievements of an earlier emperor, Trajan the model conqueror, stood as a challenge: he too had defeated the Parthians, captured Ctesiphon and turned all of Mesopotamia into a province only to have it fall apart after his death. He too had, like Severus, tried to take Hatra but had failed like Severus after his war with Niger. If Severus could take it, he could surpass Trajan.

Severus and his army arrived at Hatra probably in the late summer of 198, after he had completed his arrangements for Mesopotamia. He laid waste the territory of the Atreni, whose main city it was. They were Scenite Arabs who seem to have inhabited the southern Mesopotamian interior between the two rivers.[39] Although nominally subject to the Parthians, they were able to maintain a great deal of autonomy until the 220s. With the disappearance of the Parthian empire, they allied with Rome in 225. The alliance survived until the city was taken by the Sasanians in 241 and destroyed.[40] On the eve of Severus's attack, the city had formidable fortifications, consisting of double concentric walls. In addition, like many Near Eastern peoples, the Atreni were excellent archers and possessed effective artillery to repel besiegers. Finally, and perhaps most importantly, its climate and topography played a significant role in its defence. It lies in the desert steppe of northern Iraq and, as Dio remarks, its territory lacked the water, timber and fodder needed to support a sizeable besieging army.[41] The desert climate meant that any army operating there in the summer would suffer from extreme heat.

Despite the season, Severus began to besiege Hatra. The defenders' siege engines were effective in repelling attacks, and using clay pots filled with inflammable naphtha set on fire and destroyed the Roman siege engines. Given the lack of wood, replacing them was difficult and time-consuming. The Hatrians filled other clay pots with poisonous insects and snakes and launched them against the besieging Romans. Not only were the Roman siege engines destroyed, but they also suffered heavy casualties. The siege of 198 ended in failure and Severus had to withdraw.[42]

The failure had a strange sequel.[43] The first and less important incident involved a praetorian tribune Julius Crispus. Dio claims that Crispus, dismayed by the results of the siege, quoted some verses of Vergil in the *Aeneid* in which a soldier laments his fate and blames it on the self-centredness of his commander.[44] His quote was reported to Severus and his execution soon followed, with the informer awarded the vacant tribunate. A second casualty of the siege was Julius Laetus, the hero of the siege of Nisibis. Dio implies that Laetus' murder was motivated by his distinguished record and popularity with the soldiers which excited Severus's jealousy. There is no reason to doubt jealousy as a motivation, perhaps encouraged by Severus's close friend Plautianus who may have seen Laetus as a possible rival.[45] In addition, Severus in his frustration at the siege's failure may have been looking for someone to blame and Laetus would have been a useful scapegoat.

Probably during 198, Severus made several modifications to the borders of the eastern provinces. Syria Phoenice, created by Severus's division of the province of Syria into two parts, embraced far more than the traditionally Phoenician coast. It now included the great mountain chains of the Anti-Taurus in southeastern Turkey and Mount Hermon which forms a mountain cluster at the southern end of the Anti-Taurus. It extended inland across the southern Syrian plain and included Damascus and the important caravan city of Palmyra in the Syrian desert.[46] Parts of the province were added to Roman Arabia. Arabia had been created by the Emperor Trajan in 106. Its capital was Bostra, which was also the base for its sole legion, III Cyrenaica, which protected the northern part of the province. Under its first governor, Cornelius Palma, a new road was constructed, the *Via Nova Traiana*, which ran all the way from Bostra in the north of the province to Aila in the south on the Red Sea. It formed a link to neighbouring provinces as well as to important cities within the province. The Roman frontier now moved beyond this road, which was never a fortified barrier, into the Azraq basin in north central Jordan from which a route ran down the Wadi Sirhan in northwestern Saudi Arabia, into central Arabia and Yemen, and finally ended at the Persian Gulf. Severus made a determined effort to strengthen the military defences of the province's frontier. There was particular activity in the Wadi Sirhan depression near the town of Azraq. As has been suggested, the annexation of Mesopotamia led to the need to create stronger defences in the desert approaches and to protect desert trade routes leading north.

In 199, Severus launched another attack on Hatra. This time he seems to have made far more extensive preparations, including a large store of food and timber for building various siege engines. Once again he employed the Bithynian engineer Priscus to construct the new siege engines.[47] Despite the extensive preparations, this siege also ended in failure. The excellent Arab cavalry successfully attacked Severus's foraging expeditions. Dio singles out the excellent and effective archery of the defenders and of their artillery. There were Arab counterattacks on foragers which strained the food supply; the large army, fixed in place by the siege in the middle of an arid steppe, was particularly vulnerable to starvation. When the Romans approached the city walls, they were once again assailed by burning naphtha. The naphtha not only caused casualties among the troops but also destroyed siege engines. Dio claims that only those of Priscus survived.

In the course of the siege, the Romans finally created a breach in the outer wall, but the emperor restrained his troops from rushing in. Severus had retreat sounded to halt the soldiers from penetrating further into the city. Dio claims he was deterred by his hope that the city would come to terms to spare its temple to the Sun God and the great wealth that had accumulated from its cult and from its caravan trade as well as sparing the citizens. The emperor waited a day for it to come to terms. The next day, with no response, he ordered his troops to renew their assault. When they did so, they found that during the night the Atreni had rebuilt the wall that they had breached. Soldiers, who Dio calls the Europeans, mutinied and broke off their assault in their fury at the way the siege was being handled, while another group that Dio calls the Syrians continued their attack and suffered heavy losses as a result.

More surprisingly, after all this effort Severus broke off the siege in twenty days. The only coherent account is Dio's and it is difficult to interpret.[48] Two important questions remain. First, why did Severus not continue the assault after the breach in the outer wall had been made, and the second is why did he break off the siege after only twenty days? As to the first question, it is important to remember that the breach was only made in the outer wall and that the inner wall was presumably intact. As D.B. Campbell has pointed out, there are known Roman sieges where an initial breech was made in a relatively short time, but the rest of the siege went on for far longer.[49] He cites the siege of Jerusalem in 70 when the outer wall was pierced by the Romans in fifteen days, but a further five months were necessary to take the inner fortifications and the city.[50] This would have meant pursuing an extended siege in an unforgiving environment and against an effective defence. In the end, it most likely would have been a costly and futile exercise. There is no evidence to suggest that Hatra and Severus came to terms. Nothing redeemed the siege's failure.

These facts probably explain the shortness of the siege. Severus's attempt to extract a treaty had failed, but the renewed attack led to even more unsettling results. The so-called European troops, enraged by Severus's actions, mutinied. Dio calls them Severus's only effective troops while he disparages the Syrians who had failed to take the city. It is odd that Dio should make such a distinction, as up until this point there is no hint in our sources that such a distinction existed. It has been suggested that the troops were not Europeans in the geographical sense, but soldiers quartered at Dura-Europus.[51] Other scholars accept the term to mean soldiers from Europe and we know that Severus took a substantial number of Europeans on the campaign. It would be astonishing if a general term simply referred to the garrison of an important but mostly obscure city on the Euphrates. Adding some weight to the argument that the term Europeans is used in a geographical sense is the arrival of a Gothic auxiliary unit in Arabia. The inscription that attests its presence belongs to 208, but as G.W. Bowersock argues, it most likely arrived with the force that defeated the Parthians in Severus's second Mesopotamian campaign.[52]

With the war over and new provincial arrangements put in place, Severus returned to Nisibis and then went on to Antioch. After a short interval, he then headed south to Egypt, probably in late 200, passing through Palestine. Probably at this time he lifted the sanctions he had imposed on the province for supporting Niger.[53] It may be that Severus also granted Palmyra colonial status at this point.[54]

Entering Egypt, Severus sacrificed to the spirt of Pompey, presumably at Pelusium at the extreme northeastern mouth of the Nile on the direct route from Palestine. It was here in 48 BC that after his defeat at Pharsalus, Pompey in flight from Caesar had landed and had then been assassinated by the Ptolemaic government. There was a precedent for Severus's act. Hadrian, passing this way in 130, likewise sacrificed to the great conqueror and rebuilt his tomb.

As Severus sailed on from Pelusium towards upper Egypt, he journeyed as both an emperor and a tourist. The emperor undertook a reform of a province which had supported Niger, but which had judiciously come over to Severus's side before it was too late. The emperor concentrated his reforms on the provincial capital, Alexandria. Although the second largest city in the empire as well as being a major commercial centre, it lacked a city council. This limited the ability of the town to make independent decisions and was also a hallmark of Greek status. Alexandria prided itself on its Greekness and considered itself superior to the native Egyptian population. The city had been deprived of its council during the struggles of the Ptolemaic period. It was during this time that antagonism between Greeks and Jews intensified. The struggles between the two groups continued into the Roman period. Despite the loss of their council, the Alexandrians were used by the Romans as administrators in the province and retained important privileges such as the possibility of gaining Roman citizenship.

The city remained a volatile mix and in the 30s and 40s of the first century there was serious rioting between Greeks and the large Jewish community as well as against Roman control. In part these riots were sparked by the continued refusal of the Roman government to grant a council and the feeling that the Romans favoured the Jews at the Greeks' expense.[55]

Severus lifted the penalties under which Alexandria suffered. It was granted a city council, which began to meet during the spring of either 200 or 201. At the same time, councils were also granted to the towns that served as local administrative centres in the rest of Egypt.

Severus or his son Caracalla passed a law that allowed Jews to hold municipal office.[56] The move may have been an attempt to lighten the burden of imperial officials as the establishment of councils now meant that the council members were responsible for the collection of taxes for the central government. Thus there would be more councillors available to carry out this task. The use of the local administration as agents of the imperial government was part of the Greek and Roman liturgical system, which made the wealthy who would usually be council members responsible for various governmental functions. Allowing Jews to hold municipal office also made them liable to these liturgies.[57] The emperor's attitude to Christians was less favourable: he made conversion to Christianity a punishable offence.[58] Along with Severus's generous grants of colonial status it points to an attempt to promote uniformity in the administration of the empire. A clear signal of this was the stationing of II Parthica in Italy which for two centuries had only the Praetorian Guard and the other military stationed in the city. In addition, he gave a number of public buildings to the city showing his favour to it.

For much of the trip, the tourist replaced the administrator. It displayed another side of the emperor's personality. That aspect of Severus comes out in Dio's description of Severus's character. He emphasizes the emperor's interest in learning and his religious sensibilities.[59] The *Historia Augusta* emphasizes his pleasure in certain Egyptian religious rites and his visiting many ancient monuments.[60] His behaviour conforms to elite attitudes towards Egypt and its Pharaonic culture. The attitude was to some extent mixed with a disdain for Egyptian religion and its animal gods, a disdain probably intensified if a province was resistant to Roman control and had revolted. The Romans had had trouble not only in Alexandria but also in the countryside. Three decades earlier a major revolt had occurred during the reign of Marcus Aurelius. In 172 under the leadership of the *Boukoloi*, the term literally means herders, a major revolt broke out in the Nile delta. It is likely that this was not a revolt only of herders but rather a general rising of the people of the Nile Delta. Under the leadership of an Egyptian priest it spread to the rest of Egypt and might well have resulted in the capture of Alexandria if Avidius Cassius, the governor of Syria, had not intervened.[61]

On the other hand, there was a fascination with its culture which many thought the oldest in the world. There was a particular interest in its monuments, often expressed in the Roman period by the appearance of Nilotic motifs in Roman private and public decoration and in gardens and parks laid out in Egyptian style. Its literary counterpart was the appearance of Greek novels set in Egypt.[62] For the emperor this would have been a first visit as senators were forbidden to enter Egypt without imperial permission. Its wealth, the fact that it was a major granary for Rome and was easily defensible, made it a province that the imperial government needed to monitor. In fact, for these reasons it was the first Roman province to have a legionary garrison under an equestrian prefect's command.

In Alexandria Severus inspected the tomb of Alexander the Great. It had long been an object of special veneration for Roman magistrates and commanders. In the Republic, Roman commanders such as Pompey had modelled themselves on Alexander. When Augustus visited Alexandria in 30 BC he had the body of Alexander and its sarcophagus brought from its shrine. He adorned it with flowers and placed on it a golden crown. When invited to view the tombs of the Ptolemies, he supposedly refused to so on the grounds that he was interested in seeing a king not corpses.[63] He then locked up the tomb so that no one else could view the body. Dio mentions that Severus collected books from the tomb and from other sacred sites so as to be able to monopolize and control the sacred writings they contained. He also sacrificed to the well-known Egyptian god Serapis who had followers across the Mediterranean.[64] Interestingly, the god was a combined Greek and Egyptian deity, designed by the first Ptolemaic ruler of Egypt, Ptolemy I (303–282 BC) to bind the two groups together. Ptolemy succeeded brilliantly. Serapis became a national god worshipped by the two groups. His special significance for Rome is that he was the god who protected the grain shipments from Egypt on which the city's food supply depended. He appears on Roman coinage under Commodus and then under Severus's son Caracalla.[65]

The confiscation of books and the ban on other religious activities underscore an important side of Severus's personality: his interest in and observance of religious practice and his belief in the importance of dreams and omens. As mentioned above, it was Dio's first work on the dreams and signs that portended Septimius' accession the throne that established a bond between Dio and the emperor.[66] They or others like them found their way into Severus own autobiography as well as being inscribed on numerous statues that he dedicated.[67] It was not merely a justification of Severus's claim to be emperor but expressed a basic preoccupation of the emperor. The same interest and beliefs extended to oracles as well. Whatever practical considerations led to Severus's choice of Julia as his second wife, he may also have been motivated to marry her by her horoscope, which predicted that she would marry a king.[68] The truth of the story is not the issue, but rather its believability. The accounts of his travels are filled with his dreams, omens and his recourse to shrines and oracles. These beliefs are typical of his age. They must have been especially important to a man like Severus, who had hopes and aspirations that involved personal danger and the possibility of death. His wife and her circle were also drawn to the supernatural. Julia's interest in wonder worker Apollonius of Tyana and the biography of him by her friend Philostratus are evidence of this.[69]

In addition to these methods of predicting the future and appeasing the supernatural, Severus was also strongly drawn to astrology. He was not the first emperor to be. Augustus' successor Tiberius had been a devotee. The last of the Flavian emperors, Domitian, executed a senator because he was known to have an imperial horoscope.[70] Severus's fascination with astrology is amply demonstrated by his having painted the ceiling of the audience rooms of the palace with a representation of the heavens at his birth. Stars needed to predict his horoscope were shown in different ways in different rooms to keep anyone else from successfully predicting his horoscope.[71] Severus's most impressive building, the Septizodium, contained statues of the seven planets around a central statue of the sun.[72]

The *Historia Augusta* presents what must be a partial catalogue of the places Severus visited in his voyage down the Nile. They are the traditional tourist sites. At Memphis, the old pharaonic capital, Severus would have seen the Pyramids and visited the Sphinx. He sailed south and at Thebes, also a one-time capital of Egypt, he would have encountered the two statues of Memnon. The statues are actually of Amenhotep III, a pharaoh of the fourteenth century BC. The Greeks identified them as statues of Memnon, a mythical king of Ethiopia, who came north to help the Trojans in their war with the Greeks and was killed by Achilles. The seated colossi became a standard tourist attraction and were covered with graffiti by passing visitors.[73] One of the two statues had been damaged by an earthquake and regularly emitted a sound at the sun's rising. Severus after his visit had it repaired but by doing so silenced it.

From Thebes, Severus may have sailed south along the Nile to Philae, a small island close to the Nile's first cataract. With the building of the new Aswan High Dam its structures were relocated. It lay on the border with Lower Nubia or the northern Sudan and had a strong garrison, serving as a garrison point for the southern limit of Roman control on the Nile. Its garrison provided detachments that were sent out to points to the south in Lower Nubia that had been conquered at the end of the first century BC. It was also an attractive tourist stop, being an important religious centre for the Egyptian goddess Isis as well as other temple complexes.[74] It is likely that Severus and his family sailed back upriver and left Egypt for Syria in early autumn 200.[75]

In Antioch in 201 the 13-year-old Caracalla received the *toga virilis* which marked the transition for a male to adulthood and was designated consul with his father for the following year. The grant of the consulship exposed the emptiness of the office. In the Republic it had been the chief executive office and had marked the culmination of a political career. It now had become a reward for loyal followers of the emperor or a mechanism to bolster the standing of members of the imperial family, particularly in enhancing the position of the chosen successor. Since Caracalla had already been named Augustus, it further marked him as the chosen successor. The next year Geta, Caracalla's slightly younger brother, received his *toga virilis*. At this point Severus probably envisioned a joint rule of his two sons. It had happened with Marcus Aurelius and his fellow ruler Lucius. It is also possible that such a situation was envisioned by the first emperor Augustus for his two adopted grandsons, Gaius and Lucius. But in Augustus' case death took a hand and neither grandson survived him. It was a problem that always surfaced when there was more than one son in the imperial house. Normally, death, natural or otherwise, solved the problem. In the case of Marcus and Lucius the forbearance of Marcus permitted it.[76] In the later empire multiple emperors ruled. The work of ruling had become so arduous that one man could no longer perform it. The attempt to solidify his family's hold on power was now advertised on the coinage, which increasingly stressed eternal imperial control by Severus and his family and concord within the family.[77] The stress on family and the perpetuation of its rule increased as Severus aged. In 201 he would have been 55, a not inconsiderable age for a Roman of this period.

With his victory over the Parthians completed and the new administrative arrangements finished, Severus started for Rome. The tenth anniversary of his accession to the throne was approaching and he had a triumph to celebrate, a triumph which would enhance his own and his family's glory.

Chapter 7

Rome and Africa

oon after Severus and Caracalla entered their joint consulate in January 202 at Antioch, Severus left the city and returned to Rome. He seems to have gone overland through Asia Minor, then crossed to Byzantium. He then journeyed through Thrace where he founded a new trading centre, Forum Pizius in modern Bulgaria.[1] His later movements are unclear. Herodian claims that he visited the legionary camps in Moesia and Pannonia. As has been pointed out, there is no definite evidence for a route through the Danubian provinces, but it is more likely than not. It is hard to believe he would have failed to visit the area that supplied the majority of the Praetorian Guard that accompanied him and had played an important role in his victories. As Birley suggests, given that the Danubian legions were the single most powerful military force in the empire, he would certainly have taken the opportunity to confer with the provincial governors who commanded them. In addition, he surely would have wanted to inspect those parts of the frontier where the Romans were extending their frontiers.[2]

The emperor celebrated his arrival in Rome by giving lavish gifts to certain groups of citizens and to the Pretorian Guard.[3] Members of both groups also received distributions of gold coins, one for each of the ten years of Severus's reign.[4] These were substantial sums and the sizeable amounts were meant to honour his *decennalia* or tenth anniversary as emperor which fell on 9 April 202.[5] There were lavish celebrations as well, with games and other festivities.

Severus made a further bid to increase his popularity with the urban populace. He had been away from Rome for most of his reign which must have distanced him from the people. He also may have wanted to strengthen the Romans' loyalty to his dynasty, especially in light of the marriage of his elder son. Various grain mills were built in different parts of the city. It was a major undertaking that would not be completed until the reign of Severus Alexander, the last member of Severan dynasty, who came to the throne in 222 and was murdered in 235.

In the context of his triumphal return, he staged the marriage of Caracalla to Plautilla, the daughter of his praetorian perfect Plautianus. Both
were young. Caracalla was 13 and although her birthdate is not known his
bride was probably born about the same time as he was.[6] Dio, no friend
of her father, describes a lavish wedding which he no doubt attended. Dio
criticized Plautianus for the extravagance of his daughter's dowry. He says
he saw the parade of gifts as they made their way from the Forum to the
palace. He claimed that the prefect had given in gifts as much as would have
sufficed for the dowries of fifty women of royal rank. Then Dio attended the
wedding banquet which he describes as being partly in royal and partly in
barbaric style. There were not only cooked but also raw meats, and animals
served up while still alive. The bride assumed the title of Augusta. Coinage
for the new Augusta was soon to appear with an emphasis on Pietas, the
goddess who personified piety, and Venus. Venus must refer to hoped-for
fecundity and Pietas should be understood in a dynastic context stressing
her loyalty to the dynasty. Both Venus and Pietas also appear on the coins
of Julia Domna. One theme on Plautilla's coinage, Concordia, may reflect
problems within the imperial family.[7] It also is an important theme on
Julia's coinage. The marriage was not to be a happy one. Dio claims that
she was shameless and disgusted Caracalla, but much of the resentment
her husband felt was probably due to the actions of her father. Some of it
may have been exaggerated to explain her father's later execution and her
exile after his death.

There were extravagant games presented which Dio, who must have
attended them, has described. He gives an account of a special structure
in the shape of a boat. At a signal the structure fell apart and hundreds of
animals were released, including some that had never been seen in Rome
before. According to Dio the fantastic sum of 200,000,000 sesterces were
spent on these celebrations.[8] Their luxury is remarkable given the expenses
that the constant warfare of Severus's reign had entailed. It gives an idea
of the vast amount of wealth that flowed into the imperial treasury from
purges, confiscations and the wars in the wealthy East.

The Senate, as was customary, had awarded a triumph to the emperor
for his victories. But it is not clear if the emperor ever celebrated it. One
of its traditional ceremonies was a triumphal procession that passed
through the centre of the city and culminated in the honoured commander
ascending the steps of the Capitoline Hill to sacrifice to Jupiter for his
victory. Despite the elaborate celebrations described in the sources, there is
no reference to such a procession in Dio or Herodian. The *Historia Augusta*

claims that Severus refused the Senate's offer because of a serious case of gout that would have made standing in the chariot and then climbing the Capitoline Hill an unbearable agony. However, he did give his son permission to celebrate one for some rather shadowy successes in Judaea. Given Caracalla's age, it was clearly meant to honour Severus as well. Nothing further is known about this triumph.[9] It is likely that the celebrations mentioned by Dio and Herodian highlighted Severus's military successes and were a kind of substitute for a formal triumph.[10] Severus had already marked his victory over Parthia by taking the title of Parthicus Maximus in 198. His coinage celebrated his eastern triumphs with legends such as *Victoria Parthica Maxima* (Greatest Parthian Victory) and *Victoria Aeterna* (Eternal Victory).[11]

Severus also memorialized his victories in a more concrete fashion. He built a number of structures to line the route that triumphs customarily took. The most impressive was the enormous Septizodium at the southeast corner of the Palatine Hill where it overlooked the triumphal route. It was decorated with statues of the planetary gods and the sun. There were also statues of Severus and his family, along with those of prior Antonine emperors with whom Severus claimed kinship. The structure seems to have functioned as a monumental fountain. The façade bore an inscription in foot-high letters. It proclaimed that his right to rule was divinely ordained – a useful claim for a man who had come to power by violence. It has even been argued that Severus was creating a larger monumental zone to memorialize his reign and family. With Severus's triumphal return and the marriage of his eldest son, his *decennalia* makes a fitting context for its construction.[12]

The most visible expression of Severus's status as emperor and conqueror was the award of a triumphal arch by the Senate during the *decennalia*. It was finished and dedicated the following year.[13] It was located in the northwest corner of the Roman Forum, sited on the route that triumphs followed known as the Sacred Way, across from the triumphal arch of Augustus that also celebrated a victory over the Parthians. It thus juxtaposed Severus's victory with that of the first emperor. An even closer parallel was created by having Severus's arch imitate the three portals of Augustus. The long inscription on the attic of the arch lists Severus's victories over the Parthians, he having been awarded the title of victorious general eleven times, and praises him as defender of the state and an enlarger of its boundaries. His sons are also praised on the monument.[14] It is as much an assertion of dynastic continuity as a statement of the emperor's victories. The effect was enhanced by the bronze statue that topped the arch, portraying Severus in a four-horse chariot with his two sons flanking him on horseback. It was an obvious allusion to the triumphal parade.[15]

The reliefs on the arch portray several different scenes. There is a frieze of the triumphal procession in 202, but as mentioned earlier it is not clear that it ever took place. Although other figures appear on the arch, the two highly visible panels on each face of the arch portray scenes from the Parthian War. The first panel on the side facing the Forum shows the army setting out from camp and then liberating Nisibis. The second panel continues the campaign with the capture of Edessa and the surrender of what must have been the Parthian garrison. The other side shows the sieges of Seleucia and Ctesiphon, the final significant battle in the Parthian War.[16]

The marriage of Plautianus' daughter to the imperial heir was an extraordinary mark of imperial favour. It signalled the height to which Severus had raised his praetorian prefect. The only parallel to the height of influence that Plautianus reached is Aelius Sejanus almost two centuries earlier. Under the Emperor Tiberius, Sejanus achieved extraordinary power and promotion. But like Plautianus he was to pay a heavy price for his eminence. Raised to the consulship as a colleague of the emperor, he was executed by him in AD 31.

Like Severus, Plautianus came from Lepcis Magna and was related through his mother's family to Severus. His early career was not exceptional. It is possible that during Severus's coup in 193 he was prefect of the *vigiles* or night watch of the city. He could have been appointed by either Commodus or Pertinax. If Pertinax, he might have played some part in Laetus' conspiracy.

Whatever the circumstances, Plautianus was quick to ally himself with his relative and won Severus's trust. At the start of the war with Niger, Severus sent Plautianus to secure Niger's children.[17] He accompanied Severus in the campaign against Niger. In fact, an inscription proclaims that he accompanied Severus on all his expeditions before his downfall and death.[18] At the start of 197 he was appointed praetorian perfect and remained sole prefect except for a short interval until his death. In 197 he was awarded consular ornaments. Such ornaments signified an honorary consulship which raised him to senatorial status. He held the consulship for a second time with the emperor's older brother Geta in 203.

After the Parthian War he accompanied Severus to Egypt. Severus appointed the prefect of Egypt, Aemilius Saturninus, as Plautianus' colleague. In the sources he is little more than a cipher and was eventually murdered by Plautianus. Plautianus reduced the power of Guard tribunes to prevent the possibility of a future colleague who might limit his power.[19]

Plautianus had built up his power by forging a close relationship with Severus; it was that that gave him almost unlimited power. A source reports that he had been the boy lover of Severus, but that is doubtful. First, there is no evidence for any other such relationship in the emperor's life. Dio's picture of him as rigidly traditional in his sexual behaviour tells against such a relationship.[20] Second, attempts to blacken reputations by alleging unacceptable sexual activity were a common method of attacking political opponents. For instance, both Severus's wife Julia and Plautilla are accused in the sources of shameful sexual conduct. Women were often the victims of attacks on their sexual behaviour since they normally did not have an active political role.

During the imperial family's travels in the east, Plautianus managed to replace Julia as Severus's confidant and advisor.[21] Plautianus harassed her with continual investigations into her conduct and by using torture on her friends and confidants. These tactics were so effective that Julia ceased political activity and withdrew into the company of literary men and philosophers.[22] There is a clear sign of her loss of influence in that her friends and relatives cease to be appointed to official positions while Plautianus was almost all-powerful.[23]

Dio provides the fullest description of Plautianus' behaviour. Since Dio knew that his work would be read by contemporaries, the description of Plautianus' behaviour must be generally accurate, although probably darkened given the historian's dislike of the prefect. It must have been written after the prefect's death, when he was no longer a threat.

Plautianus' outrageous behaviour seems have been particularly evident during the period after the Second Parthian War while Severus and he were still in the East. Dio accuses him of taking what he wanted from everyone and claims that there were no limits to the man's greed. He claims that his depredations were not limited to the East; he plundered the entire empire. Dio singles out the centurions he sent to steal the horses sacred to the sun from islands of the Red Sea. Interestingly, he calls them striped horses – they were probably zebras. The action he singles out as the most egregious was the castration of one hundred Roman citizens of noble birth. He adds that he did not limit himself to boys but also castrated grown men. The mass castration was carried out so that his daughter Plautilla could have only eunuchs as her attendants. This is such an outrageous action that it is hard to not suspect that Dio is not embellishing. He also seems to have set up a number of statues larger and grander than anyone else's, including those of Severus and his sons. Apparently his name was added to the yearly oaths taken to the emperor.[24] Such self-advertisement was extremely dangerous. If he tried the emperor's patience, the result could be catastrophic for him.

Dio twice makes clear that the fault for these excesses lay with the emperor.[25] He even suggests that Plautianus had been led to believe he might become emperor, although this seems highly unlikely. Severus had his sons and the idea that he would disinherit them in favour of Plautianus seems implausible.[26] Dio's assessment of Severus's character is strongly at odds with such an idea.[27] Any explanation of the reasons for Severus's attitude towards his prefect can only be conjectural. Severus's adversarial behaviour towards the Senate must have made it difficult for the emperor to trust and confide in senators. His sons were too young for such a role. There was his brother Geta, but his lack of advancement under Severus may hint at some estrangement between the brothers. Plautianus could offer a source of support and serve as a close confidant. The emperor's isolation must have drawn him to Plautianus as someone whom he knew and who, since he was totally dependent on Severus, could be trusted.

Late in 202 or early in the following year, the imperial family including Plautilla set out for Africa in the company of Plautianus.[28] With Severus at the peak of his reputation and influence, it might have seemed a suitable time to return to his home province. It remained one of the most important provinces in the empire. It was the richest province in the western half of the empire and beginning in the second century had supplied numerous senators and equestrians active in imperial service. It also had become the most active centre of Latin literature.

Unlike neighbouring Egypt and Cyrenaica, Africa had had few imperial visitors. The only prior imperial visitor was Hadrian in 128, almost three-quarters of a century before Severus. After Severus's tour, no emperor would visit again until the end of the third century. The lack of direct imperial attention to Roman North Africa may in part be due to the lack of any important threat along its borders. Inland tribes harassed Africa proper and Mauretania, but they were never until the mid-third century an existential threat. West of Egypt and Cyrenaica only one legion and auxiliary forces held the north African littoral.

The visit must have been motivated by nostalgia and probably also by more prosaic considerations. Severus visited his hometown Lepcis, bestowing the *ius Italicum* on it, which gave it freedom from taxation. He also began a substantial programme of urban renewal and embellishment, another way of celebrating his reign and himself. The buildings were magnificent, on a scale unparalleled elsewhere in Africa. The port was rebuilt and expanded with a long colonnaded street running from the port through to a new forum. The centrepiece of the new civic centre was a temple of the imperial cult dedicated to the worship of Severus and his family.[29] Also in the forum, Severus began construction of a basilica which was completed by his son Caracalla. For the emperor probably the most important new structure was a triumphal arch. The arch was a quadriform or four-face arch, located at the traditional centre point of the city where the two main streets of the city intersected. It was erected at the time of the emperor's visit in 203. The arch, like the one in Rome, memorializes his eastern victories and the imperial family.[30] Severus then turned his attention to two other important North African cities: Carthage, the second largest city in the west, and Utica. Both were also granted the *ius Italicum*.

We hear of no special projects in Africa apart from the massive building at Lepcis. This may reflect the paucity of evidence for the trip which probably reflects its relative political unimportance. As far as Severus's attitude towards Africa is concerned, there is no evidence for any special favouritism towards the province. The strongest arguments for favouritism towards Africa and Africans have been drawn from the number of Africans who were either advisors, military commanders or occupied important posts in the imperial government. But many of the men close to Severus and later rewarded by him were not Africans. These include Cornelius Anullinus, a Spaniard and successful general who served as prefect of Rome in 196 and was awarded a second consulship (a singular honour) in 199; and Tiberius Claudius Candidus who was a Greek from Asia and commanded against Niger at the battle of Nicaea. There are many other instances of non-Africans serving with Severus and playing key roles in his success including the biographer Marius Maximus who was of Italian origin.[31] Some of these men who served Severus were African, but there is no obvious bias in their favour. The emperor's preference was for men who were closely associated with him and whom he could trust. There were also relations like his brother Septimius Geta who played important roles in his rise to power and later in his imperial service. It is well to remember that Clodius Albinus came from Hadrumentum in Africa.

A number of African senators and equestrians appear during and after Severus's reign. They reflect the wealth and increased importance of Africans evidenced by their increasing numbers in the Senate and among equestrians. The *Historia Augusta* mentions that Severus spoke with an African accent, but it is not clear if this is a fabrication or not. Dio does not mention it. More revealing is an anecdote in the *Historia Augusta* about Severus's sister's visit to Rome. The *Historia* claims that he was extremely embarrassed by her inability to speak Latin and sent her home as soon as he could.[32] That Septimius Severus was embarrassed by his sister's lack of a command of Latin argues against the idea that he promoted or was attached to some idea of a specifically African culture. In general, the culture of Roman elites was homogeneous until late in antiquity when the Greek and Roman parts of the empire began to pull apart. There is simply no evidence for significant provincial chauvinism. There was prejudice against different ethnic groups, but that did not translate into a sense of superiority, except perhaps in Italy towards provincials. People seem to have identified themselves with their cities, towns or villages, not their provinces. Witness the rivalry and boundary problems between Lepcis and Oea in Tripolitania or Antioch and Laodicea which had unpleasant consequences for the latter after the war with Niger. It was personal and family connections that seem to have mattered most.

Although there were no pressing military threats, Severus did alter the province's defensive arrangements. Probably in the course of his visit Severus divided the large African province. The imperial legate, who commanded III Augusta, the province's main military force, stationed at Lambaesis in Numidia, was made governor of the new province of Numidia.[33] In modern terms this was the area north of the Sahara that roughly corresponds to western Tunisia and eastern Algeria. The rest of the African province continued to be governed by a senatorial proconsul. Such a division seems to be part of a consistent policy of splitting large and potentially threatening provinces such as Syria and Britain into smaller entities. At the end of the third century under Diocletian this would become standard policy with smaller provinces and separation of military and civilian government. The total number of troops in Numidia and the two Mauretanias was relatively small. A reasonable estimate is about 12,000, although numbers varied over time. Despite the small number, the problem that North Africa presented was its key role in ensuring the food supply of Rome. Without it Rome faced potential shortages and perhaps famine.

The military problem the Romans faced was the defence of a large area from attacks by largely nomadic tribes on horseback. This made the auxiliary units in some ways more important than III Augusta, which was an infantry unit with a small cavalry contingent. Under Severus the southern boundaries of Roman Africa were extended far to the south into the desert. The extension seems to have been planned in advance of Severus's visit. Several years were spent by the legate of III Augustus, Quintus Anicius Faustus, who served from 197 to 201 constructing the necessary defences. He built forts along the borders of Tripolitania. They were based on the oases located along the trails leading out of the tribal areas to the south, presumably to channel nomadic wandering and exercise some control over raiding. These supplemented and extended earlier Roman fortifications in the area. The borders were also extended south in Numidia. The furthest penetration southward came in Mauretania Caesariensis where a new frontier was created before Severus's arrival. Outposts were established forward of the existing fortifications to discourage marauding bands and give early warning of approaching trouble. These changes were directed towards enhancing control of the southern tribes. They hardly formed a defensive barrier against attack.

In 203 Severus began a campaign to end tribal pressure on the cities and towns of Tripolitania. He attacked the Garamantes, the most dangerous of the tribes on the border of Tripolitania. Their territory consisted of the oases and the stream beds known as wadis in Arabic which were dry most of the year but filled with water during the rainy season in the area of the Fezzan in southwestern Libya. They were skilled agriculturists and herders. They also enjoyed a substantial source of income from trans-Sahara trade.[34] Severus's expedition was a success; it appears that it had the desired effect.[35]

Severus and his family returned to Rome shortly before 10 June 203 and would remain there until 210. With no obvious threats to his position and most of the borders of the empire at peace, he was able to stay at the capital for the longest period of his reign.

Chapter 8

The Return to Rome

The return of the imperial family to Rome was marked by festivals and celebrations, including games. Herodian stresses the frequency and magnificence of the emperor's displays. They included wild beast hunts, musical performances, mock battles and religious ceremonies imitating the famous Eleusinian Mysteries.[1] In addition, gifts of cash were distributed to the Roman people. The chronology of the victory games Severus gave is uncertain, but more likely it was given after his return from the second Parthian war in 198.[2] They were best understood as a demonstration of the regime's success. It showed that it had successfully surmounted all its challenges both internal and external.[3] Also with his advancing age and deteriorating health Severus will have been increasingly concerned to publicize his children to assure that his family would continue to dominate the empire's fortunes.[4]

The following year, 204, saw the celebration of the most important games of all, the Secular Games. The title of these games derives from their timing. They were performed to mark the transition from one *saeculum* to the next. The *saeculum* was defined as the limit of a human lifespan. This was fixed during the Roman Republic as 100 years. The idea seems to go back to pre-Roman ideas of cosmic cycles. The games in some way marked the renewal of both the state and its people. Under Augustus the time interval was changed to 110 years for political reasons. The first attested celebration of the games is in 249 BC during the First Punic War. The next celebration followed in 146 BC. A century later the games were not held. Their celebration would have fallen in the middle of the war between Caesar and Pompei, not a time for celebration.

The celebration fell under the direction of the *quindecemviri sacris faciundis* or fifteen men in charge of sacrifices. This was one of the most prestigious of Rome's religious colleges. In fixing the date of the games, they consulted a series of prophecies known as the Sibylline Books. These were a series of Greek texts probably acquired by the Romans in the sixth or fifth centuries BC. They were often consulted in times of crisis.

They did not offer predictions, but rather the religious formulas and procedures necessary to avert impending disaster or to carry out certain rituals, such as when to hold the Secular Games.

The religious focus of the games changed under the first emperor Augustus. After his victory over Antony at Actium in 31 BC, Augustus pursued a policy during the 20s BC intended to stabilize the state and make his own position unassailable. Augustus devised a formula which allowed him, the first emperor, to disguise the power of his new position and make it appear as if the old political order still survived. His absolute power was disguised in traditional Republican governmental forms. The political future of the new dynasty he had founded now seemed secure. Although without sons to succeed himself, he had married his daughter Julia to his most important lieutenant and closest friend, Marcus Agrippa. The union had produced two sons. The elder Gaius was born in 20 BC. In 18 BC Julia was pregnant with his younger brother Lucius who would be born the following year when the Secular Games were held.

We have an inscription that provides a detailed account of the Augustan games.[5] It is in the form of an address by Augustus to the College of Fifteen who were charged with the overall arrangements for the celebration of the festival. It informed the College about the new calculation of the timing of the games, now on a 110–year cycle. It also notified the college of the date of the games, new arrangements for the games, who would preside over the various stages of the proceedings, and the dates on which the games would be held. It records two edicts of the College instructing the people about the arrangements for the games and its manner of celebration, including prayers, sacrifices, banquets and the contests themselves. The inscription also includes two decrees of the Senate. These decrees were followed up by a deliberate attempt to include the populace. Before the games took place, heralds were sent out to invite them to attend festivities which 'no one had ever seen or would see again', since it would not be repeated until the present generation had passed away. To further encourage participation, Augustus had distributed torches and other equipment for purification as well as barley, wheat and beans to be offered in sacrifice.

The games and sacrifices took place over three days and nights, from the 1st to the 3rd of June. The changes that Augustus introduced altered the focus of the celebration. Originally the sacrifices were made to the gods of the underworld and had an expiatory purpose. With Augustus, the underworld gods faded from view and the sacrifices were now to deities who promised a more benevolent and fruitful future on earth, such as the goddesses associated with childbirth and to Mother Earth with her promise of fruitfulness and abundance. There were also sacrifices to Jupiter Optimus Maximus and his consort Juno Regina. Of political significance was the addition of sacrifices to Apollo who was Augustus' personal deity.[6] Accompanying the religious sacrifices were the games themselves which were theatrical competitions.

The new format that Augustus mandated placed Augustus and his son-in-law Agrippa and thereby the ruling house at the centre of the games and stressed the rebirth that they had brought Rome, renewal after overcoming a multitude of internal and external threats to the state. For instance, in previous games the consuls had offered up the main prayers; it was now Augustus and his son-in-law Agrippa, neither of whom were consuls in 17 BC, who did so. In essence, Augustus was portrayed as a second founder of Rome.

Severus disregarded differences in timing by earlier emperors and returned to the Augustan calculation of 110 years. In 204 his secular games took place 220 years after Augustus's. The choice of the Augustan cycle was one element in a deliberate identification of Severus with Augustus. As mentioned above, Severus's arch celebrating his victory over the Parthians was deliberately sited diagonally across an open plaza from Augustus's.[7]

As is the case with the Augustan games, a fragmentary inscription survives providing some details about Severus's games. The surviving fragments make it clear that he deliberately modelled his games on those of his predecessor.[8] The facts that both emperors had overcome rivals in civil wars, extended the boundaries of the empire and had celebrated victories over the Parthians were too obvious to ignore. In addition, Severus undertook a large-scale programme of temple restoration as Augustus had before him.[9] He did his best to emphasize a parallel that strengthened his claim of legitimacy, a legitimacy more precarious given Severus's rise to power as an adventurer with no prior imperial claim.

The imperial family played an active role in the staging of the games as an earlier imperial family had in the Augustan games. The Severan games consisted of three nights of sacrifice followed by seven days of theatrical contests and chariot races. During the religious ceremonies, Severus presided over the festivities and his sons played prominent roles. Julia was also conspicuous. Severus did add some personal elements to the Augustan programme. The most striking of these was the invocation of his *di patrii* or ancestral gods. These gods were the tutelary gods of his hometown Leptis.

Originally Semitic deities, they had been romanized as Bacchus and Hercules. Dio mentions that Severus built a temple to them in Rome.[10] They also appear on his coinage. The ceremony asserted the solidarity of the imperial house, but the reality was far different. The joint consulship of the two brothers beginning in January 205 presented a false picture of family unity.

Severus faced two major family problems: the relationship between his two sons and the relationship of Plautianus, his sole praetorian prefect, to himself and to his family.

Only a year separated his two sons. His marriage to Paccia had produced no children. His marriage to Julia Domna in 187 quickly proved fruitful.[11] Antoninus, at first named Septimius Bassianus, was born on 4 April 188, his younger brother Geta was born in March of the following year. No more children followed. It is hard to avoid the conclusion that with two potential heirs produced, Severus made a deliberate decision to have no more children. Interestingly, although Domna is accused of adultery and licentiousness, no such charge is made against her husband. Given the record of earlier emperors, this is unusual enough to indicate that Severus led a relatively restrained personal life.[12] Not yet emperor, he avoided a further division of property and contention between his heirs. Otherwise, it is hard to explain the absence of more children during the remaining twenty-two years of marriage. With Severus becoming emperor, the situation was more complicated and difficult. As potential successors to the throne, the relationship of the two brothers was problematic. One possibility was to share power between the brothers.

There were precedents in Roman history. During the Republic, every year with some exceptions, two men were elected consuls to share supreme power. Their power was limited by other organs of state, especially the Senate, and also by assemblies and each other. Occasionally in the late fifth and early fourth centuries BC, consuls were replaced by other magistrates, but they were also limited by the principle of shared power. In the civil wars of the last century BC the system occasionally broke down amid the turmoil of struggles. Sometimes shared command could lead to serious problems. At the end of the second century BC, the Romans faced invasions by migrating German tribes. In 105, the refusal of one of the consuls and a proconsul to cooperate at Arausio (Orange) led to the loss of between 60,000 and 80,000 men and a defeat rivalling the Roman disaster at Cannae in 216.[13]

With the establishment of the empire by Augustus, the possibility of shared supreme power once again emerged. The first emperor sired a daughter Julia, but no sons. His daughter as wife of Marcus Agrippa filled the need for an heir with her two sons. In 17 Augustus adopted both of his grandsons as his own sons. It was clear that he intended them to be his heirs and successors. Augustus took steps to single them out by the award of various titles. Each was designated consul at age of 14, to be held five years later when they reached 19.[14] They were also appointed *principes iuventutis*, that is they were named heads of the equestrian order. They also received various military commands. Augustus's intention to create them joint emperors seems clear, but before they could assume office both died.

Augustus forced his unloved successor Tiberius, whom he adopted in AD 4, to adopt Germanicus, his deceased brother's son, at the same time even though he already had a son, Drusus, who was alive and well. The reason was no doubt that Germanicus was a great nephew of Augustus and married to a granddaughter of Augustus. Both men died before they could succeed to power. This seems to have been another attempt to create dual rule.

Under the following Flavian dynasty, Vespasian, its first emperor, chose to rapidly advance his elder son Titus, who came to the throne in 79. His younger brother Domitian was resentful of the secondary role he was assigned. It has been suggested that Vespasian saw his younger son as a backup should Titus die.[15] Titus did die after only two years on the throne, and the younger brother Domitian succeeded in 81.

By a twist of fate, after the death of Domitian in 96 none of the following emperors, the so-called Antonines, had male heirs. The dynasty perpetuated itself by a series of adoptions. In the end these adoptions led to the first imperial government of two emperors with equal powers. The Emperor Hadrian, who ruled from 118 until his death in 138, seems to have played a central role bringing this about. There has been much modern dispute about his exact role and how instrumental he was in bringing about a dual monarchy.[16] When he adopted Aurelius Antoninus his successor, like Augustus he made Antoninus, who was childless, adopt two sons.[17] The younger was Lucius Ceionius Commodus; the elder, nine years his senior, was Marcus Annius Verus. On adoption, Commodus became Lucius Verus and Marcus Annius Verus became Marcus Aurelius Antoninus, the famous Marcus Aurelius.

Hadrian died shortly after the adoptions in 138. Antoninus Pius then had a relatively quiet reign with only some serious fighting in Britain and a less important conflict in Dacia. It was not a threat to Roman control in Britain, but Roman advances beyond the existing frontier by an energetic governor led to conflict. The campaign was a success and resulted in the advance of the Roman frontier north and the building of a new Antonine Wall further north.[18]

On 7 March 161 Antoninus Pius died after having recommended Marcus and his daughter Faustina, who was Marcus's wife, to his advisors and the praetorian prefects. Marcus and Lucius Verus had remained in Antoninus' household but their political careers had diverged widely. Marcus had received a series of powers which clearly marked him out as the senior successor of his adopted father. He received three consulships, the first at the age of 19. There was the marriage to the emperor's daughter and the grant of the two main imperial powers of *imperium* (the power to command, especially military forces) and tribunician power that were the principal indications that a man had been marked out as a successor. It was more than his age that led to this preference for Marcus. It seems likely that Antoninus had preferred Marcus because of his abilities. It may be that Pius had not intended a joint monarchy and it was Marcus's actions that brought it about.

The progress of Lucius Verus had not been so spectacular. He was consul twice, in 154 and then again in 161, as opposed to Marcus's three consulates. He had also held them at a later age. More importantly, he had not been granted the two crucial powers of *imperium* and tribunician power that his brother had received. At Pius's death he still remained a private citizen, while Marcus had the powers necessary to become emperor on his own.

Despite the powers granted Marcus, he was not yet formally an emperor. For this, he still needed the titles of Augustus and *imperator* as well as the office of chief priest of the state cult, the *pontifex maximus*. The Senate was ready to award the title and the office, but Marcus refused until his adopted brother Verus had also received the full powers of an emperor. The two emperors established a successful working relationship, but Marcus remained the dominant figure. Marcus, through what seems to have been a general reluctance to accept his office, reduced the sources of friction and competition between the two.[19] Verus died in 169 at the age of 39 and his early death might have played some role in averting conflict between the adopted brothers. The succession of Marcus's son Commodus might have created friction between them as he grew older.

Despite being separated by less than a year, Caracalla's career moved faster than his brother's. In 195 he had been given the title of Caesar, which marked him out as the successor to his father. Just as important was the new name Severus gave his son. The former Bassianus was now to be known as Marcus Aurelius Antoninus while his father now adopted himself into the family of Marcus, deifying Commodus despite his reputation and naming himself the divine Commodus's brother. Further honours and titles were given to Caracalla. The coinage celebrated his having received the title of *princeps iuventutis* in 196, just as Gaius and Lucius, Augustus' intended accessors, had.[20] Caracalla was also honoured by admission into all the major priestly colleges. Then in 197 *imperator designatus* or *destinatus* were added to his titles as well as particeps imperii, (partner in rule).

The final step in Caracalla's ascent to the throne was taken in the wake of the successful conclusion of the Second Parthian War. In 199 after the fall of Ctesiphon, Caracalla was named Augustus or co-emperor with his father. He was now 11. It is striking that the new emperor did not receive his *toga virilis* marking his entry into manhood until 201. At the same time, Geta was named Caesar. In 195 their mother Domna had been given the title of *mater castrorum* (mother of the military camps), further emphasizing the link between Severus's family and that of Marcus. The title also was a way to honour the army to which Severus owed so much. Two decades earlier, the same title had been awarded by Marcus to his wife Faustina.

At the same time as the honours were given to her sons, their mother Julia was given the title of *mater Augusti et Caesaris* or mother of an emperor and a Caesar. When Geta became Augustus in 209 her title was changed to *mater Augustorum* or mother of both emperors. It was a title that honoured her as the mother of Rome's rulers and also proclaimed the unity of the imperial house. Probably under Caracalla, Domna appears on coinage not only as *mater Augusti,* mother of the emperor, but also as mother of the Senate and also as mother of the nation. The last title appears for the first time with Domna and is patterned after the traditional imperial title of father of the nation.[21] Her at least symbolic importance continued after Severus's death. Her influence seems to have increased under her son. On the news of his assassination in April 217, she committed suicide by starving herself. She had been an important cultural figure as well as a significant political advisor and confidant to her husband and to her son. His assassination robbed her of her political role and condemned her to permanent insecurity and probable execution by her son's successor. Death must have seemed an attractive option.

In 202 on the family's return from their visit to Egypt, Caracalla received the honour of opening the year as consul with his father. The same year saw his marriage to Plautilla, which was celebrated with extraordinary pomp by her father Plautianus. In 204 he presided with his father at the Secular Games, a further indication that he was to be the eventual successor.

Geta remained in the background, overshadowed by his older brother. His promotion to Caesar in 198 came three years after his brother's. In 205 he held his first consulship with his brother who was then consul for the second time. It was not until 209 that he was made an Augustus over a decade later than his brother's appointment, who was only a year older. It seems clear that until 209 Severus did not envision a dual reign with both brothers rather like Vespasian, he had in mind a system where the older brother would rule while the younger would advise and help his brother and be available to replace him should he die in office. This meant that by 209 there were, at least in theory, three emperors reigning simultaneously.

The reason for the change in 209 seems to have sprung from concerns about his sons' characters. Caracalla is judged negatively by all the ancient sources. Dio claims that he embodied the negative characteristics of the three peoples who made up his ancestry, the Gauls, Syrians and Africans.[22] In a long series of passages, Dio condemns Caracalla's character repeatedly. He denounces his thirst for blood and lack of respect for learning as well as his partiality for the military.[23]

Herodian does not give a blanket condemnation of Caracalla, but his narrative makes clear the defects of his character. Revealingly, when he describes the reaction to Caracalla's assassination, he cites the Senate's pleasure at the news. He says the senators felt that a sword poised above their necks had been removed and they immediately began to move against his supporters and agents. Herodian claims that men now lived with a sense of security and a semblance of freedom that had not existed under Caracalla.[24]

The *Historia Augusta* offers the same dark picture of the emperor as the other sources. In its life of Caracalla, it pointedly summarizes the emperor's character succinctly:

> *His mode of life was evil, and he was more brutal even than his cruel father. He was gluttonous in his use of food and addicted to wine, hated by his household and detested in every camp save that of the praetorian guard.*[25]

The portrait of Geta is only slightly more positive, perhaps due to the fact that he was assassinated before he could do much harm. Both Dio and Herodian mention the dissipation of the brothers, their abuse of women and boys as well as their corruption in money matters. However, their main preoccupation was an unceasing and unbridled rivalry with each other.[26] It went so far that the claim is made by some late sources that the brothers had different mothers.[27] This is clearly untrue. It seems to have been invented by those who were hostile to Caracalla. It calls Julia his stepmother while claiming that Geta was her only child. If true, this assertion would have strengthened the claim of Geta to be the real successor of Severus.

It has been suggested that in making Geta Augustus in 209 Severus was attempting to save his younger son's life.[28] As David Potter phrases it: 'to have disinherited Geta was as good as a death sentence.'[29]

It is hard to believe the statement of the *Historia Augusta* that at the time of his death Severus was very happy that he was leaving two Antonini (his two sons) to rule the state with equal powers. Given the absence of defined powers and competences for each of his sons, it was a disaster in the making. It had only worked with Marcus Aurelius and Lucius Verus because Marcus was willing and indeed eager to make sure that it did.[30] The intense sibling rivalry and dislike amounting to hatred between the brothers was only contained by Severus's presence. With his death, a mortal struggle between the brothers was bound to develop.

About midway through Severus's stay in Rome in January 205, a major crisis struck the imperial family. It involved the praetorian prefect Fulvius Plautianus.[31] A fellow townsman of the emperor and a distant relation, he forged a very close bond with Severus. He had joined his cause in 193 and had remained with him. Appointed praetorian prefect in 197, he murdered the other prefect Quintus Aemilius Saturninus in 200. In 202 the bond between the two men and their families was strengthened by the marriage of Plautianus' daughter Plautilla to Caracalla. An increasing parade of honours for Plautianus was added to in the next year when he held the consulship of 203 with the emperor's brother Geta. Enormous wealth had also accrued to him.

Plautianus was not reticent in displaying that wealth and his position in the state. In public his conduct struck fear in bystanders. He was accompanied by a guard who made sure that no one could approach the prefect. No one was allowed to stand and stare as he went by. No one could block his right-of-way. All who encountered him had to stand aside and avert their eyes. These actions did not endear him to the Roman populace. In early 205, crowds in the Circus taunted him, remarking on his paleness and claiming it was not warranted since he had more than the three. By the three, they meant Severus and his sons.[32]

The bond between the two men seems to have been extraordinarily close. As mentioned above, there is even a claim in the Herodian that Plautianus had been the boy lover of Severus.[33] His power is clear from the recognition he received. Dio, who is no friend, compares him to Sejanus, Tiberius's powerful prefect, noting that no other prefect approached the power that these two men wielded.[34] Significantly, he was included in the imperial house in at least one inscription.[35] The sources claim that his statues outnumbered those of the emperor.[36] He was also included in the oaths sworn by soldiers and senators. Dio claims at one point that Severus led him to hope for possible succession.[37] Given Severus's concern that at least his eldest son should succeed him, this seems an unlikely interpretation of Dio's text: '*led on to greater hopes*'. It is not clear what Dio meant.

How Plautianus won such influence with Severus is unknown. His powers as prefect were immense. Not only did he control the garrison of Rome, but also in his role as prefect was of central importance in the business of government. However, their relationship highlighted one important aspect of imperial governance. Dio blames Severus for the situation. He claims that Severus yielded to his prefect in all matters with the result that Plautianus became the *de facto* emperor and Severus his subordinate, although this seems a vast exaggeration.[38] For this situation to continue, Severus would have had to allow it to do so. In the end all power was in the hands of the emperor. Even the mightiest official like Plautianus depended on the goodwill of the sovereign. If that were withdrawn, his power would evaporate, and his life would be in serious danger.

At one point the relationship had become strained, in 201 before the return to Rome. Probably while the imperial family was in Lepcis during its African visit, Severus found out that Plautianus had more statues than the emperor himself; in Dio's version or according to the *Historia Augusta* he learned that the prefect had dared to place his own statue among those of the imperial kinsmen and close connections.[39] There is no reason to see these statements as contradicting each other. More likely, they simply are different aspects of the same story. Severus's anger had a deadly consequence. The emperor ordered that some of Plautianus' statues be melted down. This was wrongly interpreted by some that Plautianus' power was at an end. The governor of Sardinia followed what he thought was an imperial order, and melted down Plautianus' statues, paying for doing so with his life. Others who had acted similarly were put on trial and punished.[40] By the return of the party to Rome the rift between the two was healed, and if anything the prefect emerged even stronger with the extravagant marriage of his daughter.

Plautianus' actions and his power made many enemies, but the most important were in the imperial family. There was first the emperor's wife Julia. The prefect made a determined effort to undermine her position at the court and to make her life a living hell. Dio states that he detested her and made his dislike public, vilifying her to the emperor.[41] He successfully ended her influence. He then brought a charge of conspiracy against her which was unsuccessful. Julia also was taunted with the usual sexual slanders that were normal in attacks on imperial women. Among them was the accusation that she had engaged in sexual relations with Caracalla.[42] This was clearly a fabrication designed to attack both Julia and her son. The success of Plautianus is evidenced by the decrease in the size of the coinage issued that featured Julia. At least for the moment, Julia dealt with the situation by withdrawing from the court and public life. She turned her attention to philosophy and literature.[43] Despite the temporary retreat, Julia remained a significant enemy to the prefect. Plautianus was also a continuing threat to her status in the imperial house and also to the succession of her sons. Herodian suggests that fearing the succession of Severus's sons, Plautianus plotted to seize power for himself.[44]

The more significant enemy of the prefect was Caracalla. The marriage to Plautilla was a disaster. Her husband would neither eat nor sleep with her. Whatever the truth, she too was accused of illicit sexual behaviour. She was in an impossible position. Her presence was a constant reminder of her father's relationship to Severus and also of his constant meddling in his life.

There must have been constant plotting and manoeuvring by mother and son to end Plautianus' power. However, we have little definite information about the manoeuvring of either side in this period. The first effective blow against Plautianus came from the emperor's dying brother P. Septimius Geta. Early in 205, knowing that death was approaching and that he therefore no longer had anything to fear from Plautianus, he revealed the truth about him.[45] Dio does not tell us what Geta revealed, but his comments earlier in the chapter hint that he hoped to do away with Severus's sons and succeed him as emperor. Given the youth of Severus's sons and his age and health, it was a plausible accusation. It is indicative of the credence that Severus gave to the accusation that immediately upon his brother's death Severus set up an honorary statue to him in the Forum. The prefect was stripped of many of his powers immediately after Geta's death.

Although there is no explicit evidence, it is hard not to believe that Julia and Caracalla, both shunted aside, urged and influenced the dying Geta to make these accusations and after his death reinforced them by repeating the charges to the emperor. Given the strong ties that bound emperor and prefect, it seems likely that the most effective way to break them apart was to claim that Plautianus was indeed planning a coup. If believed, the accusation would justify the harshest measures.

Herodian offers a story of such a plot by Plautianus. Supposedly, Plautianus summoned one of his military tribunes, Saturninus, and instructed him to make his way into the emperor's presence and do away with both him and Caracalla. As an inducement he offered him the praetorian prefecture if he succeeded. Saturninus was horrified and asked for a written document outlining the plot, so that if challenged after he had carried out the murders, he would have proof that he acted with Plautianus' permission. Trusting Saturninus, Plautianus complied.

In the presence of the emperor, Saturninus revealed the plot and showed Severus the instructions he had received from Plautianus. It is indicative of Severus's strong feelings of affection for his prefect that he still needed to be convinced. He thought the whole thing might have been a plot by Caracalla to get rid of Plautianus. A message was sent to Plautianus that the emperors were dead and to hurry to the palace. He was arrested, but even then it took further persuasion before the prefect was executed on 22 January 205.[46]

Dio has a variant of the story which is even less plausible. He is clear that the so-called coup was a fabrication, and that the real instigator of the plot was Caracalla who wanted the hated prefect removed and at the same time to be free of Plautilla whom he hated with a vengeance. Caracalla used his tutor Euodus to persuade Severus that Plautianus had engineered a coup against him and the imperial family. He came into the presence of Severus with ten centurions, one of whom was the same Saturninus, who claimed that they had been ordered to kill Severus and Caracalla and presented a written memo that supported their claim. Dio rightly dismisses the story as a fabrication, given the circumstances. Plautianus was summoned and then admitted by himself. While the prefect was denying the charge, Caracalla rushed in, took Plautianus' sword and hit him with his fist. Caracalla was ready to finish him off when Severus stopped his son and ordered an attendant to finish the job.[47] Dio had been right that the eruption of Vesuvius had portended a great change in the government.[48]

It has plausibly been suggested that the story in Herodian is to a great extent spun out of Herodian's own imagination and based on the propaganda put out after the murder to excuse the emperor and his son from blame.[49] But the similarity to the story in Dio is evident and it is best to take the story of a plot, whatever the details, as variations of an official version. Dio's version of the aftermath of the plot contains what I believe is a significant detail. After the death of Plautianus an unnamed bystander plucked a few hairs from the prefect's beard and brought them to Julia and Plautilla. It is hard not to see the proof of death as a way of informing Julia that her plot in conjunction with Caracalla against the prefect had succeeded. Plautilla understandably was devastated both with grief for her father and fear for her own future.[50]

After it was all over, Severus summoned the Senate and in his speech to it made no accusations against the dead prefect, but simply lamented the effects of pride and high position. The speech perhaps expressed the absence of anger against Plautianus, and to some degree shifted the blame to circumstances and not the individual. Some of Plautianus' supporters were tried and some were executed. Saturninus and Euodus received honours for their role in the alleged coup. Ironically, they were later executed by Caracalla. Plautilla and her brother Plautius were banished to the island of Lipari off Sicily and lived in poverty until Caracalla ascended the throne, and were executed in 211 or 212.

Plautianus had possessed so much property that a special official and department had to be appointed to handle it. His memory was cursed and his body thrown out in the street. He was finally buried by order of Severus. He was replaced by two praetorian prefects. This dual prefecture went back to Augustus. When it was replaced by a single prefect the concentration of power and the access to the emperor of the prefect made him a potential danger for the ruler. A standard Roman procedure was evoked, which was employed in the case of traitors. A determined effort was made to erase every public and private dedication to or memento of Plautianus' and his daughter's existence. To borrow the language of a later time, the prefect and his daughter had become non-persons.[51]

As Fergus Millar has pointed out, after the fall of Plautianus the text of Dio becomes anecdotal and is focused on two subjects: the bandit Bulla Felix and the growing hostility of Caracalla and Geta towards each other.[52] This probably reflects the relatively peaceful state of the empire. The other sources add sparse information and provide little help in understanding the events of the period between 205 and 208 when Severus left Rome for the last time to wage war in Britain.

Dio describes the career of an Italian bandit Bulla Felix (Bulla the Lucky), presumably a nickname, who together with a band of 600 men preyed upon travellers between Rome and Brundisium, the main Italian port for those travelling to the eastern Mediterranean.[53] The Greek historian's account illustrates just how fragile security of life and property were in Italy.[54] Dio claims that Bulla developed an extensive intelligence network that alerted him to those travelling between Rome and Brundisium. This implies a firm base of support among the population in the area he operated. Such a base of support was an absolute necessity for bandits who depended on the local people for food and other support. Once they either chose to abandon their base or were compelled to do so, they were usually doomed. One possibility open to them was an alliance with powerful men in the region who could protect and support them in exchange for using their services.[55]

Bulla was adept at avoiding pursuit and hoodwinking the authorities. After the capture of two of his men and their condemnation to death by being thrown to the wild beasts, he disguised himself, and pretending to be the governor of his own district he persuaded the men's jailers to release them. On another occasion, when his band was under pressure from a centurion who had been instructed to destroy it, he disguised himself as a local and offered to lead the centurion to his own hideout. The centurion followed and was, of course, captured. Later Bulla had the centurion brought to him and ordered his head to be publicly shaved. He then instructed the officer to inform his masters that if they fed their slaves, their slaves would not turn to brigandage. Finally, after frustrating Severus for two years, a tribune who had been sent in pursuit pressured a woman who had had sexual relations with Bulla to betray him. The bandit was captured while asleep and brought to Rome. While on trial before Papinian,[56] the praetorian prefect, he was asked why he had become a brigand and replied, 'why did you become a prefect?' – the implication being that both lines of work were of equal worth. He was convicted of brigandage and executed by being thrown to the wild beasts in the arena.

Dio has a similar though less detailed account of another bandit, Claudius, who was overrunning and ravaging Judaea and Syria during the first war against Parthia.[57] His challenge to Severus was more direct than Bulla's. Dio informs us that, in disguise and accompanied by several horsemen, he approached Severus, saluted and kissed him and then rode off and disappeared.

Dio mentions that many members of the band were imperial freedmen who had been paid badly or not paid at all.[58] Most likely these were individuals who worked on the imperial estates in Italy and not the freedmen belonging to the central administration.[59] They had likely worked as shepherds or in other low-ranking positions on the estates. The toll of the civil wars and the trials and judicial executions that followed them vastly increased imperial holdings in Italy. The ancient sources, both historical and fictional, closely associate shepherds with bandits. The association grows out of two similarities between them. Both are rural and both share a rootlessness that sets them off from the rest of the rural population who were mostly subsistence farmers.

It is in rural and mountainous areas that the state's control was weakest. Banditry was endemic in the Roman Empire and in most other ancient states. These states simply did not have the manpower or technology to adequately project their power outside urban areas. This was particularly true of provinces with mountainous regions or with few cities and towns. It is characteristic of Rome's expansion that it encouraged the formation of urban centres as a means to incorporate local elites and to exercise control. Certain provinces often characterized by large tracts of mountainous and marginal country and by internal instability were chronic centres of banditry. In Judaea, rabbinic sources indicate that banditry was endemic in the second and third centuries.[60] The hinterland of Mauretania, where Roman control was spotty, was frequently subject to extensive tribal banditry. Early in his career, Severus experienced a serious raid by Mauritanian bandits in southern Spain. In the east in southeastern Asia Minor, endemic banditry could be found in Cilicia and to its north Isauria, as well as in other areas of southern Asia Minor.

Another source of recruits for bandit bands was the displacements resulting from the civil wars that marked Severus's reign and so explain their appearance in Dio's account. Many soldiers on the losing side of these conflicts would have found themselves without employment and with few prospects in civilian life. This would have been especially true of men from Rome's professional army.[61] Added to this were deserters, and in Italy the special case of Severus's treatment of the Praetorian Guard on his arrival in Rome in 193. He summoned the existing guard and disbanded it. Dio claims that by dismissing the Italian soldiers from the Guard he ruined the youth of Italy who had to turn to brigandage and gladiatorial fighting to sustain themselves. This might explain the solitary reference to banditry in the emperor's life in the *Historia Augusta*. Describing Severus's actions in legal cases the *Historia Augusta* calls Severus an implacable enemy to bandits.[62] What emperor was not? Perhaps the description reflects his reaction to the upsurge of such activity in Italy as a result of his own actions.

Neither bandit appears in other sources. This omission probably reflects the cursory nature of much of the life of Severus in the *Historia*

Augusta and Herodian's omissions seem arbitrary, such as his leaving out the trip by the imperial family to Africa.

Stories involving bandits were certainly a staple of upper-class literature in the second and third centuries. They seem to have exerted the same attraction that modern crime and mystery novels do today. They are fascinating because they offer a glimpse into a different world which both mimics and inverts the familiar world of their readers. It is likely that fictional material has worked its way into Dio's account, such as Claudius's encounter with Severus or Bulla's tricking of imperial officials. These incidents serve as social criticism. The bandits' tricks expose the incompetence of those in authority and their failure to fulfill their responsibilities. The inclusion of these stories in Dio, besides their intrinsic appeal, may be the result of Dio's ambiguous attitude to Severus.

The account of Bulla's actions suggests another function of contemporary banditry. When he captured travellers, he only took what he needed from them and then let them go. If they were artisans, he used their skills and then let them go with a present. In the same vein are Bulla's instructions to the centurion to tell his masters to feed their slaves, adding that if they had done so there would be no bandits. Such actions fit a type of bandit first recognized by E. Hobsbawm in his work on bandits. He formulated a new category which he called the social bandit. In Hobsbawm's conception, they are peasant bandits who are stigmatized as illegal and as a threat, but in the peasant society where they operate they are perceived in a very different way. There they are seen as heroes and avengers who act in the interests of the peasants. Hence, they are protected and supported by the rural population.[63] Essentially, the social bandit is a Robin Hood figure. That the bandits were angry at the disparity in wealth and power is certainly historical, but that they robbed to support the poor and downtrodden does not seem to be supported by the evidence. There is no real indication of active opposition to the existing social order except in very special circumstances, such as in some of the slave rebellions at the close of the Republic. That people fought to escape slavery and poverty has support in the sources, but they seem to have fought to better their own situation, not to overturn the social order. A widespread class consciousness that could coalesce into a movement of the poor against the rich is unattested in the imperial period. As in the tales of Robin Hood, the social dimension is an elaboration based on wish fulfillment.

The intensity of the struggle of Caracalla and Geta increased dramatically with the removal of Plautianus and his daughter. To see it only as a struggle over who would succeed their father is to omit the irrational hatred between the two. In 205 Caracalla had been Augustus for seven years, while Geta was only Caesar. In mid–195 Caracalla's name had been changed to Antoninus to link him to Marcus Aurelius and Marcus's son Commodus. He had campaigned with his father in the east and so was well known to the army. He had been granted the honorific title 'Father of his Country' at the tender age of 11, the year after his elevation to Augustus. He had also been named 'Leader of the Youth' which marked him out as the successor to the throne. In 202 he had held his first consulship in conjunction with his father, an important honour, and then had held his second consulship with his brother in 205. He had been inducted into all the major priestly colleges. At the same time, he appears on coins as emperor designate. It is easy to understand Geta's resentment at being an obvious runner-up and his fear about his future with his hated and hateful brother as emperor.

The brothers' conduct now was a constant round of self-indulgence and ferocious competition with each other. At one point it became so fierce that during a chariot race Caracalla fell out of his chariot and broke his leg.[64]

Each of the brothers attracted a coterie of followers and supporters who encouraged them to compete with each other and so intensified the conflict between them.[65] On any rational consideration, Geta's position was so weak that his survival would depend upon his father.

Chapter 9

The Last Act

Despite some problems on the empire's borders, Severus's time in Rome was undisturbed by large-scale foreign threats. It was the continuing problems within the imperial family that claimed his attention. The rivalry and mutual hatred that marked the relationship of his two sons had not abated during the years after Plautianus's fall. If anything they seem to have grown worse. In particular, Caracalla seems to have become more and more impatient to succeed his father and to dispose of his brother, whom he seems to have detested as a possible co-emperor with what seems to have been visceral dislike, which Geta returned.

The situation was exacerbated by Severus's poor health. What Dio and Herodian describe as gout had afflicted the emperor during the Second Parthian War. It was so bad that the *Historia Augusta* claims that he turned down a triumph when he returned to Rome after the war because he would not have been able to stand in the triumphal chariot during the procession.[1] It had worsened over time. Gout is a type of inflammatory arthritis that if not permanently treated can become chronic. It can cause recurrent, severe pain. It can also over time lead to joint degeneration, which seems to have been the case for Severus.[2] He was also approaching a dangerous time of life when death was a distinct possibility, the grand climacteric. The Romans placed it in an individual's sixty-third year. Severus was either in his sixty-third year or fast approaching it, being born in 145 or 146.[3]

Adding to the worrisome situation within the imperial family and declining personal health came news of troubles in Britain. Herodian reports that the governor of Britain, probably Lucius Alfenus Senecio, was having serious troubles with the tribes north of the Roman border which now rested on Hadrian's Wall, which ran east to west across the island from Bowness on the Solway Firth in the west to Wallsend on the north bank of the Tyne in the east. He had sent a letter to Severus either requesting reinforcements or the presence of the emperor himself.[4]

Senecio, an African like the emperor, but from Cuicul (modern Djémila) in Numidia, was a senior senator and consul who had already governed the important province of Syria Coele.[5] Having already served in a consular province in the east implies that he was a man of some military experience and that the appointment was the result of present or anticipated trouble on the border. Archaeological evidence seems to suggest that there was also trouble within the province, but that conclusion is far from certain.[6] Dio provides evidence that there was unrest and fighting in Britain shortly before 208, but he seems to indicate that Senecio had matters in hand and was winning a series of victories.[7] It may be that the situation in Britain had worsened by 208 and more help was needed.

Little is known about the military situation in that year that finally persuaded the emperor to mount a major expedition. Neither Dio nor Herodian offer any help as to what motivated Severus. The *Historia Augustus* offers no help either. Dio claims that Severus wanted to remove his sons from the luxury and temptations of Rome and through the rigours of campaigning bring about a change in their lifestyles and reconcile them to each other. He also states that Severus wanted to harden the army that was being weakened through prolonged idleness.[8] Herodian adds that it was welcome news for a man with a desire for military glory. Given his health, family considerations and the desire to end his life as a conqueror were probably paramount. So Britain, where he would probably face what he may have thought was a weak tribal adversary, seemed an attractive prospect. Dio reports that before he left, his own astrological calculations and a threatening omen that were analyzed by expert interpreters predicted that he was destined to die on the expedition. If true, it is a measure of his desire to go that he was not deterred.[9]

The Roman conquest of Britain began in 43 with an invasion under the Emperor Claudius. It had involved hard fighting and several revolts, but by the 70s of the first century at least nominal Roman control extended north to just short of the Lowlands. By the late 70s the decision was taken to extend Roman control to all of Britain and perhaps Ireland.[10] During the seven-year governorship of the historian Tacitus's father-in-law Gnaeus Julius Agricola, who governed the island from 77 to 83, Roman control was extended to the whole of Britain.[11] Although details are lacking, Agricola's conquest proved ephemeral, especially as threats to imperial security and campaigns elsewhere led to the reduction of troops in Britain.

The weakening of Rome's military presence and the tribal nature of northern Britain resulted in periods of unrest and warfare between the free tribes and the Romans. There was a major conflict with the tribes in northern Britain under Hadrian in the period 117–122 which resulted in heavy Roman casualties. It was in this period that Hadrian's Wall was built.[12] It was completed in about 125, three years after the emperor had left the province. The purpose of the wall has been much debated, and several interpretations have been offered by scholars. It is best to see it as having several functions. It marked the provincial boundary and so acted as a way of controlling movement in and out of the province. It also provided a barrier behind which it would be possible to marshal troops against elusive raiders and attackers.[13] It could not have stopped a large invading army, but, like the frontier in North Africa, there was little chance that the tribes beyond the border could form such a force. It is during the period of its construction that we find linear barriers in Germany and Africa. These often follow and protect major road systems.

Even after the building of the wall had started, there was serious fighting and there is reference to a British campaign of some magnitude in the later 120s following on substantial Roman losses.[14] This presumably defensive war was followed by an advance soon after Hadrian's death in 138. Under the next emperor, Antoninus Pius, the Romans moved north into Lowland Scotland and between 139 and 142 a new barrier was constructed by the governor Q. Lollius Urbicus. The Antonine Wall was thirty-seven miles long and ran from Old Kirkpatrick on the Clyde to Bridgeness on the Forth.[15] Instead of stone, the wall was made of turf on a stone base. Unlike Hadrian's wall the new wall was constructed without any prior Roman construction in the area. It ran across the Forth-Clyde isthmus and was backed by a number of forts which were more closely integrated into the barrier system than the forts on Hadrian's wall. The lack of prior construction in the area seems to indicate that there was little prior planning and that the move was simply expansionist, which fits with the Roman conception of endless expansion.[16] Probably as a result of this expansion Urbicus was involved in a war with the local tribes that ended in a Roman victory in 142.[17]

Early in the reign of Marcus Aurelius, within twenty years of the building of the Antonine Wall, there was a withdrawal back to Hadrian's Wall, probably by 163. The reasons for this pullback are not clear. One suggestion is that with commitments elsewhere, perhaps the war against Parthia in the early 160s may have played a role. The withdrawal seems to have been orderly and unhurried. This would imply that it was not done under local pressure and makes the need for troops elsewhere a likely reason, although there was at least the threat of troubles in Britain in the 160s.[18] Much has been made of the transfer to Britain of 5,500 Sarmatian cavalry. The Sarmatians, who provided excellent cavalry, were a tribe of Iranian extraction who then lived on the Hungarian plain. They fought as allies of the usurper Avidius Cassius who had been defeated by Marcus in 175. He had them sent to Britain. One possibility is that it was a way of both using their skills and removing them far enough from their homeland so that they would no longer be a threat. The argument has also been made that, given the size of Britain's relatively enormous garrison, this was a sign of trouble. But it may be that they replaced troops moved to other frontiers and so were not a sign of an increased threat in Britain. There is no way of deciding which alternative is correct.[19]

Under Commodus in the early 180s, tribes outside Roman control launched a major assault on the province.[20] According to Dio, this was the largest and most dangerous war that Commodus fought. It seems to have begun with a crossing of Hadrian's Wall and led to widespread destruction, including the loss of a general and his army. Commodus sent Ulpius Marcellus against them. He won a crushing victory and the danger to the province passed.[21] The gravity of the crisis is signalled by the taking of a seventh imperial salutation by Commodus in 184 as well as assuming the title of Britannicus.

Internal troubles soon followed the external threat. Ulpius Marcellus, whose eccentric character is described by Dio, may have acted so harshly that he caused a mutiny among his troops.[22] The uprising had gone so far that there was a failed attempt to set up a rival emperor and it is possible that the troops sent a large deputation to Commodus to protest the policies of his praetorian prefect Perennis, which they viewed as somehow related to their problems. The deputation probably played a role in the fall of Perennis and his execution in 185. There was further trouble under Pertinax, Marcellus's successor, which almost cost him his life.[23]

In 192, Clodius Albinus was appointed governor after a successful military career. With the assassination of Commodus, he had emerged as a major contender for the imperial throne, but he was defeated and killed by Severus in the decisive battle at Lugdunum in 197. Since Albinus had moved large forces to the continent to face Severus, it would seem to have weakened the British garrison. No doubt they were sent back after Albinus's defeat with recruits to make up for their losses, but it would have taken time for the legions to reform and train these men and to rebuild morale. It used to be thought that Albinus's removal of troops led to a series of disturbances in Britain, but the evidence for this is thin. The argument for a serious disturbance rested on what was thought to be a serious breaching of Roman defences in 197, signs of destruction and long-delayed repairs carried out on Hadrian's Wall and also signs of rebellion and the destruction of forts in Wales.[24] But more recent archaeological work has made such a scenario unlikely.[25]

One further piece of evidence has been advanced to argue for large-scale problems at this time in Britain. A large payment was made by Virius Lupus, the governor who replaced Albinus, to the Maeatae who lived in southern Scotland close to the Antonine Wall.[26] From Dio's account, it appears that the Caledonians, another Celtic group north of the Maeatae, were about to ally with them, presumably to raid Roman territory. Given the weakened condition of the garrison so soon after Albinus, and Severus's preoccupation elsewhere, the fact that a governor had to buy off raiding by these groups is hardly surprising and offers no support for fighting and destruction on a large scale. Rather, increased raiding in the face of temporary Roman weakness best explains the payments and the situation in Britain.

As suggested above, what seems to have been a string of victories appears to have ended by 208. It was in the context of the changed situation that Severus set out to campaign in Britain. As had happened in the campaigns in the east, the entire imperial family set off for Britain along with senatorial advisors. The serious state of the emperor's health was evident, as for most of the journey he was carried in a litter.[27] From the evidence of coinage, Severus, his entourage and the army left Rome in the early months of 208. They proceeded north to the Channel through Gaul. It seems that the roads in Gaul had been specially renovated to accommodate the imperial passage.[28] Neither Severus's point of departure from Gaul nor where he landed in Britain are known. He then proceeded north and made his base at Eboracum (York), which later became the capital of the new province of Britannia Inferior.

We lack sufficient information to trace the course of the campaign in detail. Certainly before the civil war with Albinus, Britain had the largest garrison of any province in the empire, which points to continuing problems with tribes both inside and outside the province. The garrison consisted of the legions II Augusta based at Caerleon, XX Valeria Victrix at Chester and VI Victrix at York. The legions together with a number of auxiliary formations probably totalled about 50,000 men. This was close to one-sixth of the total armed strength of the empire. How far this paper strength corresponded to reality is unknown. Severus certainly brought additional troops with him. Most were probably battle groups drawn from the legions, which the Romans called *vexillationes*. It was less disruptive to provincial defence than removing whole legions, which would have substantially weakened a province's military forces.[29] The most likely source for these troops were the German legions. These were the same legions that had declared for him in 193 and had supported his march on Rome. It is also likely that he was accompanied by at least some troops from II Parthica along with the Praetorian Guard. Given the lack of information we have no idea about the size of the force at Severus's disposal. Herodian claims that the tribes who were to be the objects of the campaign were so overawed by the size of Roman forces that they sought peace terms.[30]

The embassy from the Maeatae and the Caledonians achieved nothing, and it seems likely that Severus at this stage did not want peace. An immediate peace would achieve little. It would not heal the rift between his sons or allow them to gain popularity with the army or give them military and administrative experience. On his own account, he probably thought of the continuation of the campaign as a way to bring peace to Britain and have a last chance to win military glory for himself. The sources say little about what he expected the campaign to achieve. Dio claims that he envisioned the subjugation of the entire island.[31] Neither Herodian nor the *Historia Augusta* offer any enlightenment. That he wanted to end any threat by the northern tribes to the province is obvious, but even Dio's statement is ambiguous as to the final fate of his conquests. The key question is, was he seeking to permanently extend the province so as to include the whole island? Scotland was not wealthy, and it would probably have cost more to garrison and administer it than it would have yielded in revenue. But the Romans for reasons of personal prestige had undertaken such conquests before. Claudius's invasion of Britain was one such project. The Greek geographer Strabo writing under Augustus wrote that if the Romans conquered Britain they would need at least one legion and some cavalry (a striking underestimation) to garrison it, which would more than offset any tribute money it might produce, and claims that this dissuaded Augustus from attempting its conquest.[32]

There is no simple answer to the question of what the emperor's intentions were and modern scholars have offered different analyses of them. Brian Campbell's suggestion is that Severus had not made a final decision at the beginning of the campaign about what he wanted to achieve. He proposes that Severus wavered between a full conquest of the north and a large-scale punitive expedition which would cow the northern tribes and secure a frontier based on Hadrian's Wall.[33] This seems a reasonable interpretation of the existing evidence.

Severus assigned different roles to his sons, probably to keep them apart and at the same time train them for their imperial responsibilities. Geta was left behind at York in charge of the civil administration. The praetorian prefect Papinian, who was an eminent jurist, had been brought along on the expedition and it is likely that his primary responsibility was to assist Geta in his administrative tasks.[34] He was also an associate of Julia and these two facts probably explain his presence, as he had no military experience.

In either late 208 or more probably during the spring of the following year, Severus and Caracalla opened the campaign against the Maeatae and their northern neighbours the Caledonians. The sources give little help in localizing these people or in characterizing them. Dio claims that the north Britons were divided into two groups: in the south, the Maeatae and to their north the Caledonians. He claims that they were not tribes but tribal confederations. Such confederations, which also developed on the German and Danubian frontiers, were in part a response to the presence of Rome. It was Roman expansion and pressure on these peoples, her introduction of new technology, both military and in the form of new social groups, that created the need and presented the opportunity for larger social entities to form. The Maeatae may have been formed relatively recently as they first appear in Roman sources at the end of the second century, while the Caledonians first appear earlier at the end of the first century and there is some evidence that they might have been formed at an even earlier date. Dio mentions that the Maeatae lived near the wall which cuts the island in half. There has been a great deal of dispute over which wall Dio meant. Was it Hadrian's Wall, the provincial boundary, or the now abandoned Antonine Wall which must still have been standing? They are separated by over one hundred miles. The general opinion is that they occupied the northern Scottish Lowlands, the Antonine Wall area, and Fife.[35] The fact that they are not heard of again after Severus's invasions may be due to the destabilizing effects of the emperor's campaign, which may have fractured the confederation into its component tribes. The only traces of them are the hill of Dumyat near Stirling and to its southwest Myot Hill, also derived from their name.[36] Politically, they seem to have had some sort of understanding with the Romans which seems to be implied by the payments they received and the captives they returned during Virius Lupus' governorship probably in 197.[37]

More is known about the Caledonians. Their centre lay in northeast Scotland. It is difficult to be any more specific. From mid-ninth century documents it has been conjectured that the Caledonians were centred in the valley of the River Tay and on Atholl.[38] They were ready to support the Maeatae against the Romans and this was a factor in Virius Lupus' buying them off.[39]

The descriptions of these Celtic peoples in Dio and Herodian are simply a patchwork of commonplaces drawn from conventional Greek and Roman views on the ethnography of northern Europeans.[40] Dio claims that the tribes inhabit trackless wastes and are nomadic, living in tents and going naked. He asserts that they go into battle on chariots. He says that their infantry fight armed with a short spear and shield as well as a dagger. Implausibly, he states that they can stay submerged with only their heads above the water for days on end.[41] Herodian's account is no more factual or informative. He adds that they love ornaments of iron which they wear around their throats and waists. This seems to reflect the Gallic torque or metal collar.[42]

There is little evidence for the social organization of these tribal peoples. The classical historians are much more concerned with continental Celtic peoples. Archaeology shows that they lived in small, dispersed communities, which suggests the absence of political centralization. However, by the Severan period larger settlements appear. Many of them contain stone and wood structures. There is little evidence of social stratification. There is also evidence for hill forts which are common all over the Celtic world. By the first century, Celtic society seems to have been characterized by a deep split between warrior chiefs and a lower class that supplied the wealth the nobility needed to maintain their dominance. Political power was concentrated in the nobles, while the lower classes seem to have had a serf-like status. Crucial to the maintenance of the nobles' power were clients who were bound to them by debt obligations. Of even greater importance were the bands of warriors that they controlled. In first century BC Gaul, such client groups could be very large. For instance, the Helvetian aristocrat Orgetorix, mentioned in Caesar's *Gallic War*, had a following of 10,000 clients.[43] Crucial to the maintenance of these warrior bands and so of aristocratic dominance was frequent raiding which enabled the individual aristocrat to distribute wealth among his followers and thereby cement their loyalty. Unlike Dio's and Herodian's descriptions of these tribes, Celtic armour and weaponry were quite sophisticated, and the equipment of continental Celts had a strong influence on the evolution of Roman military gear. Also, the picture of extreme poverty and simplicity is belied by a number of finds of high-quality Roman artefacts in their territory. Many of these pieces fall into two categories: those used for personal adornment and those connected with feasting. Both categories were connected to the elite. They provide evidence for a social hierarchy probably not too different from that among the continental Celts. There are large numbers of Roman coins, some dating to the Severan period, that have been discovered in their territory. These coins were most likely the result of Roman payments to local chiefs.[44]

There seem to have been two campaigns. The first probably took place in the spring of 209 and was jointly commanded by Severus and Caracalla, while Geta remained at York with the empress. Supply bases have been identified at Corbridge west of Newcastle, at South Shields at the mouth of the Tyne, Cramond on the Firth of Forth, and Carpow at the confluence of the Tay with the Earn between Abernethy and Newburgh near Perth. The dating of several of these bases including Carpow have been the subject of dispute. Corbridge may not be of Severan date, but it is certain that it was used and expanded during Severus's campaign. The base at South Shields was turned into a granary by Severus. Cramond, although constructed earlier, was turned into a port. The date of Carpow, a small legionary fortress, has been taken to be Severan, but may have been built under Commodus on the basis of coins found at the site.[45] It is impossible to decide, but given the meagre information we have, it is likely to have at least been used by Severus. There are also two lines of marching camps close to the east coast and running northeast. These are usually considered to date from Severus's campaigns and point to the centre of the Roman effort being in the northeast, aimed at Caledonian territory.

The sources do not provide a coherent account of the campaigns. According to Dio, in 209 Severus struck at the Caledonians. This is something of a puzzle as the Romans would have had to advance through the territory of the Maeatae to reach the Caledonii. It is possible that some of the troops could have reached their objective by sea, but marching camps and the supply bases point to the major advance being overland. Given the initial offer to surrender of these peoples at the arrival of Severus with his large army, it seems that a likely possibility was the immediate surrender of the Maeatae. This would have allowed the Romans to attack the Caledonii by marching through their territory and so explain the marching camps. Although wanting to be present for the campaign, Severus was quite ill and weak and had to be carried in a litter for most of it.

The line of camps points to an advance as far as the Moray Firth. As Birley suggests, this would reasonably explain Dio's comment that Severus had reached the extremity of Britain.[46] There seems to have been a more westerly route followed by a portion of his army. It eventually terminated at Carpow and the Tay and it has been suggested that a coin of Caracalla dating from 209 refers to a crossing and that this may refer to a pontoon bridge over the Tay.[47]

Dio emphasizes the difficulty of the campaign. He mentions the absence of roads, the numerous swamps that had to be crossed, the rivers that needed to be bridged, and the use of livestock by the enemy to hinder the Roman advance. He claims that some troops committed suicide to avoid capture. Herodian, who seems to depend in part on Dio here, essentially repeats the same basic story with certain changes in emphasis.[48] He claims that Roman casualties totalled 50,000. This is an impossible figure. It represents all of the Roman troops in Britain before the emperor's arrival. But it is probable that casualties were heavy. The descriptions point to guerilla warfare, not to large-scale engagements. This type of warfare has always presented problems for conventional armies that fought in formation like the Romans. The locals have a decided advantage in their knowledge of the country and their ability to melt back into the population. But given the limitations of ancient weapons, the inability to coordinate scattered groups and often the lack of any kind of central organization, they could rarely win a decisive victory. They could make the invader uncomfortable, but rarely could they expel him.

There is a parallel case in Caesar's conquest of Gaul. In preparation for his invasion of Britain the following year, Caesar launched an expedition against the Gallic Menapii and Morini who lived on the coast near the Channel in 55 BC. The tribes had refused to face the Romans in battle and dispersed, withdrawing into their territory that was wooded and marshy. Caesar had the woods cut down and widely ravaged their territory, destroying their villages and capturing their livestock. These measures ended his immediate difficulties with these peoples. Caesar's campaign shows decided similarities with Severus's campaign in Britain.[49] In the end the Romans were able to conquer and absorb the Gallic tribes under Augustus.

Despite the difficulties the Romans encountered during the fighting, they concluded a favourable peace treaty with the tribes, who were forced to abandon considerable tracts of land.[50] This was probably the occasion for Severus and Caracalla to assume the title of Britannicus. The victory was also marked by Geta's elevation to the rank of Augustus, which made him Caracalla's equal.

The Britons were not the only ones to cause Severus trouble. Dio says that Caracalla seemed to have been a growing problem. Severus was well aware of his plans, which included the murder of his brother and plots against his father.[51] Dio describes an attempt by Caracalla to do away with the freedman Castor, his former tutor who was now in charge of the emperor's correspondence and the imperial bedchamber. Dio gives him high praise. Caracalla had suborned several soldiers and launched his attack on Castor by claiming he was being mistreated by him and had the soldiers yell in support. The affair quickly stopped with the appearance of Severus who punished the worst offenders.

Dio adds one further story that during truce negotiations with the Caledonians in 209, when Severus and his son were riding out to parlay with them, Caracalla stopped his horse and tried to kill his father. But before he could strike, those with them cried out and Severus turned towards his son who immediately ended his attempt on his father's life. Severus, aware of what was happening, ignored it and proceeded with his negotiations. On his return to camp he summoned Castor and the praetorian prefect Papinian as well as his son. He offered Caracalla the opportunity to kill him in the presence of these two witnesses and had even placed a sword at the ready for his use. When Caracalla did nothing, he shamed him, pointed out that he was old and feeble and virtually had one foot in the grave.[52]

It is hard to know the truth of these stories. Dio, who knew Caracalla personally, intensely disliked him and the ancient tradition was no more favourable. His later behaviour shows that he had no compunction about murdering family members. The plot against Castor seems more plausible than the attack on his father. It recalls his attack of Plautianus in 205 which is not contested. No certainty is attainable about the attempt on Severus's life, but the Castor incident seems credible, perhaps lent some weight by Caracalla's execution of him when he succeeded his father. Herodian also mentions a plot by Caracalla to persuade his father's doctors and attendants to kill his father, which apparently came to nothing.[53]

For whatever reason, the treaty did not hold, and fighting was resumed in 210. First the Maeatae revolted and then the Caledonians allied with them. This time Severus was too ill to campaign and the direction of it was left to Caracalla. Severus's order to Caracalla was a quotation from Homer's *Iliad*. It was an instruction to commit genocide.[54] He wanted revenge for the broken treaties and what he probably saw as a personal insult.

The attempt to commit genocide appears in earlier accounts of Roman warfare. In the mid-second century BC the Greek historian

Polybius expressed horror at the extent of Roman cruelty during the Second Punic War. The contemporary total destruction of Carthage and Corinth bore witness to it.[55] Even the saintly Marcus Aurelius supposedly contemplated exterminating the Sarmatians and creating a new province of Sarmatia.[56] Roman frustration often resulted in extreme measures. In Severus's case a treaty he had concluded at great cost had been violated. Not only was the peace and security of the province at issue, but he also must have seen the violation as a personal insult.

Although still at York in the midst of the 210 campaign, Severus, worn out by age and disease, died on 4 February 211. Before his death he supposedly told his sons to be harmonious, enrich the soldiers and ignore everybody else.[57] It was good advice. Personal experience had made clear that the only sure support of power was military force. Appropriately, the body was dressed in his military uniform and burnt upon a pyre. To honour him, the soldiers and his sons ran around the pyre, throwing gifts on it. When all of these rites had been carried out, Caracalla and Geta lit the pyre. After cremation the ashes were placed in a vase made of purple stone and readied for its trip back to Rome.

With Severus death, Caracalla emerged dominant and ended the war,[58] although there is evidence that there was continued Roman presence beyond the wall. The sources criticize his haste to break off the campaign and return to Rome. But what stands out is the fact that peace in Britain was unbroken for the next 85 years. The defensive line once again seems to have been based on Hadrian's Wall. Under Caracalla the Wall underwent further refurbishment and construction.

Severus's death marked the beginning of a fierce succession struggle between his sons, in which Caracalla early assumed the dominant role. His eagerness to seize sole power even at the cost of his father's life is well attested. It is likely that as his health worsened Severus decided to protect Geta by elevating him to the rank of Augustus. The *Historia Augusta* claims that there was a source that claimed that Severus rejoiced at the thought that just as Pius had left two Augusti to succeed him, so he Severus was now leaving his sons as two Augusti to succeed him.[59] The source the *Historia Augusta* cites is in fact fictitious.[60] It is hard not to take this statement as ironic. The *Life* goes on to state that Severus was sorely mistaken. Even though only a year younger than his brother, Geta had always been until 209 in the background.[61] It is more likely that he had raised Geta as co-equal to Caracalla to try to protect him from his brother now that his own end was approaching. One thing that is clear is that Severus was indulgent to both his sons, although he had clear warning signs of what would happen after his own death.

Caracalla dismissed Papinian from the praetorian prefecture and began a purge of members of the imperial household. Dio mentions his own tutor Euodus as well as Castor. He also executed his former wife Plautilla and her brother Plautius, the children of Plautianus. He had hated her and her father and had made that quite plain.[62] This list of expulsions and executions shows that he intended to remove those he considered to have restrained him and his desire to take revenge. Julia, now a widow, must have tried to restrain Caracalla. Herodian claims, and it seems plausible, that he tried to win over army commanders to support him as sole emperor. In this he failed. The army proved decisive. According to Dio, it was well-disposed to Geta and refused to abandon him. That seems to have checked Caracalla's drive to eliminate his brother.[63] This must have made his desire to return to Rome even stronger. There he would have more room to manoeuvre against Geta.

The brothers and their mother accompanied the ashes of their father back to Rome. With no favourable opportunity for either brother to take advantage of the other, Geta and Caracalla pretended to be reconciled and to govern together. After the appropriate honours and deification, Severus's ashes were deposited in the Mausoleum of Hadrian, now the Castel Sant' Angelo.

Beneath the façade of reconciliation, it was clear that the struggle between the two brothers was continuing. There was even a plan to divide the empire between them; no doubt not a formal territorial division but defining areas of the empire where each could act independently of the other.[64] Geta, who may have been little different from his brother, did his own plotting and manoeuvring to remove Caracalla. Both were protected by guards at all times. Finally, Caracalla persuaded his mother to invite both Geta and himself, without their attendant guards, to a meeting of reconciliation in her own rooms. Julia was a clever and perceptive woman. It is hard to understand how she was taken in by Caracalla's ruse. Perhaps she felt that in her presence neither brother would make an attempt on the life of the other and that as their mother she might find it possible, if not to reconcile, at least to convince them that shared governance was preferable to continued struggle

But Caracalla's quest for sole rule would not be denied. He had planned to assassinate Geta at the festival of the Saturnalia in December 211 but failed. He had suborned some centurions who were posted outside his mother's rooms to attack Geta as he entered. He was struck down but managed to run to his mother begging her to save his life. It was to no avail. Geta was murdered at the age of 22. In the fury of the attack Julia was slightly wounded but, covered in her son's blood, she took no notice of her injury.

With his brother dead, Caracalla made sure of the troops in the city and proclaimed that he had killed Geta to protect himself against an assassination plot of his brother. He won over the Praetorians by promising great rewards and claiming he was defending his mother against Geta. At Alba, the camp of II Parthica, his reception by the troops was not friendly. They shut him out of the camp, claiming that they owed allegiance to both brothers. Once again, his calumnies against Geta and a money bribe swung their allegiance. At this point, he had won the support of all the troops in Italy who might have posed a threat. He then proceeded to the Senate, presumably to defend his actions, and to defame his brother. To win the Senate's allegiance he announced that he was allowing those who had been exiled to return home and pardoned some of those convicted of crimes. Then in the spirit of his father's actions after the defeat of Albinus, he initiated a widespread purge of imperial freedmen and soldiers. These presumably had favoured and supported Geta.[65]

His reign was not to prove a happy one. In some respects, it recalled that of Commodus. He did not get along with the Senate and this influenced the accounts by senators, which had always had a strong influence on the historical tradition. Eminent senators were executed or exiled. He seems to have gone out of his way to demean senators and a number of posts such as city prefecture or army commander were deliberately given to those of low birth. Taxes were increased as well as exactions to fund his numerous campaigns, which often had little justification. His affection was directed towards his troops, to whom he gave a substantial pay raise.

He was fascinated, as Roman military commanders were, by the allure of Alexander the Great.[66] He visited Alexander's tomb in Alexandria, leaving substantial numbers of gifts. But more symbolic was the fact that when he set out on his expedition against the Parthians, he made sure to land in Asia Minor where the Macedonian had landed in 336 BC, over 500 years before. He then proceeded to Troy to follow in Alexander's footsteps. There was no doubt that he was in love with soldiering, but he seems not to have possessed much in the way of strategic or tactical gifts. In 217 he ironically suffered the same fate he had once meted out to his brother. A plot against him was formed by the men of his court, tired of his erratic leadership and lack of success. Opellius Macrinus, his praetorian prefect, who felt his own life was in danger, suborned a soldier to kill him. In April 217 during a visit to the temple of the moon god outside Carrhae in Syria, Caracalla stopped and moved to the bushes to relieve himself. The soldier followed him and killed him. He was conveniently killed by the emperor's German guards so that there was no chance of his implicating others. Macrinus was the first member of a non-senatorial family to ascend the throne. Within a year, Domna, who now had lost both her sons and her influence, and who as the widow of Severus stood in imminent danger from Macrinus, committed suicide in 218. Relatives of Severus or his wife held on to power until 235. What followed them was a half-century of war and internal instability that almost destroyed the empire.

In his account of the aftermath of Albinus's defeat, Herodian mentions the division of Britain into two provinces, an upper and lower province. The lower consisted of southern England and Wales, while the upper included all of northern England, presumably as far north as Hadrian's Wall.[67] It is known from other sources that there was a difference in status between the governors of these two provinces. Lower Britain as the less threatened section of Britain was entrusted to a governor of praetorian rank and given one legion, VI Victrix, plus auxiliaries for its garrison, while the upper province was under a more senior consular governor and had a garrison of two legions, II Augusta and XX Valeria Victrix, plus other troops. However, inscriptional evidence points to a later date for the division probably under Caracalla. The matter is far from resolved. Some scholars accept Herodian's date of 197 and then try to harmonize it with the inscriptional evidence. Given Herodian's general unreliability in matters of chronology, it seems preferable to accept the inscriptional evidence.[68]

The change would mirror that conducted by Severus who reduced the number of legions under the control of the governor of Syria to lessen the threat that such a concentration of power presented to the central government. There was always tension between the power of the emperor and his governors, especially now that the influence of civil institutions had weakened. Attempts to reduce it would result by the end of the century in an increased number of smaller provinces.

Severus came to power in the first civil war to afflict the empire for over a century. His rise was contingent on the failure of Marcus Aurelius's plan for succession. The assassination of Commodus meant that the traditional dynastic bond that had bound the army and administration and the people of Rome had been broken. Since 96 and the death of Domitian, whose father came to power through a civil war that had been brought about by Nero's incompetence, there had been no hereditary succession. This had been due to chance rather than policy. No other emperors before Marcus had had a male heir and so they were forced to adopt. Marcus had one, who unfortunately proved entirely unsuitable to succeed his father. Once again assassination acted as a catalyst to cause the failure of normal government.

A coup and then assassination eliminated the candidate, Pertinax. His replacement had no sanction beyond the Senate's fear of the Praetorians. This opened the way for the armies of the provinces to intervene as they had in the earlier civil war. Of the three men who now sought the throne, Severus was the most likely to succeed. He commanded a powerful province, Pannonia Superior which opportunely was located in the most heavily defended frontier of the empire. It was a position he owed more to his political connections than to his proven military capability. His career had not involved military command on any scale. What he did have were the political skills that enabled him to build support among his fellow governors.

He showed his decisiveness in marching straight on the capital without hesitation. The opposition there was easily brushed aside. The two governors who emerged, Niger in the east and Albinus in the west, were formidable opponents. He was no warrior himself; although present on the battlefield in three battles, he only intervened once, at Lugdunum in 197, with disastrous, but not fatal results. Although not himself an experienced general, he had two crucial abilities. First, he knew how to pick successful generals who would present no political threat to himself, and second, he had the ability to bond with his troops. He presented himself to his soldiers as one of them. In the campaign against Albinus he marched at the head of the formation, bare-headed in the snow.[69] He further introduced a number of reforms to improve the soldiers' lot and expanded the military.

His treatment of the Senate was at first deferential; he promised not to take the life of any senator, but he soon abandoned this policy and instituted purges of senators who had supported his rivals. He also appointed non-senators to positions normally reserved for senators and furthered the careers of a number of equestrians. The questions about whether he favoured his fellow Africans is contested. Given the personal nature of Roman government, the fact that a number of Africans and easterners were employed by Severus does not necessarily imply any favouritism. This was also a period when the number of African and Eastern senators was increasing so that it would be hardly surprising to find them involved in government.

Dio, who was not an unalloyed admirer, notes his energy and attention to work. He is less favourable about the two wars he fought in the east. He criticizes aspects of the campaigns and questions their value.[70] He felt that they brought additional expenses and difficulties without adding much to the empire.[71] Modern scholars are divided on the usefulness of Severus's eastern campaigns.[72] But in Severus's case practical considerations were linked to personal motives of glory and conquest, a trait that Caracalla clearly inherited. Augustus had been far more successful in both civil conflict and foreign expansion. A century before, Trajan had conquered and secured more territory although not faced with civil conflict.

The British campaign seems to have been far more successful, although what Severus intended is unclear. It was not Caracalla but Severus's campaign that freed the province from major threats for the better part of a century. Herodian claimed that he won more military distinction than any other emperor, he was clearly misled by Severan propaganda.

Despite the financial drain of these campaigns, he was able to leave a substantial surplus in the treasury when he died, even after undertaking an extensive building programme in Rome and the provinces. No doubt the wealth of those purged by him formed a significant part of the treasury surplus.

For a man with such keen political sense, his plans for succession were seemingly weak. Caracalla's unfitness to rule and perhaps Geta's as well echo the career of Commodus. As in the case of Marcus Aurelius the bonds of familial affection were too strong to deny. In addition, he had seen what happened when there was no dynastic loyalty to hold the government together. In a real sense, he had no choice other than leaving the empire to his sons. He knew disaster might follow and apparently did his best to avoid it.

Severus was instrumental in discarding the façade of the traditional empire. It had depended on the ostensible partnership of Senate and emperor. True power lay with the emperor as long as he controlled the military, but he used the senators as commanders and in other vital functions. The façade had occasionally broken down. This was usually the result of the vagaries of individual emperors such as Nero and Domitian. Succession depended on the emperors. If a dynasty suddenly ended, as was the case with Nero and Domitian, there was no remedy other than civil war or the threat of violence. The use of adoption after Domitian was an expedient forced upon the emperors by chance. Once Marcus had a son, it was abandoned for the normal mechanism of hereditary succession. Unfortunately Commodus lacked the necessary qualities and was removed. What followed, as had happened after Nero, was a prolonged civil war and increasing militarization. Severus's reign simply continued and intensified the increasing militarization of the political system. It was later further intensified by the emergence of new and more threating enemies. It was that and increasing internal instability that by the end of the third century resulted in a very different Roman Empire. The supposed dying words of Severus to his sons reflected the true state of affairs: 'Preserve your concord with each other, enrich the soldiers and despise all others.' If actually spoken, these last words reflect the hard-headed realism of the dying emperor and his political insight.

Appendix

Severus and the Roman Army

T he army that Severus commanded had a long history that stretched back to the beginning of the imperial period. During the last century of the Republic, the Roman army had been a citizen militia, which, with a grant of citizenship to all Italian communities south of the Po, included almost all of Italy. There were also troops drawn from the provinces of the Empire as well as units supplied by Rome's allies, and specialist troops such as archers and slingers hired as mercenaries.

The last century BC had been wracked by civil war. The armies that fought it had been drawn mostly from Italy. Staffing them had made enormous demands upon Italian manpower. It has been estimated that in the last phase of the conflict that had begun with Caesar's assassination in 44 BC and which ended with the victory of his heir Augustus in 30, 250,000 Italians served in the armies of all sides. At the end of the war, there were sixty legions in service with a paper strength of 300,000 citizen soldiers, an unsustainable burden. Victory and the immense spoils of the conquest of Egypt meant that Augustus was now able to consolidate and rationalize Rome's military forces. He demobilized thirty-four legions, settling many of the veterans in colonies in Italy and in increasing numbers overseas. Two more legions were added to the existing twenty-six in 25 BC with the addition of a new province. The number of legions remained fixed at twenty-eight until AD 9 when three legions were destroyed by the Germans. They were not replaced by Augustus. So, in AD 14 at his death, the twenty-five legions had a nominal strength of 145,000 men. The number was too small to meet the various military and civilian tasks entrusted to the army. The number was raised to twenty-seven under Caligula.

The problems and losses caused by the first civil war in AD 68–69 resulted in some reorganization of the army and the raising of the number of legions to twenty-nine. By the end of the first century, there were thirty legions in service. This number, despite losses and replacements, remained standard until the reign of Severus.

These legions were unlike those of the Republic. Although their weapons and tactics had, with minor changes, remained basically the same, their character had changed. They were no longer a citizen militia, but a long-service professional army, for the most part stationed far away from Rome and Italy. Augustus had established this professional army at the end of the first century BC.

There is no direct evidence to explain the emperor's reform, but several factors can be suggested. In the Late Republic, competing aristocrats were able to mobilize military forces against each other and the Senate. The conflict that resulted had destroyed the state. Augustus had created a disguised military monarchy while maintaining the older Republican forms. To survive and stabilize the government, Augustus had to create strong bonds between himself and the army. These links consisted of a nexus of material and emotional ties. The emperor controlled the finances of the army. He instituted a system of retirement benefits that must have served as a strong incentive for the troops to maintain their loyalty to him and later to his successors. At the end of the service they were given either land or substantial cash bonuses. Their pay was not high, but it was guaranteed, as was the provision of food. They were also given special privileges in the making of wills and in property sales. This was especially important in a society where the vast majority of the population made its living as peasant farmers. More personal were the gifts of cash made on special occasions by the emperor to his troops.

The loyalty of the soldiers was also enhanced by various emotional and ideological measures. Numerous public monuments were constructed at Rome and in the cities of the empire to celebrate Augustus' military victories and his power. These victories ended with cash distributions to the troops. Various military celebrations were monopolized by the emperor and his family. The troops took a yearly oath not to the Roman people or to the Senate but to the emperor personally. Images of the emperor and his family were kept in a special chapel in military camps and were displayed on special occasions and anniversaries.

The aristocracy was subordinated to the emperor. Despite this, he needed its members to exercise military command in the provinces as governors and peacekeepers as well serving as commanders on imperial expeditions. An emperor possessed overwhelming authority legally through a military command granted by the senate that allowed him to subordinate almost all of Rome's military forces to himself. The one formally independent senatorial command of one legion was no threat to a man who commanded twenty-four of his own. Aristocrats now served as lieutenants under dele-gated authority, not as independent commanders.[1]

The professionalization of the legions led to a parallel development in the auxiliary forces. By the last century of the Republic, they supplied Rome's cavalry forces, infantry and various specialist troops. A large number of such units, both tribal and those supplied by various client kings, had fought in the civil war. A level of professionalization is already evident during the war with named auxiliary units engaged in prolonged overseas service. Although many of these units were disbanded at the end of fighting, cavalry formations were retained and under Augustus are found in various provinces. These and other types of units grew in number and usually maintained their continuity. Their growing importance is evident from the increase in their numbers; by the 20s AD their strength is recorded as 150,000, about equal to the number of legionaries. Rome's army of 300,000 men was more than sufficient to meet most of the threats to the empire until the end of second century.

Particularly in the second century, the legions and auxiliary formations underwent important personnel changes. Under Augustus the legions and the auxiliary formations or *auxilia* drew their recruits from different sources. In theory the legions enrolled only Roman citizens and so retained senatorial commanders. The auxilia were initially drawn from non-Romans who were not permitted to serve in the legions. Their units were regularized under Augustus and integrated into the army but retained their separate character. Their status and pay were somewhat lower than the legions, but their equipment and fighting role tended to be more and more assimilated to that of the legions, except for the cavalry.

The distinction between the citizens of the legions and the non–citizen auxiliaries had already started to disappear during the reign of Augustus as the legions began to draw some of their troops from the provinces. Those recruited were often given citizenship on their recruitment. Although local recruitment occurred in the first century, it was finally in the second that it became a general rule except in cases when totally new legions were formed. They were still raised in Italy through the reign of Marcus Aurelius. Already by the first half of the first century Italian recruitment had begun falling, and, except among the Praetorians and the Urban cohorts in Rome, had become negligible. Auxiliary units had initially been recruited locally and often bore titles which signalled their ethnic or geographic origin. For instance, in 195 and again in 197, it seems that Severus recruited a number of Edessene horse archers into his army. They formed a *numerus* or unit in Caracalla's army. Often these units were initially ethnically homogeneous, but as they moved from one base to another they began recruiting in their new posting and started to lose their ethnic character, although they kept their original titles.

The Roman navy was always the less prestigious service. In almost all of Rome's wars it was the army that had been crucial to victory. The navy had several permanent stations, at Misenum in the Bay of Naples on Italy's west coast and another fleet guarding the east coast positioned at Ravenna. There were also provincial fleets with the major ones on the Rhine and the Danube. Other squadrons were posted to Syria and Egypt. They assisted in amphibious operations and were essential for carrying supplies and other logistical support. They were used to suppress piracy and on occasion to provide supplemental troops to the army.

Augustus introduced an additional innovation: armed men in the capital. Republican commanders had an elite force, the *cohors praetoria*, composed originally of cavalry but by the late Republic it seems to have consisted mostly of infantry. Most importantly it served as a bodyguard for the commander and carried out specialized tasks. It was these units that had guarded Augustus during the civil war that became the nucleus of the Praetorian Guard. The establishment of the Guard broke the traditional ban on bearing arms within the city. Only three of the nine cohorts were stationed in the city and were quartered in diverse locations. Nonetheless, the close connection between the emperor and the monopoly of force in the city could not be clearer. These troops were marked off from the rest by higher rates of pay and easier conditions of service which highlighted the connection of service to the emperor and larger material benefits. Given their proximity to an emperor, keeping them loyal was a major concern. Their importance was manifested early. Caligula, the third emperor, was assassinated by a praetorian officer and the guard played the key role in the succession of his replacement, Claudius.

At the end of the second century, there were in the army approximately 450,000 men divided among 30 legions, 483 auxiliary formations of various sizes, these in turn were divided among infantry, cavalry and mixed cavalry and infantry units including servants. In addition, there were about 30,000 men serving in the fleets.[2] Given its size and geographic spread, the army was the single largest item in the imperial budget. By one estimate it accounted for about three-quarters of the budget, although there is no certainty given the paucity of evidence. However, even with the increase in the number of legions by 20% since Augustus, there is no evidence that by itself it was an unbearable burden.[3]

During Severus's reign a number of changes were made to the army. Some were certainly the result of his policies and others seem to be changes that began before he came to the throne but developed further in the course of his reign. They can be divided into three categories: the enlargement of the army, changes in the military command structure and alterations in conditions of service.

The dating of all of these measures is a problem. The three new legions, I, II and III, all bearing the title of Parthica may have been raised for the campaign against Niger, for the war against Albinus or for his Second Parthian War. Campbell's suggestion that it was raised for the war against Albinus seems the most likely proposal. That would date their enrolment to 197. This would have allowed I and III Parthica to immediately form the garrison of the new province of Mesopotamia created after in the Second Parthian War in197–8.

II Parthica was installed in Albanum, modern Albano Laziale, sixteen miles from Rome. This was the first armed force other than the Praetorian Guard and the naval contingents to be stationed in Italy. This meant that troops based in Italy had been increased from 11,500 to 30,000 including the naval contingent, when all the other changes he had made in the garrison of Rome are taken into account.[4] Severus now had at his disposal a core force of 16,000 professional heavy-armed infantry. We have no direct information as to why Severus made such a decision. There is no reason to suppose that he was now reducing Italy to the level of a garrisoned province as some have suggested. A more likely explanation is that the change resulted from his experience in the civil war. He had seen the inability of Salvius Julianus to resist his own advance on Italy. The larger number of troops in Italy who would be particularly closely tied to him could act as a holding force in case of invasion until help could arrive from the provinces. The other lesson of the civil wars had been the unreliability of the Praetorian Guard and their lack of fitness for service.[5] Now he would have two independent military units geographically separated from each other and under different equestrian commanders who could act as a counter to each other.

The murder of Geta by his brother offers an example. After he had murdered his brother, Caracalla went to the Praetorian camp and justified his action by claiming that he had killed Geta to foil his brother's plot against himself. He also claimed that he was protecting his mother against Geta. He then added a bribe, including an increase in pay, and promised great rewards to the Guard to further win its loyalty.[6] After winning over the Guard, Caracalla journeyed to Alba, southeast of Rome, to assure himself of the loyalty of II Parthica. At first the soldiers were not receptive. They claimed that they had also sworn allegiance to Geta and would not admit Caracalla to their camp. Finally, after once again repeating in harsh terms his lie about Geta's plot and bringing charges against him, he added a huge bribe and so won them over.[7] If nothing else, the presence of different units made a coup like Caracalla's more complicated.

Even the increased number of legions and auxiliary formations could not meet the demands created by the simultaneous threats on multiple frontiers that Rome now faced. The attempt to deal with these led to a greater use of legionary and auxiliary detachments. It also revealed the potential for flexibility in Roman military planning. The Romans called these battle groups *vexillationes* (sing, *vexillatio*). They were named after their unit standard, the *vexillum*, a flag that was suspended from a transverse bar. Although such detachments existed during the Republic, their first regular use is attested in the imperial period under Augustus. They became more important after Hadrian when Roman frontiers had become more or less stationary. They enabled emperors to dispatch expeditionary forces without denuding a province of military protection. The legionary *vexillationes* often numbered about 1,000–2,000 effectives. The auxiliary ones were normally smaller. Some of the *vexillationes* combined legionary and auxiliary troops. If battle had depleted the number of troops in a war zone, some of the detachments could be added to the local garrison, but normally the units returned to their parent formations. Until the end of the second century the general rule was that only officers of senatorial rank could command legionary *vexillationes* and equestrians led auxiliary *vexillationes*, following the normal command structure. Commanders were drawn from the parent formations of these detachments. In the theatre of operations, they were led by the theatre commander. By the reign of Severus, command of legionary detachments was no longer confined to senators; equestrians could and did command them.[8] As the above example illustrates, under Severus there was increased use of equestrians in command positions that had been previously reserved for senators. This was not a general policy but the result the specific situation.[9] As was the case with the Praetorian Guard, II Parthica in Italy was too close to Rome and too much of a potential threat to be entrusted to a senator. The danger was lessened by the appointment of an equestrian prefect who had a much smaller possibility of occupying the imperial throne. In addition, the Praetorian Guard was commanded by equestrian prefects and served as an obvious precedent. It is possible, but not certain, that the commander of II Parthica was a subordinate of the praetorian prefects. The other two Parthian legions in Mesopotamia were also placed under equestrian commanders, but it could hardly be otherwise as they were subordinate to the governor of the province who was also of equestrian status. Severus had adopted the same arrangement as Augustus had in Egypt when he placed its garrison of three legions under an equestrian prefect. In Egypt, it was the importance of the province to Rome's grain supply, its wealth and natural defenses that made it a useful base for a potential usurper. In fact there was an imperial prohibition that prevented senators from entering the province without the emperor's express permission.[10] The use of an equestrian commander in Mesopotamia may have been an expedient in a province that had to be defended as quickly as possible, since it faced potential military threats on an active frontier.

These measures should be considered in the context of Severus's concern for himself and his family. He had fought two civil wars and it should come as no surprise that he wanted to avoid another. This concern is evident in his splitting of Syria and Britain into two provinces each and thereby weakening the potential threat presented by the governors of these provinces which each had three legions and auxiliary troops, the largest garrisons of any province.

It is true that more equestrians served as governors under Severus than under earlier emperors, but provinces with legionary garrisons remained under senatorial governors with the exceptions just noted. Most positions that had been filled by senators continued to be so during his reign. The rising military expertise of equestrian officers and Severus's heavy dependence on the army pointed in the same direction of an increased equestrian presence in military and political matters. However, there seems to have been no specific policy directed against senators. He purged many of them and cowed the rest, but those he purged had been supporters of his rivals. He removed non-senatorial supporters of Niger and Albinus as well. Otherwise, he showed no special animosity towards or reluctance to employ senators in government service.

The dividing line between senator and equestrian had never been absolute. Even before Severus there had been elite equestrians who often ended their careers as senators. This makes the equestrian presence in certain senatorial posts less of an innovation than it seems. In addition, during the reign of Severus, the seven equestrians who are recorded as governing provinces in place of senators were all serving in provinces where no legionary troops were stationed. It may also be the case that the increased number of equestrians, especially in military posts, made military command a less attractive option for senators who pursued other avenues of advancement.

The sources clearly indicate that many of the senators were uneasy about Severus. They had feared him and were unhappy with the favour he showed the military. Dio, who was close to Severus, provides ample evidence of the senate's fear and dislike of the emperor. Severus's speech to the Senate after his defeat of Albinus could not have done much to endear him to the senators.[11]

> He praised the severity and cruelty of Sulla, Marius and Augustus as the safer course and deprecated the mildness of Pompey and Caesar as having proved the ruin of those very men. He introduced a sort of defence of Commodus and inveighed against the senate for dishonouring that emperor unjustly, in view of the fact that the majority of its members lived worse lives.

Another possible factor in deterring senators from military command was the increasing importance of cavalry in the army. Traditionally, the legions had been the decisive arm and still remained the most important part of the armed forces.[12] But the different tactics of Rome's enemies led to corresponding changes in the way the Romans fought. A clear indication of this is the increasing importance of cavalry and in particular of heavy cavalry in the Roman battle order. Fighting against Parthia and some of the steppe peoples, such as the Sarmatians, forced the Romans to change their tactics.

To deal with the problem of confronting the heavy cavalry of their opponents, at the beginning of the second century under the Emperor Trajan, some of the cavalry were provided with heavy thrusting spears up to 16 feet long. Probably under Trajan as well, *cataphracti* or *clibanarii*, that is armoured cavalry to match those of Rome's opponents, was introduced. The first organized unit of this heavy cavalry is attested under Trajan's successor Hadrian. Their numbers increased under Marcus Aurelius when the Romans fought both the Parthians and steppe peoples such as the Sarmatians who fought exclusively on horseback and had heavily armoured cavalry and archers.[13] Parthian armies fought in the same way. They had light cavalry, mostly archers, and heavy cavalry. The classical sources call them either *cataphracts* or *clibanarii*. The troopers were protected from head to foot with chain mail and carried a heavy thrusting spear as their main offensive weapon with a sword as secondary armament. Their horses were armoured as well.[14]

Under Severus, *vexillationes* of various types of cavalry were organized on a larger scale and became standing units. This was accompanied by an increase in the number of cavalry attached to the legions. Most Roman heavy cavalry fought with the heavy thrusting spear, but unlike their opponents had relatively little body armour. Fully armoured cataphracts were used, but in much smaller numbers.[15] Strategically, two of the most important measures Severus took were the division of Syria into two provinces and perhaps the division of Britain also into two provinces. Both of these measures grew out of the civil wars fought against Niger and Albinus. It's not clear that they conferred any strategic advantage against Rome's adversaries there. They were designed to lessen the power of governors and so make control from the centre more secure. Severus advanced Roman frontiers in North Africa, but his major contribution was the extension of Rome's frontiers into northern Mesopotamia and creating a permanent presence there, with the two new provinces Osrhoene and Mesopotamia. The effects of this extension of Roman control were and are controversial. Dio's opinion was that it worsened the situation in the East. He notes that Severus justified the new provinces as protection for Syria and so worthwhile in themselves. Dio thought otherwise, he thought that the new provinces made the situation on the eastern frontier worse. It involved Rome in constant warfare and was a continuous drain on the treasury. The new provinces yielded little in profit and were expensive to govern.[16]

Benjamin Isaac in his study of the Roman Empire's presence in the Near East offers a perceptive assessment of the effects of the acquisition of Mesopotamia.[17] He points out that the border was now closer to Ctesiphon than to Antioch. That meant longer marches for Roman troops as well as extended supply lines. It also meant that Parthian armies could more quickly and easily reach Roman territory. He notes that the Euphrates had formed a natural frontier between Rome and Parthia, but the Severan border separated communities that shared a common language and culture and had until the conquest been under Parthian control. It was an inherently unstable border that led to increased warfare which resulted in temporary gains without creating a final solution to the problem. It can be argued that the Second Parthian War further destabilized the Parthian monarchy and led to the rise of the Sassanians, also an Iranian dynasty, but much more aggressive and powerful than the Parthians.[18] Herodian mentions measures by Severus to improve the conditions of service for the troops and dates them to right after the victory over Albinus.[19] But the date of 197 is not secure. The fact that he dates the division of Britain into two provinces in the same year does not inspire confidence. In addition, the *Historia Augusta* dates the raise in pay to just after the Second Parthian War.[20] This dating makes more sense as he now had not only the wealth confiscated from Albinus's supporters but also the booty obtained from the sack of Ctesiphon and other Parthian cities.

Under Augustus the pay of a Roman soldier stood at 225 denarii – a living wage at a low subsistence level.[21] This was paid in three instalments of 75 denarii. This was calculated in aurei, the standard Roman gold coin which equalled 25 denarii. Unlike that of the standard silver coin, the *denarius*, its metal content did not decline and so maintained its value, although its weight was occasionally lowered.[22] The system was used to provide a more stable basis for military pay. The next change in pay came in 83 under Domitian who seems to have added a fourth payment of 75 denarii, increasing the soldiers' pay to 300 denarii a year. This remained the standard pay for an ordinary legionary for over a century. Praetorians and officers were paid at substantially higher rates.

The denarius, although having the same face value, despite the reduction in its silver content remained the most important Roman coin. The fall in intrinsic value of the coin did not lead to substantial inflation down to the reign of Severus. In great part, this must have been due to the fact that money played only a small part in the overall Roman economy since most of the population were subsistence farmers.

Regular deductions were made from a soldier's pay for food and clothing. There were also occasional deductions for extra supplies and replacement equipment. It seems that after the deductions had been made the soldiers had a small surplus available. It seems likely, despite the common view that auxiliary troops were paid at a lower rate than legionaries, that their pay rates were approximately the same as the legionaries.[23]

In spite of the low pay, there were additional cash benefits for the average soldier. At the end of his service, he would receive a retirement bonus of 3,000 denarii, equal to ten year's pay. There were also supplementary payments in the form of donatives or cash gifts to the soldiers. These were irregular but must have been a substantial addition to soldiers' pay. Another supplement to a soldier's pay was booty, which with the adoption of a greater defensive role by the army in the second century must have become a relatively minor part of the pay. Pay was also supplemented by illegal activities with frequent practice of extorting money and services from the provincial population for which there is good evidence.[24]

In addition to payment in cash there also began a system of payment in kind in the form of grain and other foodstuffs, and distributions. These distributions were known as the *annona militaris*. Dio implies that the *annona* was begun by Severus.[25] Essentially, it was a payment in kind consisting of grain which was no longer deducted from a soldier's pay. In essence it was a permanent raise in pay that continued until the end of the empire. It had the added benefit that since it was a payment-in-kind it was not subject to inflation or devaluation.

Unfortunately we have no figures for the pay rise that Severus granted to the troops. Alston offers the reasonable estimate of a 50% increase to 450 denarii per year. Caracalla further increased the sum to 675 denarii per year.[26] One factor that would help us in understanding the meaning and significance of Severus's pay raise and that of his son would be accurate figures for the rate of inflation in the century since Domitian's increase. Since the evidence is not good, there have been conflicting opinions about what the economic situation was. This is further complicated by the lack of an adequate series of prices, especially for the largest item in the diet, grain. There is a series of prices from Egypt, but it is unclear how representative they are of the rest of the empire, since it had an atypical economy.

Thus we cannot say whether military pay underwent a serious loss in purchasing power between 100 and 200.[27] The institution of the *annona militaris* may hint at some pressure.[28] But other factors may have played a part. Service under Severus had been hard duty for the army. The pay raise may have been both a recompense and a bribe. His son Caracalla seems to have made his raise for the same reasons. Money gifts had a long history as a way of buying military support. It had been used this way especially for the Praetorians, and the army had also been a recipient. This extended the practice to military pay. It was to have serious consequences as the third century progressed. But it is best viewed as the use of an established practice in a new way.[29] Severus conferred several other benefits on the army of which the most important was the right to marry during service. Marriage had probably been banned by Augustus for soldiers up to the rank of centurion, in effect for the rank and file and non-commissioned officers. It seems likely that it was designed to make the legions more mobile by discouraging close ties to the communities near their home bases. Such localism could be a problem as the course of the first civil war of 68–69 revealed. Our sources make a distinction between legions in the western provinces and those in the east.[30] It may be as well that such marriages were viewed as a threat to discipline. This would fit with Augustus' unrealistic concerns about the morals of civilian Roman citizens.[31] Given natural human impulses, a ban over such a large and far-flung group was never going to work.

The soldiers naturally formed relationships with local women, who were usually non-Romans. The lack of a legally recognized bond between the soldier and his de facto wife led to problems. Any child born during service was by definition illegitimate, even if the child was an offspring of a legal marriage contracted before the soldier entered service.[32] The enlistment dissolved a prior marriage for the term of the man's service. This ban applied to auxiliary formations as well.

The ban also led to a further problem. To increase the citizen population, unmarried Roman men were denied certain of the legal privileges of citizenship. They were not able to benefit from legacies or inheritances. In AD 44 this was remedied by a law of the Emperor Claudius that granted soldiers the rights of an unmarried man to inherit and to receive legacies. Other measures were also instituted to offer men who had established a lasting union with a woman to enjoy many of the privileges of married men. Despite this, the ban on marriage continued in force. By the time of Marcus Aurelius, various legal devices and privileges had led to an even closer approximation of marriage, but the final step was not taken.[33] The only literary source for Severus's lifting of the marriage ban is Herodian. He takes a dim view of the results of this and other measures Severus took on behalf of the army.[34] He viewed them as corrupting and weakening discipline and obedience. Campbell has made a persuasive argument that it was Severus who finally did away with the ban.[35] Herodian also mentions some other privileges accorded to certain soldiers, such as the permission given to centurions and to *principales,* who were soldiers given special duties that exempted them from normal camp duties and were paid at a higher rate to wear a gold ring. This was normally the mark of equestrian rank. The rank did not go with equestrian status, but it did highlight the increasing upward social mobility that the army enjoyed.

The army had always been the final arbiter of power. All emperors from Augustus onwards owed their position to military support. As early as AD 41 the Emperor Claudius had owed his accession after the assassination of his predecessor to the Praetorian Guard and had given them a handsome donative as a reward. When the normal structures of political life had broken down in 68–69, it had been the army that determined who was to succeed to the throne. In theory, the Senate had the dominant role in choosing an emperor. The system worked as long as a deceased emperor was succeeded by a blood relative or by a carefully groomed successor whose way had been prepared before he ascended the throne. When the process broke down as happened after Nero and again after Commodus, the true role of the army as the ultimate arbiter of power was revealed. Severus, having gained his throne through military violence and civil war, must have been more aware than most of the power of the military and took these and other steps to bind them to himself as closely as possible. His alleged final words about enriching the army and ignoring everyone else was the product of personal experience.[36]

Bibliography

General

Birley, A.R., *Septimius Severus: The African Emperor*, Routledge (London and New York, 2002).

Handy, M., *Die Severer und das Heer, Studien zur Alten Geschichte 10*, Verlag Antike (Berlin, 2009).

Hasebroek, J., *Untersuchungen zur Geschichte des Kaisers Septimius Severus*, Carl Winter (Heidelberg, 1921).

Hill, P.V., *The Coinage of Septimius Severus and his Family of the Mint of Rome: AD 193–217*, Spink, (London, 1964).

Murphy. G. J., *The Reign of the Emperor L. Septimius Severus from the Evidence of the Inscriptions*, St. Peters College Press, Jersey City, NJ, (Philadelphia, 1947).

Platnauer, M., *The Life and Reign of the Emperor Lucius Septimius Severus*, Oxford University Press (London, 1918).

Strobel, K., 'Strategy and Army Structure between Septimius Severus and Constantine the Great', in P.A. Erdkamp, (ed.) *A Companion to the Roman Army*, Blackwell (Oxford and Malden, MA, 2007) pp. 267–85

Introduction

Alföldy, G., 'Spain' in A.K. Bowman et al. (eds), *Cambridge Ancient History Vol. XI The High Empire AD 70–192*, Cambridge University Press (Cambridge, 2000) pp. 449–63.

Barrett. A. A., *Caligula: The Corruption of Power*, Routledge (London and New York, 1989).

Bowersock, G., *Roman Arabia*, Harvard University Press (Cambridge, MA and London, UK, 1983).

Champlin, E., *Fronto and Antonine Rome* (Cambridge, MA, 1980).

Cornell, T.J. and Lomas, K. (eds.), *Urban Society in Roman Italy*, Routledge (London and New York, 1996).

Erdkamp, P.A., 'The Food Supply of the Capital', in P.A. Erdkamp (ed.), *The Cambridge Companion to Ancient Rome*, Cambridge University Press (Cambridge, UK and New York, 2013) pp. 263–77.

Erdkamp, P.A. (ed.), *The Cambridge Companion to Ancient Rome*, Cambridge University Press (Cambridge, UK and New York, 2013).

Garnsey, P.D.A, 'Rome's African Empire Under the Principate', in P.D.A Garnsey and C.R Whittaker (eds.), *Imperialism in the Ancient World*, Cambridge University Press (Cambridge, 1978) pp. 223–37.

Glasterer, H., Local and Provincial Institutions and Government', in in A.K. Bowman, P. Garnsey and D. Rathbone. (eds), *Cambridge Ancient History, Vol. XI The High Empire AD 70–192*, Cambridge University Press (Cambridge, 2000) pp. 344–60.

Goldsworthy, A.K., *The Fall of Carthage: The Punic Wars 264–146 BC*, Cassell (London, 2000).

Haines, C.R., ed. and trans. *The Correspondence of Marcus Cornelius Fronto*, Vol. I, Loeb Classical Library, (London and New York, 1919).

Hammond. M., 'The Composition of the Roman Senate, AD 68–235', *Journal of Roman Studies 47* (1957) pp. 74–81.

Hanel, N., 'Military Camps, Canabae and Vici: The Archaeological Evidence', in P.A. Erdkamp (ed.), *A Companion to the Roman Army*, Blackwell (Malden, MA and Oxford, UK, 2007) pp. 395–416.

Hilali, A., 'Rome and Agriculture in Africa Proconsularis; Land and Hydraulic Development', *Revue Belge de Philologie et d'Histoire 91* (2013) pp. 113–25.

Hoyos, D., *The Carthaginians*, Routledge (London and New York, 2010).

Le Bohec, Y., *The Imperial Roman Army*, Hippocrene Books and B.T. Batsford (London and New York, 1994).

Markoe, G.E., *Phoenicians*, University of California Press (Berkeley and Los Angeles, 2000).

Mattingly, D., *Tripolitania*, Batsford (London, 1995).

Millar, F., 'Local Cultures in the Roman Empire: Libyan, Punic, and Latin in Roman Africa', in H.M. Cotton and G.M. Rogers (eds.,) F. Millar, *Rome, the Greek World, and the East Vol 2 of Government, Society, and Culture in the Roman Empire*, University of North Carolina (Chapel Hill and London, 2004) pp. 249–64.

Raven, S., *Roman Africa*, Routledge (New York, 1993).

Rickman, G.E., *The Corn Supply of Ancient Rome*, Oxford University Press (Oxford, 1980).

Syme, R., 'Donatus and the Like', in A.R. Birley, (ed.), R. Syme, *Roman Papers III*, Clarendon Press (Oxford, 1984) pp. 1105–19.

Whittaker, C.R., 'Africa', in A.K. Bowman, P. Garnsey and D. Rathbone (eds), *The Cambridge Ancient History Vol. XI: The High Empire AD 70–192*, (Cambridge University Press (Cambridge, 2000) pp. 514–46.

Whittaker, C.R., *Rome and its Frontiers: The Dynamics of Empire*, Routledge (London and New York, 2004).

Chapter 2: The Sources

Alföldy, G., 'Herodians Person', *Ancient Society 2* (1971) pp. 204–33.

Anderson, G., *The Second Sophistic: A Cultural Phenomenon in the Roman Empire, Routledge* (London, 1993).

Barnes, T.D., 'The Composition of Cassius Dio's "Roman History"', *Phoenix 38* (1984) pp. 240–55.

Birley, A.R., *Septimius Severus: The African Emperor*, Routledge (London and New York, 2002).

Birley. A.R., 'Marius Maximus, the Consular Biographer', in W. Haase and H. Temporini (eds.) *Aufstieg und Niedergang der Römischen Welt 2, 34.3* (Berlin and New York, 1997) pp. 2678–757.

Broderson, K 'Appian und sein Werk', in W. Haase and H. Temporini (eds.), *Aufstieg und Niedergang der römischen Welt 2.34.1* (Berlin and New York, 1993) pp. 339–63.

Carson R.A.G. and Hill P.V. (eds.), *Coins of the Roman Empire in the British Museum .5. 1, Pertinax to Elagabalus*, Second Edition, British Museum (London, 1975).

Cornell, T. J. (ed.), *The Fragments of the Roman Historians, Vol. I*. Oxford University Press (Oxford, 2013).

Easterling, P.E. and Kenney, E.J., (eds.), *The Cambridge History of Greek Literature*, Cambridge University Press (Cambridge, UK and New York, 1984).

Gorski, G.L. and Packer, J.E., *The Roman Forum: A Reconstruction and Architectural Guide*, Cambridge University Press (New York, 2015).

Gowing, M, 'Dio's Name', *Classical Philology 85* (1990) pp. 49–54.

Hill, P.V., *The Coinage of Septimius Severus and his Family of the Mint of Rome* (London 1964).

Hopkins, K., *Death and Renewal, Sociological Studies in Roman History Vol. 2* (Cambridge and New York, 1983).

Hose, M., 'Cassius Dio: A Senator and Historian in the Age of Anxiety', in J. Marincola, J. (ed.) *A Companion to Greek and Roman Historiography* Vol. II, Blackwell (Malden, MA and Oxford, 2007) pp. 461–7.

Kemezis, *Greek Narratives of the Roman Empire under the Severans*: Cassius *Dio, Philostratus and Herodian*, Cambridge University Press (Cambridge, UK, 2014).

Klebs, E. and Dessau, H. (eds.), *Prosopographia Imperii Romani* (Berlin, 1897).

Lusnia, S.S., 'Urban Planning and Sculptural Display in Severan Rome: Reconstructing the Septizodium and Its Role in Dynastic Politics', American Journal of Archaeology 108 (2004) pp. 517–44.

Millar, F., *A Study of Cassius Dio*, Clarendon Press (Oxford, 1964).

Murphy, G.J., *The Reign of the Emperor L. Septimius Severus from the Evidence of the Inscriptions*, St. Peters College Press, Jersey City, NJ (Philadelphia, 1947).

Richardson, Jr., L *A New Topographical Dictionary of Ancient Rome*, The Johns Hopkins Press (London and Baltimore, 1992).

Roxan, M.M., *Roman Military Diplomas I*, Institute of Archaeology, University of London; no. 2 (1978).

Sage, M., 'The Historical Works of Tacitus', in W. Haase and H. Temporini (eds.), *Aufstieg und Niedergang der Römischen Welt 2.33.2* (Berlin and New York, 1990) pp. 851–1030.

Syme, R., *Ammianus and the Historia Augusta*, The Clarendon Press (Oxford, 1968).

Wallace-Hadrill, A., *Suetonius: The Scholar and his Caesars* (London, 1983).

Whittaker, C.R., *Herodian*, Loeb Classical Library, William Heinemann and Harvard University Press (London and Cambridge MA, 1969).

Chapter 3: Prelude

Ball, W., *Rome in the East*, Routledge (London and New York, 2000).

Birley, A.R., 'The Wars and Revolts' in M. van Ackeren (ed.), *A Companion to Marcus Aurelius*, Wiley-Blackwell (Malden, MA and Oxford, UK, 2012) pp 217–33.

Birley, A.R., *Marcus Aurelius: A Biography*, Routledge (London and New York, 1987).

Bodard, G. and Roueché, C. (eds.), *Inscriptions of Roman Tripolitania*, Electronic edition, Kings College London (London, 2009).

Braund, D., *Rome and the Friendly King*, Croom Helm (London and New York, 1984).

Di Vita, A., 'Leptis Magna: Die Heimatstadt des Septimius Severus in Nordafrika', *Antike Welt 27* (1996) pp. 173–90.

Di Vita-Evrard, G., 'Un nouveau proconsul d'Afrique, parent de Septime Sévère: Cassius Septimius Severus' *Mélanges de l'école française de Rome 75* (1963) pp. 389–414.

Gilhaus. L, 'Equites and Senators as Agents of Trade: Urban Culture and Elite Self-Representation in Thaumgadi and Lepcis Magna (Second-Third

Centuries AD' in A. Bokern (ed.) *Proceedings of the Second Annual Archaeology Conference, Goethe University in* Frankfurt 29 March–1 April 2012, Oxbow, (Oxford, 2013) pp. 21–36.

Hekster, O., 'Commodus-Hercules: The People's Princeps', *Scripta Classica Israelica 20*, (2001) pp. 51–83.

Hekster, O., 'The Roman Empire after His Death' in M. van Ackeren (ed.), *A Companion to Marcus Aurelius*, Wiley-Blackwell (Malden, MA and Oxford, UK, 2012) pp. 234–48.

Hekster, O., *Commodus: An Emperor at the Crossroads*, Dutch Monographs on Ancient History and Archaeology, 23. Brill, (Leiden, 2002).

Hopkins, M.K., 'The Age of Roman Girls at Marriage', *Population Studies 18* (1965) pp. 309–27.

Levick, B., *Julia Domna, Syrian Empress*, Routledge (London and New York, 2007).

Millar, F., *The Emperor in the Roman World*, (31 BC–AD 337), Duckworth (London, 1977).

Millar, M., 'Empire, Community and Culture in the Roman Near East: Greeks, Syrians, Jews and Arabs', *Journal of Jewish Studies 38* (1987) pp. 143–62.

North, J.A., *Roman Religion*, Oxford University Press (Oxford, UK, 2000).

Pollard, N., *Soldiers, Cities, and Civilians in Roman Syria*, University of Michigan Press (Ann Arbor, 2000).

Potter, D.S., *The Roman Empire at Bay, AD 180–395*, Routledge (London and New York, 2004).

Saller, R.P., *Personal Patronage under the Early Empire*, Cambridge University Press (Cambridge and New York, 1982).

Trundle, M., *Greek Mercenaries from the Late Archaic Period to Alexander*, Routledge (London and New York, 2004).

Veyne, P., *Bread and Circuses*, Penguin (London, 1992).

Wiedemann, T., *Emperors and Gladiators*, Routledge (London and New York, 1992).

Chapter 4: Things Fall Apart

Barnes, T.D., 'A Senator from Hadrumetum, and Three Others', in *Bonner Historia Augusta Colloquium 1968–1969* (Bonn, 1970), pp. 45–58.

Boteva, D., 'Legati Augusti pro praetore Moesiae inferioris A.D. 193–217/218', *Zeitschrift für Papyrologie und Epigraphik 110* (1996) pp. 239–40.

Campbell, B., 'The Severan Dynasty', in A.K. Bowman, P. Garnsey and A. Cameron (eds.), *Cambridge Ancient History XII; The Crisis of Empire, AD 193–337*, Cambridge University Press (Cambridge, UK, 2005) pp. 1–27.

Dessau, H., *Inscriptiones Latinae Selectae*, 3 vols, Weidmann (Berlin, 1892).

Dickie, M.W., *Magic and Magicians in the Greco-Roman World*, Routledge (London and New York, 2001).

Freis, H.B., *Die Cohortes Urbanae*, Epigraphische Studien 2 (1967).

Griffin, M., 'Nerva to Hadrian', in A.K. Bowman, P. Garnsey and D. Rathbone (eds), *The Cambridge Ancient History XI: The High Empire, A.D. 70–192*, Cambridge University Press (Cambridge, 2000) pp. 84–130.

Hasebroek, J., *Untersuchungen zur Geschichte des Kaisers Septimius Severus*, Carl Winter (Heidelberg, 1921).

Jones, B.W., *The Emperor Domitian*, Routledge (London and New York, 1992).

Lendon, J.E., *Empire of Honour*, Oxford University Press (Oxford and New York, 1997).

McLynn, F., *Marcus Aurelius: A Life*, Da Capo Press (Cambridge, MA, 2009).

Wellesley, K., *The Year of the Four Emperors*, Third Edition, Routledge (London and New York, 2003).

Chapter 5 Civil Wars: Act1

Birley, A.R., 'Hadrian to the Antonines' in A.K. Bowman, and P. Garnsey and D. Rathbone (eds.), *The Cambridge Ancient History: The High Empire, AD 70–192*, Cambridge University Press (Cambridge, UK and New York, 2000) pp. 132–94.

Boatwright, M.T., 'Faustina the Younger, Mater Castrorum' in R. Frei-Stolba, A. Bielman and O. Bianchi. (eds), *Les femmes entre sphère privée et sphère publique*, Peter Lang (Bern, 2003) pp. 249–68.

Campbell, B., *Greek and Roman Military Writers: Select Readings*, Routledge (London and New York, 2004).

Durry, M., 'Les cohortes prétoriennes', *Bulletin d' École Française de Rome 146* (Paris, 1938)

Gradoni, M., 'The Parthian Campaigns of Septimius Severus: Causes, and Roles in Dynastic Legitimation', in E.C. De Sena, (ed.), *The Roman Empire During the Severan Dynasty: Case Studies in History, Art, Architecture, Economy and Literature*, Gorgias Press (New York, 2013) pp. 3–23.

Kovacs, P., *Marcus Aurelius's Rain Miracle and the Marcomannic Wars*, Mnemosyne 308, Brill (Leiden and Boston, 2009).

MacMullen, R., *Enemies of the Roman Order*, Harvard University Press (Cambridge, MA, 1966).

Magie, D., *Roman Rule in Asia Minor to the End of the Third Century after Christ Vol I*, Princeton University Press (Princeton, NJ, 1950).

Mennen, I., *Power and Status in the Roman Empire, AD 193–284*, Brill, (Leiden and Boston, 2011).

Millar, F., *The Roman Near East 31 BC–AD 337*, Harvard University Press (Cambridge, MA and London, 1993).

Platnauer, M., *The Life and Reign of the Emperor Lucius Septimius Severus*, Oxford University Press, (Oxford, 1918).

Ross, S.K., *Roman Edessa*, Routledge (London and New York, 2001).

Sage, M.M., 'Eusebius and the Rain Miracle'. *Historia 36*, 1987, pp. 96–113.

Southern, P., *The Roman Empire from Severus to Constantine*, Routledge (London and New York, 2004).

Speidel, M., 'Valerius Valerianus in Charge of Septimius Severus's Mesopotamian Campaign', *Classical Philology 80* (1985) pp. 321–6.

Chapter 6 The Civil Wars; Act 2

Birley, A.R., *Septimius Severus: The African Emperor*, Routledge, (London and New York, 2002).

Birley, A.R., *The Roman Government of Britain*, Oxford University Press (Oxford, UK and New York, 2005).

Hasebroek, J., *Untersuchungen zur Geschichte des Kaisers Septimius Severus*, Carl Winter (Heidelberg, 1921).

Platnauer, M., *The Life and Reign of the Emperor Lucius Septimius Severus*, Oxford University Press (London, 1918).

Sage, M.M., *The Army of the Roman Republic*, Pen & Sword, (Barnsley, UK, 2018).

Salway, P., Roman Britain, Oxford University Press (Oxford, UK and New York, 1981).

Scullard, H.H., *Festivals and Ceremonies of the Roman Republic*, Thames and Hudson (London, 1981).

Chapter 7: Encore: War in the East and Sightseeing in Egypt

Barnes, T.D., 'Legislation against the Christians', *Journal of Roman Studies 58* (1968) pp. 32–50.

Bennett, J., *Trajan, Optimus Princeps*, Routledge (London and New York, 1997).

Bowman, A.K., 'Egypt from Septimius Severus to the Death of Constantine', in A.K. Bowman, P. Garnsey, and A. Cameron, A. (eds.), *The Cambridge Ancient History Vol. XII, The Crisis of Empire AD 193–337*, Cambridge University Press (Cambridge, UK and New York, 2005) pp. 313–26.

Campbell D.B., 'What Happened at Hatra? The Problem of the Severan Siege Operations' in P. Freeman and D. Kennedy (eds.), *The Defence of the Roman and Byzantine East, BAR International Series 297* (1968) pp. 51–8.

Debevoise, N.C., *A Political History of Parthia*, University of Chicago Press (Chicago, 1938).

Edwell, P.M., *Between Rome and Persia*, Routledge, (London and New York, 2008).

Grimal, P., *The Concise Dictionary of Classical Mythology*, Basil Blackwell (Oxford, UK, 1990).

Harker, A., *Loyalty and Dissidence in Roman Egypt*, Cambridge University Press (Cambridge UK and New York, 2008).

Isaac, B., *The Limits of Empire* rev. ed., Oxford University Press (Oxford, 1990).

Kennedy, D.L., 'European Soldiers and the Severan Siege of Hatra', in P. W. Freeman and D.L. Kennedy (eds.), *The Defense of the Roman and Byzantine East*, (Oxford, 1986) pp. 397–409.

Kennedy, D.L., 'The Garrisoning of Mesopotamia in the Late Antonine and Early Severan Period', *Antichthon 21* (1987) pp. 57–66.

Lloyd, A.B., The Reception of Pharaonic Egypt in Classical Antiquity' in A.B. Lloyd (ed.), *A Companion to Ancient Egypt* Vol I, Wiley-Blackwell (Malden, MA and Oxford, UK, 2010) pp. 1078–85.

Lockwood, A., *Six-Legged Soldiers: Using Insects as Weapons of War*, Oxford University Press (Oxford, 2008).

Rostovtzeff, M.I., 'The Parthian Shot', *American Journal of Archaeology 47* (1943) pp. 174–87.

Speidel. M., "Europeans'– Syrian Elite Troops at Dura-Europos and Hatra', in M. Speidel, *Roman Armies Studies* I, J.C. Gieben (Amsterdam, 1984) pp. 301–9.

Wheeler, E.L., 'The Army and the Limes in the East' in P.A. Erdkamp (ed.) *A Companion to the Roman Army*, Blackwell, (Oxford, UK and Malden, MA, 2007) pp. 235–66.

Yarshater, E. (ed.), *The Cambridge History of Iran* Vol. 3.2, Cambridge University Press (Cambridge, UK, 1983).

Chapter 8: Rome and Africa

Cartwright, M., 'The Arch of Septimius Severus', *Ancient History Encyclopedia*, retrieved from https://76.15.1 and 77.www.ancient.eu/article/502/ (June 29, 2013).

Kleiner. F.S., *A History of Roman Art, Enhanced Edition*, Wadsworth Cengage Learning (Boston, MA, 2010).

Price. S.R.F, 'The Place of Religion: Rome in the early Empire', in A.K. Bowman, E. Champlin and A. Lintott (eds.), *The Cambridge Ancient History, Vol. X: The Augustan Empire, 43 B.C—A.D. 69*, Cambridge University Press (Cambridge, UK 1996) pp. 812–47.

Rowan, C., 'The Public Image of the Severan Women', *Papers of the British School at Rome 79* (2011) pp. 241–73.

Torelli, M., 'Topography and Archaeology of Republican Rome', in N. Rosenstein and R. Morstein-Marx (eds.) *A Companion to the Roman Republic*, Blackwell (Malden, MA and Oxford, UK, 2006) pp. 81–101.

Varner, E.R., *Mutilation and Transformation, Damnatio Memoriae and Roman Imperial Portraiture*, Brill (Leiden and Boston, 2004).

Chapter 9 The Return to Rome

Barnes, T.D., 'Aspects of the Severan Empire, Part I: Severus as a New Augustus', *New England Classical Journal 35* (2008) pp. 259–67.

Galinsky, K., 'Continuity and Change: Religion in the Augustan Semi-Century', in J. Rüpke (ed.), *A Companion to Roman Religion*, Blackwell (Malden, MA and Oxford, 2007) pp. 71–92.

Gorrie, C., 'Julia Domna's Building Patronage, Imperial Family Roles and the Severan Revival of Moral Legislation', *Historia 53* (2004) pp. 61–72.

Grünewald, T., *Bandits in the Roman Empire: Myth and Reality*, Trans. J.D. Drinkwater, Routledge (London and New York, 2004).

Isaac. B., 'Bandits in Judaea and Arabia', *Harvard Studies in Classical Philology 88* (1984) pp. 171–203.

Pighi, G.B., *De ludis saecularibus populi Romani Quiritium libri sex*, Schippers (Amsterdam, 1965).

Shaw B.D., 'Bandits in the Roman Empire', *Past & Present 105*, (1984) pp. 3–52.

Chapter 10: The Last Act

Breeze, D.J., *Roman Scotland*, Batsford (London, 1996).

Casey, J., 'Who Built Carpow? Review of Events in Britain in the Reigns of Commodus', Britannia 41 (2010) pp. 225–35.

Crow, J., 'The Northern Frontier of Britain from Trajan to Antoninus Pius: Roman Builders and Native Britons', in M. Todd (ed.), *A Companion to Roman Britain*, Blackwell (Malden, MA and Oxford, UK, 2002) pp. 114–35.

Frank. R.I. 'The Dangers of Peace', *Prudentia 8* (1976) pp. 1–7.

Frere, S., *Britannia*, Book Club Associates (London, 1967).

Hodgson, N., 'The British Expedition of Septimius Severus', *Britannia 45* (2014) pp. 31–51.

Mattingly, D., *An Imperial Possession: Britain in the Roman Empire*, Penguin (London, 2007).

Maxwell G., 'The Roman Penetration of the North in the Late First Century AD' in M. Todd (ed.), *A Companion to Roman Britain*, Blackwell (Malden, MA and Oxford, 2002) pp.75–90.

Salway, P., *Roman Britain, A Very Short Introduction*, Oxford University Press (Oxford, 2015).

The Arthritis Foundation, 'What is Gout?', www.arthritis.org/about-arthritis/types/gout/what-is-gout.php

Appendix: Severus and the Roman Army

Alston, R., 'Roman Military Pay from Caesar to Diocletian', *Journal of Roman Studies 84* (1994) pp. 113–23.

Campbell, B., 'The Marriage of Soldiers under the Empire', *Journal of Roman Studies 68* (1978) pp. 153–66.

Cornell T.J., 'The End of Roman Imperial Expansion', in J. Rich and G. Shipley (eds.), *War and Society in the Roman World*, Routledge (London, 1993) pp. 139–70.

Develin, R., 'The Army Pay Rises under Severus and Caracalla, and the Question of Annona Militaris', *Latomus 30* (1971) pp. 687–95.

Duncan-Jones, R., *The Economy of the Roman Empire: Quantitative Studies*, Cambridge University Press, (Cambridge, UK and New York, 1982).

Griffin, M., 'The Flavians', in A.K. Bowman, P. Garnsey and D. Rathbone (eds), *The Cambridge Ancient History Vol. XI: The High Empire AD 70–192*, pp. 1–83.

Handy, M., *Die Severi und das Heer*, Verlag Antike (Berlin, 2009).

Kehne, P., 'War and Peacetime Logistics: Supplying Imperial Armies in the East and the West', in P.A. Erdkamp (ed.), *A Companion to the Roman Army* Blackwell, (Oxford and Malden, MA, 2007) pp. 323–38.

Phang, S. E., *The Marriage of Roman Soldiers (13 BC–AD 235): Law and Family in the Roman Imperial Army*, Leiden (2001).

Pollard, N., 'The Roman Army', in D.S. Potter (ed.), *A Companion to the Roman Empire*, Blackwell (Malden, MA and Oxford, 2006) pp. 206–27.

Strobel, Z.K., 'Strategy and Army Structure between Septimius Severus and Constantine the Great', in P.A. Erdkamp, (ed.) *A Companion to the Roman Army*, Blackwell, (Malden, MA and Oxford, 2007) pp. 267–85.

Yarshater. E. (ed.), *The Cambridge History of Iran Vol 3.1: The Achaemenid, Parthian and Sasanian Periods*, Cambridge University Press (Cambridge and New York, 1983).

Notes

Introduction

1. M. Hammond, 'The Composition of the Roman Senate, AD 68–235', *Journal of Roman Studies* 47 (1957) p. 77
2. For a general study of Fronto, see E. Champlin, *Fronto and Antonine Rome* (Cambridge, MA, 1980).
3. R. Syme, 'Donatus' and the Like', in A.R. Birley, (ed.), R. Syme, *Roman Papers III*, Clarendon Press (Oxford, 1984) p. 1113.
4. C.R. Whittaker, 'Africa', in A.K. Bowman et al. (eds), *The Cambridge Ancient History Vol. XI: The High Empire AD 70–192*, (Cambridge University Press (Cambridge, 2000) p. 517.
5. Letter 2.10, C.R. Haines, ed. and trans. *The Correspondence of Marcus Cornelius Fronto*, Vol. I, Loeb Classical Library, (London and New York, 1919) p. 137.
6. Life of Severus 19.9. Apuleius, also from Africa, a major writer and contemporary of Fronto excuses his mistakes by labelling himself a speaker of an uncouth and foreign language. There is also an anecdote claiming that Severus sent his sister back to Africa because of her terrible Latin (*Life of Severus* 17.2), but this says more about language proficiency than the effect of accent.
7. The first is Elagabalus (218–222) and the second was Alexander Severus (222–235).
8. For all three Punic Wars A.K. Goldsworthy, *The Fall of Carthage: The Punic Wars 264–146 BC*, Cassell (London, 2000) offers a useful summary and discussion.
9. P. Erdkamp, 'The Food Supply of the Capital', in P. Erdkamp (ed.), *The Cambridge Companion to Ancient Rome*, Cambridge University Press (2013) p. 270.
10. It was a seaport located near modern Teboulba in Tunisia.
11. This was the colony founded by Gaius Gracchus at the site of Carthage. His death in 121 in an internal political struggle in Rome led to the abandonment of the colony.

12. An *ala*, or cavalry unit, of Gaetuli is mentioned as serving in Palestine and Arabia in the first century, consisting of horsemen and camel riders, see G. Bowersock, *Roman Arabia*, Harvard University Press (Cambridge, MA, and London, UK, 1983) p. 107.

13. On the Phoenicians and Phoenician colonization, see G.E. Markoe, *Phoenicians*, University of California Press (Berkeley and Los Angeles, 2000).

14. Cyrenaica was the eastern district of Libya bordering Egypt. It took its name from the Greek colony of Cyrene founded there in the later part of the seventh century.

15. It is not clear if the name referred to actual intermarriage or was a geographical reference. See D. Hoyos, *The Carthaginians*, Routledge (London, UK and New York, 2010) p. 17.

16. F. Millar, 'Local Cultures in the Roman Empire: Libyan, Punic, and Latin in Roman Africa', in H.M. Cotton and G.M. Rogers (eds.). F. Millar, 'Rome, the Greek World, and the East' in Vol 2 of *Government, Society, and Culture in the Roman Empire*, p, 262.

17. Whittaker, *Roman Africa* p. 603

18. See above pp. ix–x.

19. S. Raven, *Roman Africa*, Routledge (New York, 1993) pp. 59–61.

20. A revolt broke out under Claudius (Aurelius Victor, *The Caesars* 4. And Dio 60.9.6).

21. A.A. Barrett, *Caligula: The Corruption of Power*, Routledge (London and New York, 1989) pp. 115–19.

22. Latin status was a bundle of judicial rights of which the most important was the granting of Roman citizenship to the towns' magistrates on completion of their term of office.

23. Pliny, *Natural History* 18.35.

24. Whittaker, *Cambridge Ancient History Vol. XI* p. 540.

25. See p. 30.

26. On *canabae* see, N. Hanel, 'Military Camps, Canabae and Vici: The Archaeological Evidence', in P. Erdkamp (ed.), A *Companion to the Roman Army*, Blackwell Publishing (Malden, MA and Oxford, UK, 2007) pp. 410–13.

27. The literary sources indicate trouble with the Moors but lack detail, some of which is supplied by inscriptions. On the second raid see ILS 2354 and G. Alföldy, 'Spain' in *Cambridge Ancient History, Vol. XI* p. 460.

28. A.A. Barrett, *Caligula; The Corruption of Power*, Routledge (London and New York, 1989) pp. 119–20

29. For this analysis see Y. Le Bohec, *The Imperial Roman Army*, Hippocrene Books and B.T. Batsford (London and New York, 1994). p. 82. For a detailed treatment of the legion, see Le Bohec's *La IIIe Légion Auguste*, Éditions de CNRS, (Paris, 1989).

30. Such units of non-Roman citizens had been regularized by Augustus. They consisted of both mounted troops forming an *ala* (plural *alae*), infantry cohorts and also combined arms units. Their nominal strength varied between 500 and 1,000 men.

31. C.R. Whittaker, *Cambridge Ancient History, Vol. XI* p. 525.

32. For the characterization of the frontier as a transitional zone rather than a barrier see C.R. Whittaker, *Rome and its Frontiers: The Dynamics of Empire*. Routledge (London and New York, 2004) p. 6

33. This grant is recorded on the famous Tabula Banasitana, (*L'Année Epigraphique* 1971 n.534) See H. Glasterer, 'Local and Provincial Institutions and Government', in *The Cambridge Ancient History Vol. XI*, p. 363.

34. On the economy of Roman African see C.R. Whittaker *The Cambridge Ancient History XI* pp. 531–546, S. Raven, *Rome in Africa* pp. 79–99, D. Mattingly, *Tripolitania*, B.T. Batsford Ltd, (London, 1995) pp. 224–53 and A. Hilali, 'Rome and Agriculture in Africa Proconsularis; Land and Hydraulic Development' *Revue Belge de Philologie et d'histoire* 91 (2013) pp. 113–25.

35. Natural History 18.51.22.

36. Hilali, p. 113.

37. Whittaker p. 536, The amount of the grain imported has been subject to divergent estimates by modern scholars. On this problem, see N. Morley, 'Population Size and Social Structure' in P. Erdkamp (ed.), The *Cambridge Companion to Ancient Rome*, Cambridge University Press (Cambridge, UK and New York, 2013) pp. 36–9.

38. Josephus, *The Jewish War* 2. 383–5.

39. C.R. Whittaker, *Cambridge Ancient History Vol. XI* p. 536.

40. Dio 73.13.

41. G.E. Rickman, *The Corn Supply of Ancient Rome*, Oxford University Press (Oxford, UK, 1980).

42. C.R. Whittaker *Cambridge Ancient History Vol. XI* pp. 534–5.

43. Tacitus, *Histories* 4.50.

44. For a useful summary of the requirements and distribution of olive cultivation in Roman Africa, see S. Raven, *Rome in Africa* p. 92.

45. C.R. Whittaker, *Cambridge Ancient History XII* p. 537.

46. See the survey in P.D.A Garnsey, 'Rome's African Empire Under the Principate', in Garnsey and Whittaker (eds.), *Imperialism in the Ancient World*, CUP (Cambridge, 1978) pp. 223–37

47. On the trans-Saharan trade see D. Mattingly, *Tripolitania*, p. 156. He argues for the small contribution it made to African wealth.

48. T.J. Cornell and K. Lomas (eds.), *Urban Society in Roman Italy*, UCL Press (London, 1995) p. 14.

Chapter 1: Sources

1. For his first name or praenomen see M.M. Roxan, Roman Military Diplomas I, Institute of Archaeology, University of London; no. 2 (1978) N. 133. For a discussion of Dio's name, see. A.M. Gowing, 'Dio's Name', *Classical Philology 85* (1990) 49–54.

2. For a useful summary of Dio's life and career see M. Hose, 'Cassius Dio: A Senator and Historian in the Age of Anxiety', in J. Marincola (ed.) *A Companion to Greek and Roman Historiography Vol. II*, Blackwell (Malden, MA and Oxford, UK, 2007) 461–7, especially. 462. The best general treatment of Dio and his history is F. Millar, *A Study of Cassius Dio*, Clarendon Press, (Oxford, 1964).

3. Dio 73.4.2.

4. 80.2.2. The best discussion of Dio's senatorial career is T.D. Barnes, 'The Composition of Cassius Dio's "Roman History"' *Phoenix* 38 (1984) 242–3.

5. K. Hopkins, *Death and Renewal, Sociological Studies in Roman History Vol. 2* (Cambridge UK and New York, 1983) 145.

6. M. Sage, 'The Historical Works of Tacitus', in W. Haase and H. Temporini (eds.), *Aufstieg und Niedergang der Römischen Welt 33.2*, 962–963.

7. A. Wallace-Hadrill, *Suetonius: The Scholar and his Caesars* (London, 1983).

8. K. Broderson, "Appian und sein Werk", in W. Haase and H. Temporini (eds.), *Aufstieg und Niedergang der römischen Welt 2.34.1* (1993) 339–63

9. On the fascination of the Greek past for second century AD Greek writers see G. Anderson, *The Second Sophistic: A Cultural Phenomenon in the Roman Empire*, Routledge (London, 1993) p. 125.

10. Perhaps the most important third century Greek historian was the Athenian Herennius Dexippus who lived from c.210 to 273 and wrote several histories including a history of the world until 270 and a general

history of the barbarian invasions among others. Unfortunately, only citations of his work in other authors remain. On Dexippus see F. Millar, 'P. Herennius Dexippus: the Greek World and the Third-Century Invasions,' JRS 59 (1969) 12–29 who notes a number of other historical works in Greek. Christian works begin to be of use, most importantly, the Church history by Eusebius of Caesarea. On Eusebius see T.D. Barnes, *Constantine and Eusebius*, Harvard University Press Reprint (Cambridge, MA, 2006).

11. Dio, 73.22.3. The emperor shared the typical pagan religious belief of his day that dreams and omens were of divine origin and revealed the future. Severus in his autobiography described the dream and portents that encouraged him to seize power (Herodian 2.9.4–7). Dio was also a believer, See Millar, *A Study of Cassius Dio*, pp. 179–80.

12. The Composition of Cassius Dio's 'Roman History', Phoenix 38 (1984) p. 246

13. Dio 76.7.3 contradicts Severus's account in his autobiography of the death of his rival Albinus. The autobiography is also mentioned by other sources, but we know little about the autobiography, not even whether it was written in Latin or Greek

14. See below, pp. 8–9.

15. Philostratus, *Lives of the Sophists* 2.24, M.J. Moscovich, *Cassius Dio's Palace Sources for the Reign of Septimius Severus*' p. 357 suggests that Dio might have used his work although there is no mention of him in the text. This is not impossible, but doubtful. It would have made more sense to consult military men who had participated in the various expeditions.

16. See below pp. 100–101.

17. 74.4.

18. 74.14.1–2.

19. See esp. p.148.

20. 77.16–17. T.D. Barnes, *The Composition*, p. 253 argues that the contradictions in the views Dio expresses are the result of a mixture of his earlier laudatory account of Severus in Dio's account of the civil war and a later change of heart in the full-scale history when he had experienced Severus as a ruler. This thesis neglects to account for the rather positive view expressed in Dio's assessment of the emperor after his death.

21. Dio 72.36.4.

22. Herodian 1.1.4. For the *Historia Augusta* see below pp. 7–8. There is an important two-volume edition and English translation of Herodian with extensive notes, C.R. Whittaker, *Herodian*, Loeb Classical Library,

William Heinemann and Harvard UP (London and Cambridge MA, 1969).

23. A. Kemezis, *Greek Narratives of The Roman Empire under the Severans: Cassius Dio, Philostratus and Herodian*, (Cambridge University Press, 2014) p. 2

24. See the argument of Whittaker, Herodian pp. ix–xix.

25. 1.2.5.

26. 1.2.5.

27. For instance, G. Alföldy, 'Herodians Person', *Ancient Society 2* (1971) pp. 227–33.

28. P. xxxiii.

29. 1.2.5.

30. 2.9.4–7. It has been suggested that the account was written after Severus's final victory in the civil wars in February 197, so Whittaker, Herodian Vol. I p. 199.

31. For this work see p. 8 below.

32. 3.5.1.

33. 3.9.3.

34. *Septimus Severus: The African Emperor*, rev. ed. Routledge (London and New York, 1999) p. 204.

35. Herodian I, p.xxxix.

36. R. Syme, *Ammianus and the Historia Augusta*, The Clarendon Press (Oxford, 1968) pp. 207–8. It is worth quoting Syme's description of the author in full. 'The author of the HA was clever, but sly and silly, cynical and irresponsible; a rogue grammaticus alert for oddities of fact or language; a fancier of clothing and decoration, an art connoisseur in a small way; a fancier also of all *curiosa*, including the religious, but devoid of strong inner beliefs; and, above all, a collector with an untidy mind. His limitations help to reveal him. A character of this sort might not strain belief, if history or fiction conjured him up from the underworld of letters in some other clime or season.'

37. 28.4.14–15.

38. Severus 2.4. The biographer claims the autobiography omits mention of Severus's first wife. It also seems likely that the omens portending Severus's imperial future were drawn from the autobiography as well. There are further references to it in the Lives of Niger (4.7–5.1 and Albinus 7.1).

39. *Septimius Severus: The African Emperor* p. 203.

40. For reasonable doubts about the identification of the Severan general with the author of the biographies, see T.J. Cornell (ed.), *The Fragments*

of the Roman Historians, Vol. I, Oxford University Press (Oxford, 2013), pp. 603–644.

41. On Niger, see below p. 77, on Albinus see below p. 72.
42. See the entry in *Prosopographia Imperii Romani* 2 308 M.
43. For a detailed study of the biographer, see A.R. Birley, 'Marius Maximus, the Consular Biographer', *Aufstieg und Niedergang der Römischen Welt* II, 34.3 (1997) 2678–2757 and T.J. Cornell (ed.), *The Fragments of the Roman Historians*, (OUP, 2014), p. 606.
44. *Severus* 15.6.
45. *Probus* 2.6–7.
46. *The Forty Tyrants*. 1.1–2. There are further references in the life of Hadrian 5.2.
47. For a summary of Philostratus' works see P.E. Easterling et al (eds), *The Cambridge History of Greek Literature*, Cambridge UP (Cambridge, UK, and New York, 1984) pp. 655–8. On the relationship between Julia Domna and Philostratus see, B. Levick, Julia Domna pp. 108–111.
48. *Lives of the Sophists* 5.20.
49. G.J. Murphy, *The Reign of the Emperor L. Septimius Severus from the Evidence of the Inscriptions*, Jersey City, NJ, St. Peters College Press (Philadelphia, 1947).
50. BMC 5 p. 21 7–25, The standard catalogue is *H. Mattingly, Coins of the Roman Empire in the British Museum* Vol. V, Trustees of the British Museum (London, 1965). Also see P.V. Hill, *The Coinage of Septimius Severus and his Family of the Mint of Rome* (London 1964).
51. We know that Severus had a picture of the heavens painted on the ceiling of his palace. On public display there was a version that was accurate in all respects but for the actual position of the stars at the moment of his birth, so that people would not know exactly when he would die. A fully accurate version was depicted in his private apartments (Dio 76.11.1).
52. The Septizodium has been seen as a large fountain, but there is no trace of water at the site and it is more likely that it was intended as a setting for the statuary on display there, see L. Richardson, Jr., *A New Topographical Dictionary of Ancient Rome*, The Johns Hopkins Press (London and Baltimore, 1992), p. 350. See also, S.S. Lusnia, 'Urban Planning and Sculptural Display in Severan Rome: Reconstructing the Septizodium and Its Role in Dynastic Politics', *American Journal of Archaeology* 108 (2004) pp. 517–544.
53. For a description of the arch and its sculptural decoration see G.I. Gorski and J.E. Packer, *The Roman Forum: A Reconstruction and Architectural*

Guide, CUP (New York, 2015) pp. 135–146. Whether Severus celebrated a triumph is uncertain. See M. Beard, *The Roman Triumph*, Harvard University Press (Cambridge, MA and London, 2007) p. 363, note 30.

54. M.L. Popkin, *The Architecture of the Roman Triumph*, CUP, (New York, 2016) p. 135.

Chapter 2: Prelude

1. The *Historia Augusta*, Severus 1.3 gives a date of 146. However, Dio a more trustworthy source, at 76.17.4 gives his age at death as 65 and that works out to 145 and that is the date now generally accepted.
2. See Introduction, p. xvii.
3. A.B. Birley, *Septimius Severus* p. 34.
4. The section on Tripolitania and the history of Lepcis is heavily indebted to D. Mattingly, *Tripolitania*.
5. A. Birley, *Septimius Severus* p. 3. The ancients labelled these gulfs as the Greater (Sidra) and the Lesser Syrtis (Gabès). The city whose wonderfully preserved ruins lie within the boundaries of Khoms, Libya, east of Tripoli was abandoned under the pressure of Arab raids in the mid-seventh century AD.
6. See Introduction, pp. xx–xxi.
7. {Caesar} *The African War* 97.
8. For the topography and agricultural potential of the area see D. Mattingly, *Tripolitania*, pp. 7–14.
9. See Introduction, p.xx for Lepcis' struggle with Oea in 69. Local rivalries between cities were frequent.
10. *Apology* 98. This may not have been true, but it must have been believable in a trial and therefore indicative of the prevalence of Punic.
11. Severus 1.4 and 15.7.
12. A.R. Birley, *Septimius Severus* p. 9. The Punic of these inscriptions is written in an alphabet called Neo-Punic which is a cursive form of the older Punic script.
13. F. Millar, 'Local Cultures in the Roman Empire: Libyan, Punic, and Latin in Roman Africa', in H.M. Cotton and G.M. Rogers (eds.), F. Millar, *Rome, the Greek World, and the East* Vol 2, University of North Carolina Press (Chapel Hill and London, 2004) p. 253–4. Millar suggests using Libyan but points out that no ancient source uses the name.

14. See A.R. Birley, *Septimius Severus* p. 12. The numen was the active force in a person or thing that when used of an emperor signified his divine essence. It was often used in public oaths. The first altar to the numen of Augustus had been dedicated by his successor in 6 AD (Tacitus, Annals 1.73.3).

15. For the practice see P. Veyne, *Bread and Circuses*, Penguin (London, 1992).

16. For building at Lepcis see the summary account of A. Di Vita, 'Leptis Magna: Die Heimatstadt des Septimius Severus in Nordafrika', *Antike Welt* 27 (1996) pp. 173–190. The article contains excellent pictures of the remains.

17. D. Mattingly, *Tripolitania* p. 90.

18. Freedom from taxation was rare. During the Empire the number of cities with such a status declined.

19. By this period the term Latin no longer had any ethnic significance, but rather it indicated a judicial status.

20. In the second century the award of title as a colony was an honour and had administrative consequences, but no new settlers were involved.

21. The term equestrian, although derived from the early Roman cavalry, no longer had the same meaning. Equestrians now formed the social order just below that of senators and shared many personal and familial ties with them. From Augustus on, they were employed in various administrative posts, especially those that were sensitive and might have proven a threat to the emperor if occupied by a senator. They also provided a crucial augmentation of administrative personnel.

22. L. Gilhaus, 'Equites and Senators as Agents of Trade: Urban Culture and Elite Self-Representation in Thaumgadi and Lepcis Magna (Second-Third Centuries AD', in A. Bokern, *Proceedings of the Second Annual Archaeology Conference*, Goethe University in Frankfurt 29 March-1 April 2012, Oxbow Books, (Oxford, 2013) pp. 21–36.

23. D. Mattingly, *Tripolitania* p. 100.

24. T.D. Barnes, 'The Family and Career of Septimius Severus', *Historia* 16 (1967) pp. 89–90.

25. A.R. Birley, *Septimius Severus* p. 18, thinks that the family which had property in Italy had taken the Roman clan name – Septimius. T.D. Barnes, *The Family* p. 90, argues based on the tribe of Severus's family that the family was ultimately of Italian origin.

26. *Silvae*, 4.5.54f.

27. As pointed out by R.P. Saller in *Personal Patronage under the Early Empire*, CUP (Cambridge and New York, 1982) pp. 176–7, note 156.
28. *Historia Augusta, Severus*, 1.2.
29. For the sister see above p. 14.
30. *Severus* 1.4.
31. 77.16.1.
32. *Epitome de Caesaribus* 20.8.
33. *Severus* 1.5 The *Life* mistakenly assigns a second consulship to Septimius Severus's great uncle; this is incorrect.
34. There were six military tribunes in each legion who acted as assistants to the commander. Five of the six were of equestrian rank, the sixth senatorial.
35. *Severus* 2.3. A.R. Birley, *Septimius Severus* p. 40.
36. *Inscriptions of Roman Tripolitania* 541.b
37. *Severus* 2.1–2.
38. *Historia Augusta, Marcus Aurelius* 21.1. Also, *Cambridge Ancient History XI* p. 460.
39. *Mélanges de l'école française de Rome* (1963) 398.
40. *Severus* 4.1. A.B. Birley, *Septimius Severus* p. 50.
41. The marriage is mentioned by the Historia Augusta, *Severus* 3.2. The *Historia Augusta* (3.2) also claims that she was omitted from the autobiography that Severus wrote at the end of the civil wars. For references and details see A.R. Birley, *Septimius Severus* p. 225 n. 56.
42. The exact date is unknown and there have been various suggestions.
43. For the conditions of Greek mercenary service see M. Trundle, *Greek Mercenaries from the Late Archaic Period to Alexander*, Routledge (London and New York, 2004).
44. Severus 3.5. See A.R. Birley, *Septimius Severus* p. 55.
45. P.M. Edsall, *Between Rome and Persia*, Routledge (London and New York, 2007) pp. 24–26.
46. Zeugma played an outstanding role on the eastern frontier. It was located at the crossing of two major ancient highways linking the Syrian coast and Asian Turkey with Mesopotamia. It was also an easy crossing point on the river. It had frequently been used by the Parthians for invasions of Syria.
47. Samosata's ruins lay on the west bank of the Euphrates within the former location of the Turkish city of Samsat. The site was flooded by the building of the Ataturk Dam in 1989.

48. N. Pollard, *Soldiers, Cities, and Civilians in Roman Syria*, University of Michigan Press (Ann Arbor, 2000). pp. 16–24.

49. T.D. Barnes, 'The Family and Career of Septimius Severus' p. 92. n. 44. Barnes suggests that his command in Syria ran from 180 to 183.

50. The title of Caesar was an indication that the individual so named would succeed to the throne after the death of the incumbent.

51. For a short summary see A.R. Birley, 'The Wars and Revolts' in M. van Ackeren (ed.), *A Companion to Marcus Aurelius*, Wiley-Blackwell (Malden, MA and Oxford, UK, 2012) pp. 222–230.

52. 72 36.4. The theme of the change from gold to iron is also repeated in *Historia Augusta* Marcus Aurelius 36.4. It is a commonplace.

53. Dio 72.1.1–2.

54. *Historia Augusta, Commodus* 1.7. This may have been the opinion of the emperor's contemporary Marius Maximus who is mentioned as a source several times in the *Life*, for example at 15.4. Herodian, especially 1. 6.2 2 and 17.12, seems to follow Dio in the sense that he too sees the young man's character corrupted by his associates. This is, of course, a standard motive in depictions of the development of tyrants.

55. A.R. Birley, *Septimius Severus* p. 60.

56. Herodian 1.6.1.6.1–2 and *Commodus* 3.5.

57. For Commodus's reign see O. Hekster, 'Commodus: An Emperor at the Crossroads', *Dutch Monographs on Ancient history and Archaeology*, 23. Brill, (Leiden, 2002). Hekster tries occasionally successfully to rehabilitate Commodus.

58. *Commodus* 3.6.

59. Roman noblemen could also have a *cubicularius* who attended them in their bedrooms. For the influence of chamberlains in the second century see F. Millar, 'Emperors at Work', *Journal of Roman Studies* 57 (1967) p. 15.

60. On the political circumstances surrounding the marriage see A.R. Birley, *Marcus Aurelius: A Biography*, Routledge (London and New York, 1987) pp. 161–2.

61. *Commodus* 4.4, Dio 72.4.4–5, and Herodian, 1.4–6 Herodian is quite negative as regards the conspiracy and traces the emperor's hostility to the Senate to this conspiracy.

62. Dio 73.12.2.

63. Dio 73.5.2.

64. *Commodus* 4.5.

65. On Ulpius Marcellus and the events in Britain see A.R. Birley, *The Roman Government of Britain*, OUP (Oxford, UK and New York, 2005) pp. 162–70.
66. 1.9.1–6.
67. *Commodus* 6.1–3. The narrative gives no explanation as to why Commodus would have paid any attention to the complaints of these men.
68. 73.9.2–10.1.
69. *Cambridge Ancient History XI*, p. 188.
70. Phrygians were often synonymous with slaves in classical Greek and Roman worlds.
71. On the importance of imperial freedmen in imperial administration, see F. Millar, *The Emperor in the Roman World, (31 BC–AD 337)*, Duckworth (London, 1977) pp. 69–83.
72. Dio 73 .2.
73. 73.4.
74. *Commodus* 5.6.
75. 1.8.2.
76. T.D. Barnes, *Family and Career* p. 92, n.47 adds supporting evidence for the veracity of the time at Athens which appears in no other source. For Dio and Severus's interest in education see 76.16.1.
77. *Severus* 3.7.
78. See above p. 20.
79. Dio 73.4.1., *Historia Augusta Pertinax* 3.6 and 8–10.
80. D. Potter, *The Roman Empire at Bay* p. 91.
81. O. Hekster, 'The Roman Empire after His Death' pp. 237–8.
82. See the comments of Dio at 72.12. He is followed by the *Historia Augusta, Commodus* 6.6–12 and Herodian 1.12.4–5. Herodian claims he had organized a conspiracy to replace Commodus. This seems a fiction or a misunderstanding. No freedman could have become emperor.
83. D. Potter, The *Roman Empire at Bay* p. 90.
84. A cardinal imperial virtue was to keep freedmen in their place, Pliny, *Panegyricus* 88.1–2.
85. Historia Augusta, *Severus* 3.8. For the chronology, see T.D. Barnes, Family and Career, p. 93.
86. For an excellent account of her life and importance see. B. Levick, *Julia Domna, Syrian Empress*, Routledge (London and New York, 2007).
87. For Emesa see W. Ball, *Rome in the East*, Routledge (London and New York, 2000) pp. 33–47.

88. F. Millar, 'Empire, Community and Culture in the Roman Near East: Greeks, Syrians, Jews and Arabs', *Journal of Jewish Studies* 38 (1987) p. 152.

89. Josephus, *The Jewish War* 3.4.2.

90. For client kings in general see D. Braund, *Rome and the Friendly King*, Croom Helm (London and New York, 1984).

91. 3.9.

92. Dio 72.23.2 and p. 4 above.

93. B. Levick, *Julia Domna* p. 30.

94. Levick, *Julia Domna* p. 30 notes that it is possible that it was acquired from one of the governors of Syria instead.

95. Levick, *Julia Domna*, p. 23 n. 1.

96. Roman girls married much earlier than their male counterparts. The early teens possibly before 15 seems to have been the most normal age for girls in elite marriages. On this see M.K. Hopkins, 'The Age of Roman Girls at Marriage', *Population Studies* 18 (1965) pp. 309–27.

97. *Historia Augusta*, *Severus* 4.2.

98. A. R. Birley, *Septimius Severus* p. 34 suggests that since the governor. Sextus Calpurnius Agricola was probably an African he may have been persuaded by a mutual acquaintance to give Geta the position.

99. Dio 55.24.2.

100. T. D. Barnes, 'Family and Career' p. 95 argues for a different chronology. The key to Geta's career is *Inscriptions of Roman Tripolitania* n 541 in G Bodard and Charlotte Roueché (eds), Electronic edition, Kings College London, 2009.

101. Dio 73. 21.1–2, and *Commodus* 7.4–8.

102. Herodian 1.14.7.

103. J.A. North, *Roman Religion*, Oxford University Press (Oxford, UK, 2000).

104. For an attempt to provide a rational explanation for his behaviour see O. Hekster, 'Commodus-Hercules: The People's Princeps', *Scripta Classica Israelica*, vol. 20, (2001), pp. 51–83.

105. Dio 73. 15.2 and Historia Augusta *Commodus* 15.2.

106. For an explanation of his behaviour see T. Wiedemann, *Emperors and Gladiators*, Routledge (London and New York, 1992) p. 110.

107. *Historia Augusta Pertinax* 4.4.

108. Dio 72. 22. 1–2.

109. Herodian 1.16.3–1.17.11.

110. *Commodus* 18–19.

Chapter 3: Things Fall Apart

1. The Antonine Dynasty traditionally runs from the accession of Nerva in 96 AD to the death of Commodus in 192.
2. On the civil war following Nero's death in June 68, see. K. Wellesley, *The Year of the Four Emperors*, Routledge (London and New York, 2003).
3. B.W. Jones, *The Emperor Domitian*, Routledge (London and New York, 1992).
4. Jones, *Domitian* pp. 193–6.
5. Se A R. Birley, *Marcus Aurelius: A Biography*, Appendix 2: The Antonine Dynasty, Routledge (London and New York, 1987) pp. 232–48.
6. For Pertinax's origin and previous career see pp. 24–25.
7. On the urban cohorts, see H. Freis, *Die Cohortes Urbanae*, Epigraphische Studien 2 (1967).
8. *Pertinax* 4.4.
9. Dio 74.1.2.
10. 2.3.1. As Whittaker p. 144 notes in his commentary some aristocrats in the Senate did cause him problems.
11. 2.1.10.
12. The same problem with the guard surfaced after the assassination of Domitian, Suetonius, *Domitian* 23.1, Dio 68.3.3.
13. For the British mutiny under Pertinax see above p. 25.
14. T.D. Barnes, *Family and Career*, p. 89.
15. This evidence is used by A.R. Birley, *Septimius Severus* p. 83–4. For what it is worth, the *Historia Augusta*'s life of Albinus claims that Pertinax was killed on Albinus's advice (1.1). This is probably an invention as the life is largely fiction.
16. 74 [73]. 2. 5–6.
17. *Historia Augusta, Pertinax* 10.8, Dio 74 [73]. 8.1
18. J. Hasebroek, *Untersuchungen zur Geschichte des Kaisers Septimius Severus*, Carl Winter (Heidelberg, 1921) p. 17, an old but still useful study of the *Historia Augusta* life of Severus and various historical problems connected with his reign.
19. *Historia Augusta*, Pertinax 3.5.
20. F. McLynn, *Marcus Aurelius: A Life*, Da Capo Press (Cambridge, MA, 2009), p. 435.
21. M. Griffin, 'Nerva to the Antonines', in *Cambridge Ancient History XI* pp. 84–5.

22. *Historia Augusta, Didius Julianus* 2.7 and Do 74.12.1. See the perceptive remarks on the troops feeling for Commodus by M.P. Speidel, 'Commodus the God-Emperor and the Army', *Journal of Roman Studies* 83 (1993) p. 113.

23. Praetorians already had a much higher rate of pay than ordinary legionaries. Normal pay amounted to 4,000 sestertii per year without taking into account donatives and other perquisites. See, G.R. Watson, *The Roman Soldier*, Cornell University Press (Ithaca, 1969) p. 98.

24. Dio 74 [73] 1 and *Historia Augusta*, Pertinax 3.7 for the pretended illness of Commodus.

25. *Historia Augusta*, Pertinax 3.8.

26. 2.2.5.

27. 74 [73].2.

28. Such a refusal of power had become an imperial ritual since Augustus, see Dio 53.11.

29. *Historia Augusta*, Commodus 18.3–19.9.

30. It is a telling detail that reveals the importance of the soldiers; in thanking the Senate Pertinax also thanked Laetus. *Historia Augusta, Pertinax* 5.1.

31. Dio 74.2.1.

32. *Historia Augusta, Pertinax* 6.3.

33. *Historia Augusta, Pertinax* 6.4.

34. *Historia Augusta, Marcus* 17.4–5.

35. *Historia Augusta, Pertinax* 6.9–11.

36. *Historia Augusta, Pertinax* 9 with a discussion of Pertinax's reputation for greed.

37. 2.4.6–9.

38. Dio 74.8.1–2.

39. Dio 74.8.2. *Historia Augusta, Pertinax* 10.1.

40. *Pertinax* 5.2.

41. See p.39

42. 74.9.1–2.

43. 74.10.1–2.

44. The Tungrians formed an auxiliary cohort of a thousand men. So Tausius was not part of the guard.

45. *Pertinax* 11.1–13. The life gives the number of soldiers as 300 rather than Dio's 200.

46. Herodian 2.4.1.

47. The figure is given by Dio 74.10.3. *Historia Augusta, Pertinax* 15.7 claims two months.
48. He probably reflects the opinions of Marius Maximus whom he cites repeatedly in the life.
49. 74.10.3.
50. *Historia Augusta, Pertinax* 10.9.
51. *Historia Augusta, Julianus* 2.5, Dio's version is that in his greed and lust for power he made his way to the camp to contest the imperial nomination. This agrees with the extremely negative portrait that he gives of Julianus. As F. Millar, *A Study of Cassius Dio* remarks Herodian's account of these matters is mostly invention.
52. *Historia Augusta, Marcus Aurelius* 7.9. B. Campbell, *The Emperor and the Roman Army 31 BC–AD 235*, Clarendon Press (Oxford, UK, 1984). pp. 166–171 on the history of donatives offered to the Praetorians.
53. *Julianus* 3.2.
54. A. Appelbaum, 'Another Look at the Assassination of Pertinax and the Accession of Julianus', *Classical Philology* 102 (2007) pp. 199–207 argues that Julianus was involved in the death of Pertinax – there is no evidence for this assertion – and also claims that no auction took place. The second point seems to split hairs. The two men offered money gifts in competition with each other. That seems close enough to an auction to explain Dio's use of the term.
55. Dio 74.11.5.
56. Crucial for the reconstruction of his career are the early chapters of the life in the *Historia Augusta* and an inscription, see *Inscriptiones Latinae Selectae* 412. There are some slight differences in detail between them.
57. 74.12.2.
58. *Historia Augusta* 9.1 and Herodian 2.6.6. The description of his character in the *Historia Augusta* is much more nuanced than that of Dio, see 9.1–2.
59. Dio 74.16.5.
60. 74.13.1.
61. *Julianus* 3.8–10.
62. *Historia Augusta, Julianus* 4.8.
63. 74.13.5., *Historia Augusta, Julianus* 4.7.
64. D. Potter, *The Roman Empire at Bay* p. 101.2.7.2.
65. 74.14.1. Herodian 2.7.1.
66. His coins are of lower weight than Pertinax's.

67. *Histories* 1.4.
68. The beginning and end dates of Geta's governorship are uncertain. For a recent attempt to fix them, see D. Boteva, 'Legati Augusti pro praetore Moesiae inferioris A.D. 193–217/218', *Zeitschrift für Papyrologie und Epigraphik* 110 (1996) pp. 239–40.
69. The 1 April date is the suggestion of A.R. Birley, *Septimius Severus* p. 155.
70. J. Hasebroek, *Untersuchungen* pp. 21–24. B. Campbell, *Cambridge Ancient History* XII p3 n. 3 points out that the coinage indicates that Severus was supported by about fifteen legions.
71. For this date see E.W. Whittaker's edition of Herodian p. 224. Support is provided by the fact that when Severus held the Secular Games, which supposedly were only held every 100 years, he began the games on 1 June.
72. T.D. Barnes, *The Family and Career* p. 103.
73. The *Historia Augusta*'s life of Albinus is not particularly trustworthy. It cites and uses Herodian and probably Dio. But for details absent from both, reliability has to be evaluated on a case by case basis.
74. Most scholars accept the African origins of Albinus, but T.D. Barnes, 'A Senator from Hadrumetum, and Three Others', in *Bonner Historia Augusta Colloquium* 1968–1969 (Bonn, 1970), 45–58, argues for an Italian origin.
75. For Dacia, see Dio 72. 8. 1–6.
76. Herodian 2.11.1.
77. Dio 75.4–5 lists various honours that Severus gave to Pertinax along with an elaborate description of the funeral. *Historia Augusta, Severus* 5.4 claims he was universally regarded as the avenger of Pertinax.
78. Dio 73.8.1. He saw service in Dacia at the same time as Albinus. For his service in Gaul, see *Historia Augusta, Niger* 3.3. It claims that he was friendly with Septimius Severus who was there as his superior. Given the generally untrustworthy nature of the life, it can only be used with caution.
79. 75.6.1.
80. See J.E. Lendon, *Empire of Honour*, OUP (Oxford and New York, 1997) p. 110. However, the *Historia Augusta* claims that he owed his appointment to Narcissus, who would go on to strangle Commodus. *Pescennius* 1.5.
81. 75.6.1.
82. *Niger* 6.,10, and 6.7–8.

83. 2.7.5.
84. His coinage also reflects his attempt to project what may have been a well-deserved reputation for fairness.
85. Dio 75.13.5, *Historia Augusta, Pescennius* 2.1 and *Julianus* 5.1.
86. On the length of time it took for Niger to learn of the situation at Rome and of Severus's proclamation see the useful note of C.R. Whittaker, *Herodian* Vol. 1 p. 185 note 4.
87. *Historia Augusta, Severus* 5.8 and *Niger* 2.4.
88. 74.16.1, *Historia Augusta, Julianus* 5.3.
89. *Historia Augusta, Julianus* 5.5.
90. *Historia Augusta, Julianus* 5.1.
91. *Historia Augusta, Severus* 5.6.
92. 74.16.1–4.
93. Dio 74.16.5.
94. For a list see C.R. Whittaker, *Herodian* p. 219 n.1.
95. It now begins to appear on his coinage. See Whittaker, *Herodian* p. 222 n.2.
96. Apparently the new prefect was not acceptable.
97. Julianus 7.9.
98. 74.16.5.
99. M.W. Dickie, *Magic and Magicians in the Greco-Roman World*, Routledge (London and New York, 2001).
100. *Historia Augusta, Severus* 3.9 and B. Levick, *Julia Domna* p. 29–30.
101. See above p. 27.
102. Dio 74.17.
103. *Julianus* 8.8.
104. Dio 74.17.5 and *Historia Augusta, Julianus* 9.3.

Chapter 4: The Civil Wars: Act I

1. After he was securely established and had no need to justify his rule, the name of Pertinax disappears from his titles.
2. This is supported by the detailed study of M. Durry, *Les cohortes prétoriennes, Bulletin d' École Française de Rome* 146 (Paris, 1938) especially p. 12ff.
3. 74.16.3.
4. Dio 75.1.26.
5. For further discussion of Severus's military reforms, see the appendix.
6. 3.13.4.

7. 75.3–5., *Historia Augusta, Severus* 7.1–3 and Herodian 2.14.1.

8. F. Millar, *A Study of Cassius Dio* p. 139 suggests it was the separate work on Severus's civil and foreign wars published before the history of Rome.

9. Dio 75.2.1.

10. *Historia Augusta, Julianus* 4.10.

11. His account of the funeral 75.4.2–5.5. The obit for Pertinax 75.5.6–7. Such funerals go back to the Republican period and were based on those of the Republican censor. *Historia Augusta, Pertinax* 15.1.

12. 46.46.7.

13. *Historia Augusta*, Severus 8.6–7.

14. See above p. 45.

15. Herodian 2.14.6.

16. *Historia Augusta, Severus* 8. 9. Dio is silent on the matter.

17. Birley, *Septimius Severus* p. 108.

18. *Historia Augusta, Severus* 8.15. After Niger's death the *Historia Augusta* claims that Severus allowed Niger's children to go into exile.

19. On Maximus see above pp. 8–9. The expedition is not in the literary sources. It only appears in a *Corpus Inscriptionum Latinarum* (CIL) VI, 1450.

20. The choice of Candidus may have been determined by the fact that he probably was commanding a legion in Pannonia at the time of the beginning of the war with Niger. For this suggestion see I. Mennen, *Power and Status in the Roman Empire, AD 193–284* p. 197.

21. For his career see ILS 1140, Brill (Leiden and Boston, 2011) p. 197, especially n.15.

22. Dio 75.6.4.

23. Tacitus, *Annals* 16.13.

24. For these rivalries see the orations of Dio Chrysostom, especially Oration 38. For the problem in general see the summary of R. Mac-Mullen, *Enemies of the Roman Order,* Harvard University Press (Cambridge, MA, 1966) pp. 185–9.

25. 3.2.10.

26. 75.6.5–6. The *Historia Augusta*'s life of Severus is both lacking in detail and confused about the fighting. For an attempt to localize the battle see M. Platnauer, *The Life and Reign of the Emperor Lucius Septimius Severus* pp. 86, note 2.

27. 76.17.3–6.

28. *Septimius Severus* p. 49.

29. For his career see *Prosopographia Imperii Romani* C1322.
30. C.R. Whittaker, *Herodian I* p. 267 n.2.
31. For an excellent description of the pass see D. Magie, *Roman Rule in Asia Minor to the End of the Third Century after Christ Vol I*, Princeton University Press (Princeton, NJ, 1950) p. 276
32. C.R. Whittaker *Herodian* I p. 270.
33. 2.3.8.
34. There has been a long controversy over which of the modern rivers in the area was the ancient Pinarus. More recent opinion identifies it with the Payas rather than the Deli Çay.
35. There is a partially legible career inscription for Valerianus from Caesarea Maritima in Palestine, *Année Epigraphique* (1966), 495.
36. For this suggestion and a detailed reconstruction of the inscription cited in note 33 see M. Speidel, 'Valerius Valerianus in Charge of Septimius Severus's Mesopotamian Campaign', *Classical Philology* 80 (1985) 321–6.
37. A formation with some similarities is described in Flavius Arrianus' account of his expedition against the tribe of the Alans as governor of Cappadocia in 135 AD. See Flavius Arrianus, *Ectaxis contra Alanos* 11–31. It is translated by B. Campbell, *Greek and Roman Military Writers: Select Readings*, Routledge (London and New York, 2004) pp. 128–131
38. 75.7.2–3.
39. For the Rain Miracle see P. Kovacs, 'Marcus Aurelius's Rain Miracle and the Marcomannic Wars', *Mnemosyne* 308, Brill (Leiden and Boston, 2009). For the Christian aspects, M.M. Sage, 'Eusebius and the Rain Miracle', *Historia* 36, 1987, pp. 96–113.
40. See above pp. 58–9. D.S. Potter, *The Roman Empire at Bay* p. 109 thinks that Dio and Herodian are both describing the same battle and thinks as Dio does that it was the decisive one at Issus.
41. The decisive character of Valentinus' attack is now generally accepted, so M. Platnauer, *The Life and Reign of the Emperor Lucius Septimius Severus*, OUP (Oxford, UK, 1918) p. 88 or A.R. Birley, *Septimius Severus* p. 113.
42. 75.8.1. Herodian's account at 3.4.5 lacks detail and is written for rhetorical effect, not accuracy.
43. D.S. Potter, *The Roman Empire at Bay* p. 104.
44. 3.8.7–8.
45. *Historia Augusta, Niger* 10 gives a much more positive view of Niger as a commander.
46. Dio 75.8.3.

47. P. Southern, *The Roman Empire* p. 33.
48. Herodian 3.6.98 and Whittaker's note.
49. *Historia Augusta, Severus* 9.5.
50. M. Platnauer, *Septimius Severus* p. 91.
51. 3.4.8–9.
52. 75.8.4.
53. The assumption of the title imperator is a useful chronological marker. In the Republic it had been given to the victorious commander by his soldiers on the field of battle and then confirmed by the Senate; from Augustus, it was assumed by the reigning emperor as part of his titles. This use led to numbered grants which can be used to date events from coins and inscriptions.
54. This was done in 194, presumably soon after his arrival, as a number of milestones mentioning the new province name Severus still with the title of imperator IV. In the next year he became imperator V.
55. F. Millar, *The Roman Near East 31 BC–AD 337*, Harvard University Press (Cambridge, MA and London, 1993) pp. 121–4.
56. For a discussion of the revolt, see A.R. Birley, 'Hadrian to the Antonines' in A.K. Bowman, P. Garnsey and D. Rathbone (eds.), *The Cambridge Ancient History: The High Empire, AD 70–192*, CUP (Cambridge, UK and New York, 2000) pp. 176–81.
57. For the history of Edessa see S.K. Ross, *Roman Edessa*, Routledge (London and New York, 2001).
58. Scenite refers to their practice of living in tents or skenae in Greek.
59. Dio 76.1.2.
60. 3.4.6.
61. For a discussion of Severus's reasons see M. Gradoni, 'The Parthian Campaigns of Septimius Severus: Causes, and Roles in Dynastic Legitimation', in E.C. De Sena, (ed.), *The Roman Empire During the Severan Dynasty: Case Studies in History, Art, Architecture, Economy And Literature*, Gorgias Press (New York, 2013) pp. 7–9.
62. A. Birley, *Septimius Severus* p. 116.
63. Unfortunately the site was vandalized by ISIS in April 2015. However, the BBC has reported that the damage is less than was at first thought.
64. 68.31.
65. Herodian 3.5.1 although mentioning Severus's grievances against the eastern kingdoms omits the expedition of 195. He only narrates Severus's later expedition in 198/9.

66. *Arrian,Anabasis* 6.26 places it in the Gedrosian desert, today south-western Pakistan and southeastern Iran. It is hard to judge the truth of the Alexander story and equally that of Severus's own story. It may be that Severus modelled himself on the anecdote, which he would have thought to be authentic.
67. Dio 75.3.2.
68. I. Mennen, *Power and Status* p. 300.
69. The ancient use of the term 'Arab' is imprecise. It sometimes refers to the inhabitants of Mesopotamia as well as those of Arabia. For a discussion of the term, see Ross, *Roman Edessa* p. 48.
70. Dio 75.3.2. Probus is unknown and does not appear elsewhere in the sources.
71. Se above p. 59.
72. For this suggestion see M. Speidel, 'Valerius Valerianus', p. 326.
73. Dio 79.16.2.
74. For a discussion of the settlement see S.K. Ross, *Roman Edessa* pp. 49–54.
75. *Historia Augusta*, *Severus* 9.10–11.
76. Dio's description is at 75.10–11. A similar description occurs at Herodian 3.6.9.
77. Dio 75.12.3–14.1.
78. Its city status was restored later in Severus's reign.
79. 75.14.2.
80. Dio 71.10.5 and *Historia Augusta*, *Marcus* 26.8. It also appears on coinage, most of which was minted after her death in 176.
81. M.T. Boatwright, 'Faustina the Younger, Mater Castrorum' in R. Frei–Stolba, A. Bielman and O. Bianchi (eds), *Les femmes entre sphère privée et sphère publique*, Peter Lang (Bern, 2003) p. 250.
82. See above p. 51.
83. For the date see C.R. Whittaker, *Herodian* I pp. 286–7.
84. B. Levick, *Julia Domna* p. 42.
85. Herodian 3.5.8 and *Historia Augusta*, Clodius Albinus 8.
86. 3.5.2.

Chapter 5: The Civil Wars: Act 2

1. On the festival of the Saturnalia see H.H. Scullard, *Festivals and Ceremonies of the Roman Republic*, Thames and Hudson (London, 1981) pp. 205–7.

2. For Cleander see above pp. 25–6. For the games as a venue of communication between the emperor and the masses see F. Millar, *The Emperor in the Roman World*, new ed., (Bristol Classical Press, 1992) pp. 368–75.

3. *Historia Augusta, Severus* 10.1 and Niger 6. 1.

4. See above p. 23.

5. Dio 73.9.2a.

6. Dio 73.2^2–4. It is a puzzle how such a large number of troops could have left Britain unhindered. Birley, *The Roman Government* p. 169 suggests that they may have been sent to round up deserters on the Continent whose number had reached serious proportions because of military problems in Gaul and Germany.

7. Dio 76.6.2.

8. *Inscriptiones Latinae Selectae* 419.

9. 75.5.

10. See above p. 69.

11. Herodian 3.6.10. It is not clear who the commander of the force was. Some think it was C. Julius Pacatianus, who was also governor of the new province of Osrhoene. Fabius Cilo has also been suggested. The problem revolves around the date of the formation of the province.

12. *Inscriptiones Latinae Selectae 1140.*

13. *Historia Augusta, Severus* 11.1.

14. *Severus* 11.2.

15. For this translation of Dio see A.J. Graham, 'The Numbers at Lugdunum', *Historia* 27 (1978) pp. 625–8.

16. P. Salway, *Roman Britain*, OUP (Oxford, UK and New York, 1981) pp. 221–2.

17. There is disagreement over who this Laetus was. At the battle Herodian (3.7.4) and Dio (76,6.8) mention a Laetus and his decisive role in the conflict. Commanders with the name Laetus occur at several points in the narratives of Severus's reign. C.R. Whittaker in his note to the passage (p. 299), in my view correctly, assumes that the same commander (Julius Laetus) is meant in each passage. The alleged treachery by Laetus at the battle was most probably invented after 198 when Severus executed Laetus for treachery on his later eastern campaign.

18. M. Sage, *The Army of the Roman Republic*, Pen & Sword (Barnsley, UK, 2018) pp. 209–13.

19. Dio 76.7.3.

20. *Historia Augusta, Severus* 11.6.

21. *Inscriptiones Latinae Selectae* 1140.

22. *Historia Augusta, Severus* 12.5–6.
23. *Historia Augusta, Severus* 9.3 and Dio 75.9.
24. These will be discussed in detail in the appendix on Severus and the army, p. 123ff.
25. Herodian 3.8.4–5.
26. Dio 76.8.1–4 and *Historia Augusta Severus* 13 lists forty-one senators. For the numbers see Platnauer, *Life and Reign* p. 113 n.1.
27. Severus 14.1.
28. D.S. Potter, *The Roman Empire at Bay* p. 112.
29. 76.7.1–2.
30. Herodian 3.5.2.
31. 76.8.5
32. Herodian 3.8.9.

Chapter 6: Encore: War in the East and Sightseeing in Egypt

1. The coinage and imperial acclamations (IX and X) point to a departure probably in late summer 197.
2. Dio 76.9.1.
3. Herodian 3.1.2. He had promised to raise forces for him.
4. B. Isaac, *The Limits of Empire* rev. ed., OUP (Oxford, 1990) pp. 10–11.
5. For a short summary of the history of Ctesiphon, see J. Kröger, 'Ctesiphon', *Encyclopedia Iranica* Vol. 6.4 pp. 446–8. The article is also available at iranicaonline.org/articles/ctesiphon.
6. J. Bennett, *Trajan, Optimus Princeps*, Routledge (London and New York, 1997) pp. 201–203.
7. A.R. Birley, *Marcus Aurelius: A Biography* rev. ed., Routledge (London and New York, 1987) p. 140.
8. For Hatra, see below pp. 84–5. Elymais was located at the head of the Persian Gulf. Gordyene was located south of Lake Van in eastern Turkey.
9. On the structure and administration of the Parthian Empire see among others, V.G. Lukonin 'Political, Social and Administrative Institutions: Taxes and Trade', in E. Yarshater (ed.), *The Cambridge History of Iran* Vol.3.2, CUP (Cambridge, UK, 1983) pp. 681–746.
10. E. Yarshater (ed.), 'Introduction', *The Cambridge History of Iran Vol.3.1*, CUP (Cambridge, UK, 1983) p. xxx.
11. M.I. Rostovtzeff, 'The Parthian Shot', *American Journal of Archaeology* 47 (1943) pp. 174–187.

12. For a short account and analysis see M. Sage, *The Roman Republican Army: A Sourcebook, Routledge* (London and New York, 2008) pp. 258–63.
13. E.L. Wheeler, 'The Army and the Limes in the East' in P.A. Erdkamp (ed.) *A Companion to the Roman Army*, Blackwell, (Oxford, UK and Malden, MA, 2007) p. 260.
14. E.L. Wheeler, 'The Legion as Phalanx', *Chiron* 9 (1979) pp. 303–18.
15. M. Gradoni, 'The Parthian Campaigns of Septimius Severus: Causes, and Roles in Dynastic Legitimation', in E.C. De Sena (ed.), *The Roman Empire During the Severan Dynasty: Case Studies in History, Art, Architecture, Economy and Literature*, Gorgias Press (NY, 2013) p. 10.
16. On Parthian fighting abilities see A.K. Goldsworthy, *The Roman Army at War 100 BC–AD 200* (Oxford, 1996) pp. 66–8.
17. Dio 76. 9.1.
18. N.C. Debevoise, *A Political History of Parthia*, UCP (Chicago, 1938) p. 258.
19. *Ibid.* p259.
20. D.L. Kennedy, 'The Garrisoning of Mesopotamia in the Late Antonine and Early Severan Period', *Antichthon* 21 (1987) pp. 59–61.
21. For the establishment of the legions see Dio 55.24.2.
22. *Severus* 15.1.
23. 3.9.1.
24. 75.3.2–3.
25. 68.17.1. Interestingly Dio claims that Trajan's motivation was the desire for glory. See B. Isaac, *The Limits of Empire* p. 51 who calls attention to the fact that there were those at Rome who did not see the need for endless imperial expansion.
26. Isaac, The *Limits of Empire* p. 15.
27. N. Pollard, *Soldiers, Cities, and Civilians in Roman Syria*, University of Michigan Press (Ann Arbor, 2000) p. 58.
28. B, Levick, *Julia Domna* p. 48.
29. *Inscriptiones Latinae Selectae* 456.
30. *Severus* 15.2.
31. S.K. Ross, *Roman Edessa,* Routledge (London and New York, 2001) p. 67–8.
32. Herodian 3.9.2.
33. A.R. Birley, *Septimius Severus* p. 129.
34. Dio 76.9.3.
35. M.K. Gradoni, 'The Parthian Campaigns of Septimius Severus: Causes and Roles in Dynastic Legitimation' p. 10–11. Gradoni also points to

technical changes such as the use of Near Eastern auxilia units as also important in enhancing Roman striking power in the region.

36. Dio 76.9.3.
37. Herodian 3.9.11.
38. On the garrisoning of the province and the locations of its legions, see Kennedy, D.L., 'The Garrisoning of Mesopotamia in the Late Antonine and Early Severan Period', *Antichthon* 21 (1987) pp. 57–66.
39. See A.N. Sherwin White, *Racial Prejudice in Imperial Rome*, Cambridge University Press (Cambridge, 1967).
40. P.M. Edwell, *Between Rome and Persia*, Routledge, (London and New York, 2008) p. 155.
41. 68.311.
42. For these details see Herodian 3.9.5. Whittaker in his note on this passage p. 319 dismisses the insects as an 'old campaigner's story'. In fact insects have been used as war weapons throughout recorded history to attack the enemy with diseases. See J.A. Lockwood, *Six-Legged Soldiers: Using Insects as Weapons of War*, Oxford University Press (Oxford, 2008). As Whittaker (p.319) notes, the events are misplaced in 195.
43. 76.10.2–3.
44. Aeneid 11.371–3.
45. A.R. Birley, *Septimius Severus* p. 131 on the basis *of Historia Augusta, Severus* 15.6 suggests the murder was done at the instigation of Severus's powerful praetorian prefect Plautianus who was hunting supporters of Niger.
46. F. Millar, *The Roman Near East 31 BC–AD 337*, Harvard University Press (Cambridge, MA and London, 1993) p. 296.
47. For Priscus, see 75.11.2.
48. 76.12.1–13.1.
49. D.B. Campbell, 'What Happened at Hatra? The Problem of the Severan Siege Operations'. In P. Freeman and D. Kennedy (eds.), *The Defence of the Roman and Byzantine East, BAR International Series* 297 (1968) p. 52
50. Josephus, *The Jewish War* 5.7.2.
51. M. Speidel., '"Europeans" – Syrian Elite Troops at Dura-Europos and Hatra' in M. Speidel, *Roman Armies Studies* I, J.C. Gieben (Amsterdam, 1984) pp. 301–9. The traditional view is defended by D.L. Kennedy, '"European" Soldiers and the Severan Siege of Hatra', in P.W. Freeman and D.L. Kennedy (ed.), *Defence of the Roman and Byzantine East*, (Oxford, 1986) pp. 397–409.

52. *Roman Arabia*, Harvard University Press (Cambridge, MA and London, UK) p. 120.
53. *Historia Augusta, Severus*, 14.6.
54. See F. Millar, *The Roman Near East* p. 143.
55. See A. Harker, *Loyalty and Dissidence in Roman Egypt*, CUP (Cambridge UK and New York, 2008).
56. A. Harker, Loyalty and Dissidence pp. 132–3.
57. A.K. Bowman, 'Egypt from Septimius Severus to the Death of Constantine', in A.K. Bowman, P. Garnsey, and A. Cameron, A. (eds.), *The Cambridge Ancient History Vol. XII, The Crisis of Empire AD 193–337*, CUP (Cambridge, UK and New York, 2005) p. 318.
58. Eusebius, *Ecclesiastical History* 5.6 and 6.1. On Severus and the Christians, see T.D. Barnes, 'Legislation against the Christians', *Journal of Roman Studies* 58 (1968) pp. 40–41.
59. 77.16.1.
60. *Historia Augusta. Severus* 17.3.
61. Dio 71.4. On Avidius Cassius see p. 62.
62. A.B. Lloyd, 'The Reception of Pharaonic Egypt in Classical Antiquity' in A.B. Lloyd (ed.*)*, *A Companion to Ancient Egypt Vol I*, Wiley-Blackwell (Malden, MA and Oxford, UK, 2010) pp. 1078–85.
63. Suetonius, *Augustus* 18.1.
64. *Historia Augusta, Severus*, 17.3.
65. B. Levick, *Julia Domna* pp. 125–6.
66. See above p. 4.
67. Herodian 2.9.4.
68. *Historia Augusta, Severus* 3.9
69. See above pp. 9–10.
70. Suetonius, *Domitian* 10.
71. Dio 77.11.1.
72. See above p. 32.
73. P. Grimal, *The Concise Dictionary of Classical Mythology*, Basil Blackwell (Oxford, UK, 1990) p. 268.
74. N. Pollard, 'Military Institutions and Warfare: Graeco-Roman', in A.B. Lloyd (ed.), *A Companion to Ancient Egypt Volume I*, Wiley-Blackwell (Malden, MA and Oxford, UK, 2007), p. 455.
75. For the chronology see A.R., Birley, *Septimius Severus* p. 139.
76. See A.R. Birley, *Marcus Aurelius, A Biography*, Rev. ed., Routledge (New York, 2001) p. 49ff.
77. C.R. Whittaker, *Herodian* p. 325.

Chapter 7: Rome and Africa

1. *Inscriptiones Graecae in Bulgaria Repertae* III.1690.
2. A.R. Birley, *Septimius Severus* pp. 143–4.
3. These were the citizens who had the right to receive free grain.
4. The gold aureus equalled 25 denarii or 100 sestertii. Trying to find the modern values of ancient coins is a notoriously difficult subject. Some light can be thrown on it by looking at yearly military pay which was probably 300 denarii at this time for the legions and the Pretorians probably twice as much.
5. There is some uncertainty about the date when the celebration took place. The official date is 9 April, but some scholars think that Severus did not reach Rome until later in the year and suggest 9 June 193.
6. Her age is based on the average age of marriage for elite women of about 13–15.
7. C. Rowan, 'The Public Image of the Severan Women', *Papers of the British School at Rome* 79 (2011) p. 256.
8. 77.1.1.
9. *Severus* 16.6–7.
10. See M. Platnauer, *Life and Reign* p. 125.
11. Hasebroek, *Septimius Severus* pp. 99–100.
12. For detailed discussion see S.S. Lusnia, 'Urban Planning and Sculptural Display in Severan Rome: Reconstructing the Septizodium and its Role in Dynastic Politics', *American Journal of Archaeology* 108 (2004) pp. 517–44.
13. There was an earlier arch erected at Issus to commemorate Severus's victory over Niger.
14. The words commemorating Geta were removed during the reign of Caracalla. This was part of a systematic attempt to erase all public and private references to Geta and all representations of him. On this, see E.R. Varner, *Mutilation and Transformation, Damnatio Memoriae and Roman Imperial Portraiture*, Brill (Leiden and Boston, MSA, 2004) pp. 168–84. On the arch see p. 175.
15. F.S. Kleiner, *A History of Roman Art, Enhanced Edition*, Wadsworth Cengage Learning (Boston, MA, 2010) pp. 238–40.
16. M. Cartwright, 'The Arch of Septimius Severus', *Ancient History Encyclopedia*, retrieved from ttps://76.15.1 and 77 ancient.eu/article/502/ (29 June 2013).
17. *Historia Augusta, Severus* 6.10.

18. *Inscriptiones Latinae Selectae* 456.
19. Dio 76.14.2.
20. 77.16.4.
21. Dio 76.15.6–7.
22. See above pp. 9–10.
23. B. Levick, *Julia Domna* p. 71.
24. 76.14.3–7.
25. 76.15.1 and 77.2.3.
26. 77.4.5, and Herodian at 3.10.7.
27. 77.17.1.
28. Philostratus, *Lives of the Sophists* 2.20. The visit is omitted by all the other sources.
29. For a short summary of the imperial cult, see S.R.F Price, 'The place of religion: Rome in the early Empire', *The Cambridge Ancient History, Vol. X*: The Augustan Empire, 43 B.C.–A.D. 69, Cambridge University Press (Cambridge, 1996) UK p. 837–41.
30. F.S. Kleiner, *A History of Roman Art, Enhanced Edition*, Wadsworth Cengage Learning (Boston, MA, 2010) pp. 250–2.
31. For a detailed analysis see T.D. Barnes, 'The Family and Career of Septimius Severus', *Historia* 16 (1967) pp. 87–107.
32. *Severus* 15.7 and 19.9.
33. See Introduction p. xviii.
34. *Historia Augusta, Severus* 18.3.
35. For a discussion of the expedition see A.R. Birley, *Septimius Severus* p. 151.

Chapter 8: The Return to Rome

1. The Eleusinian Mysteries was an annual celebration held at the town of Eleusis in Athenian territory honouring the goddesses Demeter and Persephone. It was in origin an agricultural fertility cult. The initiation into the cult was structured as a series of revealed mysteries which also guaranteed that the initiand would have a special reward in the afterlife.
2. Herodian 3.8.9–10.
3. See the perceptive comments of D.S. Potter, *The Roman Empire at Bay* p. 119.
4. Even a cursory glance at the coinage makes this preoccupation clear. See C. Gorrie, 'Julia Domna's Building Patronage, Imperial Family Roles and the Severan Revival of Moral Legislation', *Historia* 53 (2004) p. 61.

5. *Corpus Inscriptionum Latinarum* VI, 32323.
6. K. Galinsky, 'Continuity and Change: Religion in the Augustan Semi-Century', in J. Rüpke (ed.), *A Companion to Roman Religion*, Blackwell Publishing (Malden, MA and Oxford, UK, 2007) pp. 75–6.
7. G.J. Gorski and J.E. Packer, *The Roman Forum A Reconstruction and Architectural Guide*, CUP (2015) p. 135.
8. For the text of the Severan fragments see G.B. Pighi, *De ludis saecularibus populi Romani Quiritium libri sex*, Schippers (Amsterdam, 1965) p. 142. For a detailed discussion of earlier emperors' games and their relevance to Severus, see T.D. Barnes, 'Aspects of the Severan Empire, Part I: Severus as a New Augustus', *New England Classical Journal* 35 (2008) pp. 259–67.
9. *Historia Augusta, Severus* 23.1.
10. 77.16.3.
11. See above p. 28.
12. For Julia's sexual irregularities see for instance *Historia Augusta, Severus* 18.8 or Aurelius Victor 20.23. The charge of illicit sexual behaviour was a standard way of discrediting imperial women. It was used against Caracalla's wife Plautilla as well. Dio (77.3.1) calls her a woman without shame. See the comments of B, Levick, *Julia Domna* p. 33.
13. M.M. Sage, *The Army of the Roman Republic*, Introduction p. xii, Pen & Sword Military (Barnsley, UK, 2018).
14. Augustus, *Res Gestae* 14.
15. B. Levick, *Julia Domna* p. 83.
16. See F. McLynn, *Marcus Aurelius: A Life*, Da Capo Press (Cambridge, MA, 2009) pp. 36–7.
17. Antoninus had had two sons who both died young.
18. A.R. Birley, 'Hadrian to the Antonines', *Cambridge Ancient History XI: The High Empire AD 70–192* (Cambridge UK and New York, 2000) pp. 151–2.
19. A.R. Birley, *Cambridge Ancient History XI* pp. 156–7.
20. For instance, *British Museum Coins of the Roman Empire 5:* 198–9, nos. 228–39, among others.
21. See B. Levick, *Julia Domna* pp. 93–4.
22. 78.6.1a.
23. This begins at 78.6.1 and extends to 11.7.
24. 5.2.1–2.
25. Caracalla 9.3.3. Strangely it paints a much more positive picture of the emperor's childhood and early youth: 1.3 3 *'He himself in his boyhood*

was winsome and clever, respectful to his parents and courteous to his parents' friends, beloved by the people, popular with the senate, and well able to further his own interests in winning affection.'

26. Dio 77.7.1–2 and Herodian 3.10.3–4.
27. Aurelius Victor, *De Caesaribus* 21: 2–3; Eutropius, *Breviarium* 8,20,1 and Anon. *Epitome de Caesaribus* 21.5.
28. B, Levick, *Julia Domna* p. 84.
29. D.S. Potter, *The Roman Empire at Bay* p. 133.
30. See above p. 110.
31. See above p. 82.
32. Dio 77.2.2–3.
33. 3.10.6
34. 58.14.1.
35. *L'Année Épigraphique 1944.* N.74.
36. Dio 76.14.7
37. 77.4.5.
38. 76.15.1.
39. *Historia Augusta, Severus* 14.5, and Dio 76.16.2. That the venue of the incident was Lepcis is the likely suggestion of A.R. Birley, *Septimius Severus* p. 154.
40. Dio 76.16.2.
41. Dio 76.15.6.
42. *Historia Augusta, Severus* 21.7.
43. Dio 76.15.7.
44. 3.11.1–2.
45. Dio 77.2,4
46. Herodian 3.11.4–12.
47. 77.3–4.
48. 77.2.1–2.
49. A.R. Birley, *Septimius Severus* p. 163.
50. Dio 77.4.4.
51. On the process see E.R. Varner, *Mutilation and Transformation* pp. 161–8.
52. F. Millar, *Dio Cassius* p, 147.
53. 77.10.
54. T. Grünewald, *Bandits in the Roman Empire: Myth and Reality*, Trans. J.D. Drinkwater, Routledge (London and New York, 2004) p. 110.
55. B.D. Shaw, *Bandits*, p. 356–7.
56. He was one of the greatest of Roman jurists.
57. 75.2.4.

58. 77.4.
59. A.R. Birley, *Septimius Severus* pp. 169.
60. B. Isaac, 'Bandits in Judaea and Arabia', *Harvard Studies in Classical Philology* 88 (1984) p. 183.
61. B.D. Shaw, 'Bandits in the Roman Empire' in R. Osbourne (ed.), *Studies in Ancient Greek and Roman Society*, CUP (Cambridge, UK and New York, 2004) pp. 349–54.
62. *Historia Augusta, Severus* 18.6.
63. *Bandits*, new ed., New Press, (New York, 2000).
64. Dio 77.7. 1–3.
65. Herodian 3.13.6.

Chapter 9: The Last Act

1. Severus 16.6, 18.9 and Dio 77.16.1. Herodian (3.11.1) is not specific but he clearly refers to gout.
2. The Arthritis Foundation, *What is Gout?*
3. These years of danger recurred every seven years but the one in the sixty-third year was the most dangerous.
4. 3.14.1
5. On Syria Coele see p. 62 above.
6. A.R. Birley, *Septimius Severus* p. 172
7. 77.10.6. This consideration, as well as the view that Herodian's account of the reign is of poor quality, has led Birley (p. 172) to reject the letter's authenticity. As an added argument he cites other instances where Herodian uses a letter to an emperor to explain his arrival at a theatre of war as a topos or commonplace. We know that governors routinely issued reports and sent letters to the imperial administration, so the fact that such letters appear in other narratives is hardly surprising. The most important objection is surely the problem of *cui bono* or why introduce a letter at all? It adds little to the drama.
8. 77.11.1. The notion of the destructiveness of excessive peace is an old Roman commonplace. See, R.I. Frank, 'The Dangers of Peace', *Prudentia* 8 (1976) pp. 1–7 and Michael Sage *The Roman Army of the Republic* p. ix.
9. 77.11.1–2.
10. D. Mattingly, *An Imperial Possession: Britain in the Roman Empire*, Penguin (London, 2007) p. 118.
11. *Op. cit.* pp. 117–19.

12. The only ancient source to mention Hadrian as the builder of the wall is *Historia Augusta, Hadrian* 11.2. Other later imperial sources ascribe the wall to Septimius Severus, for example Eutropius, *Breviarium* 19. It may reflect the extensive renovations and building undertaken by Alfenus Senecio in 205–7.

13. J. Crow, 'The Northern Frontier of Britain from Trajan to Antoninus Pius: Roman Builders and Native Britons', in M. Todd (ed.), *A Companion to Roman Britain*, Blackwell Publishing (Malden, MA and Oxford, UK, 2002) pp. 130–1.

14. See D. Mattingly, p. 120.

15. *Historia Augusta, Antoninus Pius* 5. For a description of the wall with excellent photos and illustrations, see D.J. Breeze, *Roman Scotland*, Batsford (London, 1996) pp. 63–9.

16. So the famous words of Jupiter in Aeneid 1.278–9: 'His ego nec metas rerum nec tempora pono, imperium sine fine dedi', that is, 'I place no limits of time or space on (the Romans), I have given them empire without end.'

17. See A.R. Birley, *The Roman Government* p. 137.

18. *Historia Augusta, Marcus Aurelius* 8 and 22.

19. For the first alternative see D. Mattingly, *An Imperial Possession* p. 122. The second alternative is suggested by A.R. Birley, *Marcus Aurelius* p. 190.

20. Dio 73.8.2.

21. The exact status of the fallen general is unclear. He was either a governor or a legionary legate, presumably of VI Victrix which was closest to the wall of the three British legions.

22. The odd thing is that Marcellus, on the usual chronology, had been governor since 177 and it was only seven years later that such behaviour led to the outbreak of a mutiny.

23. See above p. 70.

24. S. Frere, *Britannia*, Book Club Associates (London, 1967) pp. 167–8.

25. P. Salway, *Roman Britain, A Very Short Introduction*, OUP (Oxford, UK, 2015) p. 58.

26. Dio 76.5.4.

27. Herodian 3.14.3.

28. J. Hasebroek, ss p. 141–2.

29. Legionary vexillations or detachments assembled for military campaigns were considerably larger than those used for other purposes. They could consist of 1,000 or 2,000 men drawn from several legions on campaign.

Of course, such detachments could be much smaller depending on the assignment and when not involved in a campaign. Auxiliary vexillationes were also used. Both types of units would occasionally be left in the province where they served and form part of its garrison.

30. 3.14.4.
31. 77.13.1. As Birley *Septimius Severus* p. 174 points out, Dio used the same words to describe Severus's goal in Mesopotamia.
32. *Geography* 4.5.3.
33. B. Campbell, 'The Severan Dynasty' in A.K Bowman, P. Garnsey, and A. Cameron, (eds.), *The Cambridge Ancient History Vol. XII, The Crisis of Empire AD 193–337*, CUP (2005) p. 8.
34. Dio 77.14. 5–6.
35. N. Hodgson, 'The British Expedition of Septimius Severus', *Britannia* 45 (2014) p. 34.
36. D. Breeze, *Roman Scotland* p. 110.
37. Dio 76.5.4.
38. G. Maxwell, 'The Roman Penetration of the north in the Late First Century AD' in M. Todd (ed.), *A Companion to Roman Britain* p. 79.
39. Dio 76.5.4.
40. F. Millar, *A Study of Cassius Dio* p. 149. Severus seems to have circumnavigated the island. Dio gives measurements for the length and breadth of Britain. His figures are 951 miles long and its widest extent of 308 and narrowest of 40 (77.12.5). He repeated the circumnavigation by Agricola who had governed Britain about a century before (*Agricola* 38.4).
41. 77.12.1–4.
42. 3.14.7.
43. Caesar, *Gallic War* 1.4.2.
44. See N. Hodgson, 'The British Expedition of Septimius Severus' p. 34 and D. Mattingly, *An Imperial Possession* p. 437–9.
45. J. Casey, 'Who Built Carpow? Review of Events in Britain in the Reigns of Commodus', *Britannia* 41 (2010) pp. 225–8.
46. Dio 77.13.4
47. A.R. Birley, *Septimius Severus* pp. 180–1.
48. Dio 77.13.1–4 and Herodian 3.14.10.
49. *Gallic War* 3.28.
50. Dio 77.13.4.
51. 77.14.1.
52. 77.14.1–7.

53. 3.15.2.
54. Severus Dio 77.15.1. The *Iliad* quotation is 6.55–59.
55. 10.15.4ff.
56. Dio 71.16.1 and A.R. Birley *Marcus Aurelius* p. 254.
57. Dio 77.15.2. Dio claims he is giving his exact words.
58. It is hard to discern any action by Geta during this period.
59. *Severus* 20.1.
60. R. Syme, *Ammianus and the Historia Augusta*, OUP (Oxford, 1968) p. 60.
61. See above p. 92.
62. Dio 78.1.1. Herodian 3.15.4 describes a much more extensive purge.
63. 78.1.3.
64. Herodian 4.3.5–7.
65. Dio 78.4.1.
66. Dio 77.7.
67. 3.8.2.
68. See the excellent discussion of the matter in A.R. Birley, *The Roman Government of Britain* pp. 333–6.
69. Herodian 3.6.10.
70. 76.9.4–5.
71. 76.3.3.
72. See the remarks of B. Isaac, *The Limits of Empire* p. 15.

Appendix: Severus and the Roman Army

1. The governor of Africa was the only senatorial governor to control a legion; that anomaly ended under Caligula.
2. P. Kehne, 'War and Peacetime Logistics: Supplying Imperial Armies in the East and the West', in P.A. Erdkamp (ed.), *A Companion to the Roman Army*, Blackwell, (Oxford and Malden, MA, 2007) p. 325.
3. T. Cornell, 'The End of Roman Imperial Expansion', in J. Rich and G. Shipley (eds.), *War and Society in the Roman World*, Routledge (London, 1993) p. 148.
4. P. Southern, *The Roman Empire* p. 294 note 43.
5. See above Julianus.
6. Herodian 4.4.4–7.
7. *Historia Augusta, Caracalla* 2.7–8.
8. For a more detailed discussion of *vexillationes* see A.K. Goldsworthy, *The Roman Army at War, 100 BC–AD 200*, Clarendon Press (Oxford, 1996) pp. 27–8.

9. See the discussion of B. Campbell in *Cambridge Ancient History XII* pp. 9 and 12–13.
10. Tacitus, *Annals* 2.59.
11. 79.7.1–2.
12. See the criticism of Roman tactics and the role of the legions in D.S. Potter, *The Roman Empire at Bay* pp. 128–30.
13. M. Handy, *Die Severi und das Heer* pp. 179–80.
14. M. Sage, *The Republican Roman Army: A Sourcebook*, Routledge (New York and London, 2008) p. 259.
15. K. Strobel, 'Strategy and Army Structure between Septimius Severus and Constantine the Great', in P.A. Erdkamp, (ed.) *A Companion to the Roman Army*, Blackwell, (Oxford and Malden, MA, 2007) pp. 273–5.
16. 75.3.2–3.
17. *The Limits of Empire: The Roman Army in the East* rev. ed., Clarendon Press (Oxford, 1990) p. 15.
18. On the Sassanians, see E. Yarshater (ed.), *The Cambridge History of Iran Vol 3.1: The Achaemenid, Parthian and Sasanian Periods*, CUP (Cambridge and New York, 1983) pp. 116–80.
19. 3.8.4–5.
20. *Severus* 17.1.
21. The most convincing study of the problem is R. Alston, 'Roman Military Pay from Caesar to Diocletian', *Journal of Roman Studies* 84 (1994) pp. 113–23.
22. For instance, by Didius Julianus in financial straits after the extravagances of Commodus and by Caracalla.
23. R. Alston, 'Military Pay', p. 122.
24. For the corruption and extortion, see the summary of evidence in N. Pollard, 'The Roman Army', in D. S. Potter (ed.), *A Companion to the Roman Empire*, Blackwell Publishing (Malden, MA and Oxford, UK, 2006) pp. 223–225.
25. Dio 78.43.2.
26. 'Military Pay', p. 115.
27. For the rise in Egyptian grain prices see R. Duncan-Jones, *The Economy of the Roman Empire: Quantitative Studies*, CUP (Cambridge, UK and New York, 1982) pp. 145–6 and Appendix 7.
28. For the ascription of the annona to Septimius Severus, see R. Develin, 'The Army Pay Rises under Severus and Caracalla, and the Question of Annona militaris', *Latomus* 30 (1971) pp 694–5.
29. D.S. Potter, *Roman Empire at Bay* p. 130.

30. See the analysis of the relation between the future emperor Vespasian and the eastern legions in M. Griffin, 'The Flavians', *Cambridge Ancient History Vol. XI, The High Empire, A.D. 70–192*, (2000) pp. 33–9. She points out that the eastern legions by the last quarter of the first century already contained a number of soldiers drawn from the eastern provinces.
31. A crucial article on the subject is that of B. Campbell, 'The Marriage of Soldiers under the Empire', *Journal of Roman Studies* 68 (1978) pp. 153–66. See also, S.E. Phang, *The Marriage of Roman Soldiers (13 BC–AD 235): Law and Family in the Roman Imperial Army* (Leiden, 2001).
32. B. Campbell, *Marriage of Soldiers* p. 155.
33. D.S. Potter *The Roman Empire at Bay* p. 131 thinks that the persistence of the ban was the result of a continuing view of the army as an all-male institution where loyalty was owed by the troops to their comrades and to the emperor.
34. 3.8.4–5.
35. See note 32 above.
36. Dio 77.15.2.

Index